THE CENTURIES OF SANTA FE

THE CENTURIES OF

SANTA FE

BY

PAUL HORGAN

William Gannon
Santa Fe, New Mexico
1976

TO
DON BERKE

CONTENTS

PREFACE TO THE 1976 EDITION

SANTA FE IS ONE OF THOSE AMERICAN CITIES—New
Orleans, San Antonio, Boston—whose past is always sought
out by visitors. Our other ports of call for tourists hold out
modern interest: expressions of the latest technology, the ingenuities and comforts made possible by dense commerce, expressions of the arts in great museums, concert halls, theatre seasons,
hotels, offerings of night life for all tastes. Such urbanisms
require constant change, renewal, the tyranny of novelty, to
keep them exciting and therefore attractive to trade.

But Santa Fe's great possession is her historic heritage—over
three and a half centuries of it; and it is her pride that many
direct evidences of her old times are still clearly visible today.
That this is so is no accident of neglect. The city's historic
face has been preserved in modern times only by devoted
vigilance on the part of citizens who saw that, once erased,
evidences of the past can never be wholly reclaimed.

Change as progress has always been a part of the American
social creed, particularly in the name of commerce. Like any
other town, Santa Fe must live on business—and business is
concerned mostly with the immediate: let the old look, the
old ways, yield to up-to-date ingenuities and conveniences to
which customers will respond. Time and again, efforts were
made to convert Santa Fe's native architecture and social atmosphere into the national commonplaces of commercial styles.
But time and again, these efforts were contained by those who
knew that Santa Fe's visible heritage was her most precious
attribute, and they succeeded in preserving the most characteristic backgrounds against which the episodes of this book
are enacted.

The core of the city and many of its irregularly radiating
streets speak eloquently of the earlier centuries, even back to
the founding year of 1610. Where the modern urban styles

have been implanted—supermarkets, thruways, condominiums, and the rest—they are located on the periphery. In the struggle between profitable, ever-changing convenience and the enduring visible evidences of the Indian, the Latin, and the Anglo-American civilizations of New Mexico, Santa Fe has preserved her historic values; and it is in honor of these values that this book, first issued through two decades in several other editions, now appears in still another. Its chapters, unfolding urgent concerns and passions of Santa Fe's centuries, are enclosed in a past which is still there to be seen by anyone who will let the metaphorical, as well as the actual, sunlight of Santa Fe reveal it to him.

P.H.

January, 1976

PREFACE

THIS IS A BOOK OF SCENES AND PORTRAITS from three centuries of
a society—the society of Santa Fe in New Mexico, that city which
was for so long the northernmost capital of Spain in the New
World. Since its foundation in 1610 it has known a great variety
of social life, and an enlivening contrast, and a commingling, of
several different races—the aboriginal Indian, the Spanish, the
Mexican, and the Anglo-American.

This volume tries to describe that life in the sequence of time
during periods of significant change and throughout a succession
of conquests from early Spanish colonial times to the present
century.

Rising eastward in great fantastic terraces from the Rio Grande
in northern New Mexico, the land opens into the grand plain of
Santa Fe at an altitude of seven thousand feet. It is girt by
formidable spurs of the Rocky Mountains—the Jemez range far
to the west, the Sangre de Cristo nearer on the east. To the north
lie other ranges, hidden from the plain by intricately eroded
foothills.

Vision receives it all with a sense of new power. The earth
seems near to the heavens, and in the light of sun, moon or stars,
even its distant features can be discerned strangely well—by
night, in all their flowing contours, by day in all their color. Blue
of mountains, rosy exposed soil, silver greens of desert growth,
transparent stains cast by high-sailing clouds, sharp dottings of
evergreen shrubs and trees, yellow fields of summer sunflowers,
bright-shadowed snow of winter—all stand forth against the brilliant open sky.

Using real traditions, events, and many real persons, I have wanted to bring alive the historical realities of the past rather in the way of the documentary film, in which we see true experience over the shoulder, as it were, of a protagonist who is also a participant with whom the reader may identify himself. In order to make this process of identification more inviting, I have kept each of my protagonists anonymous. But each, as a composite character, is as typical of his period as I could make him, and his experiences are suggested in every case by historical records and archives where in evocative power rest so many fragments of past lives. To my observers I have ascribed many views which appear as direct quotations. In a given case, while such quotations may not always come from a single source identifiable with my individual observer, they are all drawn from historical sources of the appropriate period. As my character is composite, so too is the nature of his quoted remarks or opinions. On the other hand, where an historical individual is identified by name, all actions and direct quotations attributed to him are his alone, and are transcribed from true sources.

To such elements of personality and experience out of other times I add my own impressions of Santa Fe acquired since 1915. As to its form, the result might be called a sequence of historical sketches.

I acknowledge with gratitude the generous help I have had from many other students of my subject, and from custodians of its material in libraries and museums.

First I must name with warm respect the late Mr. Nicholas Wreden, under whose editorship I accepted the assignment to describe the society of Santa Fe, and with whom the design and method of the book were determined upon. It was his suggestion —which I followed—that I should enlarge and adapt the approach to historical life in Santa Fe demonstrated in my earlier, much smaller book of sketches called *From the Royal City*, long since out of print.

My thanks go to: the officers and staff members of the Museum of New Mexico at Santa Fe who gave me fullest access to the rich archives, records, and library collections in their care—Mr. Boas Long, director, Mr. Albert Ely, Dr. Arthur H. O. Anderson, Miss Rosita Roybal, Mrs. Albert Ely, former librarian, Miss Gertrude Hill, librarian, and Mrs. Corwin, Mrs. McManaman, and Miss Rambo, of her staff; Mr. Donald Gallup, curator of American literature, Mr. Archibald Hanna, custodian of the Western Americana collections, and Mr. Robert F. Metzdorf, curator of manuscripts, of the Yale University Library; Mr. Witter Bynner; Fray Angelico Chavez, OFM; Mr. J. Brinckerhoff Jackson; Mr. Robert Hunt; the library staff of the New Mexico Military Institute; and Mrs. E. Dana Johnson for the access she granted me to the photographs and other pictorial materials of Santa Fe assembled by her late husband, and Mr. John Gaw Meem for bringing these to my knowledge. A detailed record of my indebtedness to authors of both published and unpublished works may be seen in my bibliography.

P.H.

"Santa Fe . . . The residence of the Governour, and a pretty Garrison . . . And this hath no such Wonders in it, but what an easie Faith may give credit to. . . ."

—Peter Heylin, *Cosmography*, the Fourth Book, Part II, Containing the Cosmography and History of America, and all the Principal Kingdoms, Provinces, Seas, and Islands in it. A.D. 1666

THE CENTURIES OF SANTA FE

BOOK ONE:

UNDER SPAIN

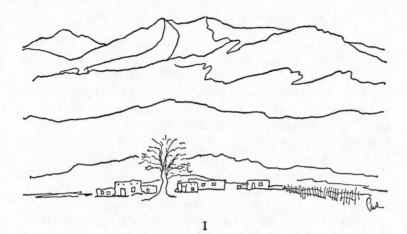

I

The Royal Notary: 1620

i.

WHEN WOULD HE see the city?

It lay, they said, at the base of those mountains which at sundown recalled the blood of Christ (he crossed himself). They rose up beyond the great plain over which he moved, now in an afternoon of late October in the year 1620.

Alone, he would have spurred his horse to ride swiftly toward the mountains until he should see the seat of the kingdom of New Mexico, the City of Santa Fe. Was it named for the original Santa Fe in Spain? He recalled how King Ferdinand and Queen Isabella had come to Granada to attack the last stronghold of the Moorish infidel, and had pitched their camp opposite to it, and had named their camp Santa Fe—Holy Faith. . . . A town had grown from it. He invoked both his memory and his imagination. As the New Mexican settlement was a Spanish city, the property of his lord King Philip III, perhaps, like Seville, it would show domes, or, like Segovia, towers, or, like Avila, fortress walls, or, like them all, palaces inscrutable with grilled windows and great paneled gates, and crowded market places, and deeply rutted streets where coaches rocked along almost touching houses on either side.

3

But he was not alone, for his pace was governed by the priggish walk of sheep. He was traveling from the City of Mexico with a dispatch and supply train of two-wheeled freight carts accompanied by a flock of sheep, a small herd of cattle, and extra strings of horses for the soldiers, the herders, the wagoners, and himself, the young Spanish gentleman who proposed to join the colony at Santa Fe. Checking both his impatience and his imagination he rode at a walk. This was wise for his horse's sake, for the train had just completed an exhausting climb over an escarpment called La Bajada. It had taken half a day for the company to wrack and haul their equipment up a rocky trail that doubled back and forth on the face of the escarpment until they came level on the plain of Santa Fe to see the mountains, if not the city, of their goal. The road was easier now. A sense of revived animation seemed to go through the other travelers now that the end of their journey of six months was near. The young gentleman asked whether they would reach the city before sundown, and was sorry to hear that they would not. But there was a waning moon, and the stars would actually shed light if the sky remained clear, and the drivers knew the way. They preferred to push on tonight, even if they must arrive late, rather than camp on the plain and come to their haven in the morning.

So darkness came before he could see any sign of the city. Where were its lights, then? he asked, and was told that there were no lights. Most people went to bed by firelight, and those who had candles, or Moorish lamps that burned oil, never burned them late, except perhaps for a secretary in the Government Palace working at papers, for tallow and oil were hard to come by, and must not be wasted. Such information made him thoughtful. A royal city, with a palace, that was yet so poor? A chill threaded along his bones. The night was suddenly cold. The starlight was icy. Ahead of him the dwindled moon was rising. In its waning, it seemed to take a portion of light out of his future, as he marched ahead into the impersonal darkness. Such travel seemed to penetrate only time, the passing hours of night.

And then—where had he been looking not to notice this?—the mountains seemed much nearer in their dark crouching bulk on the starry sky. Someone at the head of the train made a thin cry of news. There was a small river to ford. On the far right of the column as it began to cross the stream was a huddle of dim forms like earthen boxes. They were houses in a little group above the creek, the Santa Fe creek, and these were the first habitations of the city, asleep and silent and dark.

But from their shadows dogs came dancing forward to challenge the travelers. They sounded hostile in their duty. Across the creek there was at last something for the new colonist to see—rising above a level line of low roofs, a thread of smoke faintly lighted by its own invisible origin. The train wound across the creek and came among houses. At the end of a lane there was an opening, and now the firelight showed itself coming from a bonfire where a single sentry kept himself warm. His post was in front of a long, low building with blunt towers at each end. The train advanced from the lane into a great plaza formed by more buildings set out in a long rectangle.

The sentry came forward. The trainmaster spoke to him. The new colonist rode up to hear their exchange, which made him think of the sort of welcome barked by the dogs. There was, it appeared, nothing in the sentry's orders that governed the accommodation of a supply train arriving by night. On the other hand, it seemed to the trainmaster that when a supply train came once every two years, and took six months to do it, it must not very much matter what time of day or night it might arrive.

The Spanish mind illustrated itself in both points of view—the blindly official and the acidly practical.

The small conflict raised a further commotion beyond the sound of the train and its animals. People awoke in the houses and came forth. From the Government Palace behind the sentry an officer appeared, then soldiers. Someone threw logs on the fire to bring wafts of rosy light over the whole plaza and its throng of people and animals.

For some while the newest colonist was ignored, until the trainmaster thought to find him in the wavering shadows and bring him to the captain of the guard. Presently an Indian servant was told off to help him dispose his animals for the night, and then to lead him to a corner of a barrack room at one end of the palace where he might throw down a saddle blanket upon which to sleep. Soldiers of the guard slept all about him. The floor was earthen, hard, and cold. In the dark he saw a small square window of sky and stars. A bitter little wind came through cracks in its frame of mica panes, bearing a fragrance of burning pine from the sentry fire in the plaza. It was like incense. His mind moved to pray. Behind the phrases of his devotions which drifted absently on the surface of his thought, he recognized that his heart was heavy. He viewed as ominous all circumstances of his entry into the royal city of the north, where he had come to find amid towers and domes his fortune and found instead only himself, imprisoned in a mountain vacancy, at night, in the dark. Lying long awake though he ached for sleep, he took a measure of solemn comfort, not from the virtue, but from the familiarity, of who he was.

ii.

By all his twenty-seven years of life he was accustomed to the idea that he was a "son of somebody"—*hidalgo*. He was a native of the town of Zalamea de la Serena in Estremadura, in Spain, where his father, still living, was a provincial member of the minor nobility. He was not especially tall, but with his slim horseman's legs he seemed so, and he bore himself as though he were. He had a long, narrow head with lean cheeks and deep-set black eyes. His hair and beard were chestnut-colored with russet lights in them. He kept his beard trimmed close. He looked any age between twenty-five and forty-five. In repose his face looked sadly severe, and he rarely smiled, but when he laughed he did so rather harshly, with an air of surprise at himself for being moved to open expression of his feelings.

When he could, he ate enormously, but showed little fat as a result. His clothes sat well on him, and, if they were threadbare, they were made of the best materials. His hands were his finest feature. They were long, pale—for he went always gloved—and strong. They revealed his aptitude for hard labor, and also for the fine graces of penmanship, of which he believed himself a master by inclination and training.

At fifteen he was entered in the University of Salamanca, where he spent seven years reading in civil law, waiting to discover if he would find a career as a civil servant or as a priest. At the end of that time his father, unable after several seasons of extreme drought in Estremadura to pay his university fees, advised him to proceed to Madrid in search of employment and a wife. He became an agent of affairs, collecting small commissions through his ability to compose unreadable contracts for men of business, and presently he earned the title of royal notary, with a desk in a corner of a government office where he spent the day copying documents in his fine hand. The only women he met were familiars of taverns, none of whom he regarded as a "daughter of somebody." He was accordingly not moved to marry.

Though in his work he became so practiced that he did not have to read the sense of what he copied in order to produce accurate as well as beautiful pages, some of which he had reason to think went on up to be studied by the King himself, one day he read with his mind as well as with his eye the words on a certain requisition from the viceroy at Mexico City in New Spain. Among other needs, it asked the King for assignment to Mexico of six royal notaries to assist with the growing volume of secretarial work in the viceregal offices. Something stirred in him. It was like a vision. It was like a thrust of love in his breast. "Virgin America," it seemed to say, speaking to him as to a bridegroom. He must go to the Indies, like so many Spaniards before him. He was twenty-four when he made this discovery of his desire and applied for its fulfillment. Almost a year passed before the King approved the requisition designating those to be sent. The notary was appointed.

He sailed with the spring fleet in 1618 from the Guadalquivir at Seville. He knew the voyage would take three months. The fleets went twice a year in a regularly established commerce, meeting every danger before they landed at Veracruz. Discovering that there would be no chaplain on his ship—an important vessel nearly sixty feet long and in burden nearly one hundred ten tons—he took care to confess himself before sailing, vowing more earnestly than usual to keep himself in a state of sanctifying grace, in order to meet death properly if it should take him at sea. The world around him, though it was real, was not so terribly real to him as the world that awaited his soul after death. He thanked God for His mercy that He had provided him through His Divine Son Jesus Christ with the means to salvation in eternity. However much in his daily failings he might betray the Divine Love that was his by heritage and conviction, the notary was never forgetful in even the smallest act that he was the master of choice between good and evil, under a system of faith that explained, evaluated, and composed all life, natural and supernatural. Under its terms, no matter what might befall him, he would never be in doubt about the design of the world and his place in it. It was a tremendous possession, and he held it in common with everyone he knew.

The ocean voyage called for patience and ingenuity on the part of all on board. The ship was crowded. Its quarters below decks stank with foul air. The planking overhead was too close to permit anyone to stand fully erect. Rats and vermin abounded. Most passengers brought stores of food for themselves—cheese, hard biscuits, salted beef, a little olive oil and wine. On stormy days all were forced to remain below, while the ship's timbers made wracking sounds, and the carved, gilded castle at the stern shuddered visibly under stress, and the rigging sighed in the wind. On fine days, diversions sprang up on deck—mock bullfights, real cockfights so long as game chickens remained uneaten, recitations, and improvised theatricals. The notary knew a poem and was called upon to give it on many occasions. In a spell of calm, when the vessel drifted, men and boys went overside for a swim. When he had nothing else to do, the royal notary settled down to read one or the other of two books he had bought at second hand. One was a compilation of lives of the saints, the other a tale of chivalrous adventure, both printed in the previous century by Jacob Cromberger and Sons, of Seville. And then at last there were shore birds, and new scents upon the wind, and the green edge of New Spain, which extended as far as the eye could see and farther than the mind could know.

A civil servant of the Crown, the royal notary received preferred treatment in his journey from the coast to the City of Mexico. Once there, he found himself only another clerk in another dim office in a stone palace. Now he copied papers dealing with colonial affairs that were to be forwarded to the Council of the Indies at home in Madrid. Because these were matters new to him, he read as he copied, and was dismayed to discover how many of them conveyed distressing news—news of poverty, of continuous warfare with natives, of bitter argument between officers of government and colonists and ecclesiastical authorities, and of critical need for money, food, domestic animals, arms, ammunition, clothing, families, soldiers, and priests, for all of which His Most Catholic Majesty was repeatedly petitioned by the governors and captains general of not one but many provinces and colonial kingdoms of New Spain. New Mexico was among these. Where was the wealth of the Indies, that was supposed to flow homeward in a golden stream?

The royal notary found it hard to say. How unflattering it was to his own intelligence to admit that he had expected rather more of the new world. In the City of Mexico he found only a lesser Madrid activated by the same official duties, the same rigid restrictions, the same formalities as at home. Where was the grand continent, like an Amazon, waiting to be taken in passion until it should return to him great wealth with which to redeem his father's fortunes and to bring the royal notary himself a great position, and perhaps, before a pious end, the style of marquis . . . ?

There were perhaps five thousand Spaniards in the vice-regal capital, and among them he found a handful of companions from whom he gradually acquired the habits of license. Though gambling was forbidden, he discovered how and where to gamble. In the dark earthen streets at night he became a roisterer, free with his banter, his temper, and the sword which like all men he habitually wore. There were scrapes and warnings, homilies from his confessor, an icy official reproof from his superior in the secretarial bureau where he earned his salary of maravedis. His case was familiar enough to the more experienced civil servants under the viceroy, who had seen generations of youths come out from Spain, some of whom seemed to change their natures in the colonies.

Finally, to avoid indictment for the unruly behavior which kindness must attribute to released animal spirits and severity to latent criminal tendencies, the royal notary was advised to take his choice between military service against Indians in the Philippine Islands and appointment to the staff of the governor of the kingdom of New Mexico, at Santa Fe. If neither assignment carried lasting opprobrium, both were frankly disciplinary, as measures of further education for a career in the royal service.

He chose Santa Fe. The journey of half a year which took him there gave him opportunity for long thoughts. Many a young man before him had been a fool, but he took small comfort from the observation. With a sort of bitter energy he met the hardships of the crawling journey, feeling that by his endurance he was in a sense expiating the weakness of character he had displayed in Mexico. The journey hardened him in body and mind. He was secretly proud that in the land he crossed and the kingdom where he would live every able-bodied man had to be a soldier.

In the single cottonwood cart which had been assigned

to him in the wagon train he carried a suit of full armor
which he had bought cheaply from a man his size who had
lately returned from the frontiers in Yucatan. It included
a coat of chain mail, a casque with beaver, a padded
chamois jacket, a pair of cuisses to cover his thighs, a pair
of daggers, and a caparison with armor for his favorite
horse. On the trail he carried a harquebus, a pair of daggers,
and his sword. His best clothes were packed in the cart.
For travel he wore a wide-brimmed hat of bottle-green felt,
pinned up with three white plumes; a doublet of brown
felt, slashed and padded; a voluminous shirt of white Hol-
land linen; leather trunks and codpiece, laced with silver
threaded thongs; thick worsted hose of chocolate brown
striped with black; and hip boots of black cordovan leather
that hugged his thighs when he rode, and, when he walked,
were richly crushed down to his calves. His spurs were new,
of heavy silver and brass, chased with meaningless designs.
Over all this he threw a cloak of French broadcloth, wine
red in color, and lined with blue velvet. It was his garment
by day, his coverlet by night.

Sometimes as he fell asleep on his journey or as on his
first night in Santa Fe, the great new land would wheel
past his half-dreaming vision in a succession of sun-toasted
deserts, and vapor-blue mountains, and little green thread-
ings of water courses with trees; and he would think of
Spain, for the kingdoms of New Spain and New Mexico,
however strange their ways, resembled his fatherland, but
an endless Spain, as the new kingdoms were so vastly greater
in size. Endless Spain—as he was a small, living part of it,
so it was his all in terms of his life in the world.

iii.

When he awoke the next morning he dreaded to open his
eyes for fear of what he must see, the sight of this forgotten
village which would surely be the grave of his ambition.
But when at last he came out to confront his destiny he was
pierced by his first breaths of the mountain air, and he
was shaken by his first vision of the land about him. The

light was like that in a diamond. It sparkled along the trees of the creek bed. Foothills rising away from the city were pale rosy tan. Beyond them the mountains by which last night he had been imprisoned were now great screens of airy blue. A fleeting sense of well-being struck deeply into him.

He went to the corral beyond the palace to see to his horses. His Indian servant of the night before, a small young man wrapped in a white cotton blanket, greeted him, saying in Spanish,

"Saturday, Sunday, Monday."

"What?"

"Thursday, Wednesday," added the Indian, and fell silent, having used all his European words. The royal notary laughed. After they fed the horses, he gave the Indian a small bronze coin—a mistake he would never make again, for before the morning was over he discovered that in Santa Fe hardly any money circulated among the Spaniards, and certainly none ever reached the Indians.

He learned much else. At the palace the governor received him in an earthen room hung with skins and native blankets, and kept him standing while he read the papers that included his orders of appointment. There was a feeling of the court about the interview, even in this clay palace, so sparely furnished, and so thinly guarded. But the governor and even the notary in his own humble place in the royal service carried their state within them, and as representatives of the Crown they could display ceremony in their manners, no matter where. Before dismissing him to his duties, which would be executed at a narrow table in a room two doors away, the governor, expecting and so receiving no comments, made a few remarks of information about the kingdom of New Mexico over which he reigned.

There was only one Spanish city—the city of Santa Fe. It contained about fifty families, of whom most of the males were soldiers. Their military duties were twofold—to defend the colony and its Crown establishment in the governor's person, and to defend the peaceable Pueblo Indians who

lived in terraced towns against attacks by several other Indian
nations whose fighters came in roving bands mounted on
little prairie horses. These horses, it appeared, were descendants of those animals stolen eighty years ago from the
Spanish soldiers under General Francisco Vásquez de Coronado—the conqueror who had abandoned New Mexico in
1542 after two years' residence on the Rio Grande del Norte.
There were two views about how to control the raiding
Indians.

One was set forth in a direct command of the King re-
quiring that, if any conquest of them was undertaken, it
must be performed not by soldiers and colonists but by
Franciscan friars, who must go alone to convert them. This
royal order dated from over twenty years ago.

The other view was that of the governor and the colonists
—that only punishment by military means could be effective.
With so few soldiers, however, this course presented difficulties. Again and again Santa Fe had asked for reinforcements, but neither Mexico City nor Madrid could visualize
the realities so far away, and no substantial aid had ever
come.

In consequence, as could be imagined—the governor spoke
the tongue of all governments—there was some doubt in
terms of policy "as to whether the colony of New Mexico
should, or, in fact, could, be maintained." Many residents
were eager to abandon it. It was maintained for one reason
alone, and, if the royal notary thought this was to sustain
the prestige of the Crown, he was wrong. The reason was
this: that since the settlements in 1598, great numbers of
Pueblo Indians had been converted and baptized, and they
could not now be deserted. So the friars remained at their
missions in the scattered Indian cities, and the garrison at
Santa Fe remained to protect them. To mollify disaffected
colonists, all had been officially granted the use of Indian
labor and produce, receiving of course no money, but only
equivalent values in corn and woven cloths. If this was
"unpromising," it was nevertheless, said the governor, the
fact.

As for the city itself, the newly arrived notary would soon see that it consisted of two groups of dwellings. One was formally laid out in relation to the plaza, of which the palace was the most prominent feature. All was "proper and convenient," the houses square, all standing in line or at right angles to one another, and most enclosing their own patios. Each householder had his fields assigned to him for cultivation. Water was drawn through ditches from the creek. It was odd, said the governor: the Moors had always irrigated so, and the Spaniards at home, but here the Indians in their Rio Grande towns did the same thing. But to continue—the other group of dwellings lay across the creek, where lived the Mexican Indians who served the Spaniards as expeditioners, carters, and the like. They had their own chapel, dedicated to Saint Michael. The rest of the people went to mass in the parish church dedicated to Our Lady of the Assumption at the east end of the plaza. It was a poor church, rather like a large *jacal.* One day the parish would have to build a better one—assuming that the city would be able to maintain itself.

It would be in many ways a pity to abandon it, for it stood upon a beautiful site, as the notary may have noticed. It had, evidently, long been regarded as a desirable site, for when the city was laid out in 1610 the early settlers found walls of earlier Indian towns still standing right there. Indeed, some walls, though parts of ruins, were in such good repair that when this very palace was built, they were made use of as they stood. Of course, everything was built of adobes, and it was one of the most curious things in a most curious land that such material should weather so well and last so long. Some attribute of the climate must be responsible. If the governor might be permitted an irony, perhaps that very climate was the most—if not the only—useful discovery yet made in the natural features of that land where so much else had been expected, if not promised.

But it was a vast land, and the notary might be served if he had some notion of its cosmography. Having traveled north from the City of Mexico he must know by his own observation how things lay in New Spain. Farther to the north beyond Santa Fe, how far none could say with any precision, lay the North Sea, by which Tartary could be reached. To the east were the limitless plains of the cattle, where, according to Indians who turned out to be liars, were reported huge cities filled with gold and a river like a flowing lake on which a native king voyaged in a vessel bearing a gold prow. Florida, said the governor, lay just beyond. Going westward from Santa Fe you would come to the South Sea, opposite Cathay and India. To reach the harbors on the west coast of New Mexico, where you would find Indians called the Californios, you had to march for weeks. Still, commerce with China might develop like that between New Spain and the Philippines, and, after all, the first governor of the kingdom of New Mexico had had a royal contract permitting him to bring two ships a year to his own New Mexican seaports, if he could establish these.

In the western marches many extraordinary matters had been reported to a friar by Indians a few years ago. The governor seasoned such reports with a grain of salt, for perhaps two reasons. One was that Indians were really the most elusive creatures when you tried to find out anything from them—they seemed to tell you what they thought you wanted to hear, rather than the flat fact. The other was that friars had their own devices, and—the notary was astonished at the impious tone of the governor—any civil officer who paid them much heed was a fool. Half the time friars behaved less like Spaniards than like Indians, whom they spoiled with all sorts of unrealistic attentions and favors, as though Indians were actually worthy of civil privileges equal to those of the colonists. Anyhow, to get back to the marvels in the west—there were supposed to be natives whose ears dragged on the ground, and others who had only one foot, and others who slept under water, and others who slept in trees, and others who fed only on the smell of food, and others who were ruled by a pair of giant Amazon sisters, and others whose male members were long enough to wrap four times around the body.

All of it sounded like the sort of courteous rubbish often conveyed by Indians, and, on hearing such things, the viceroy the Marquis of Montesclaros wrote to the King, saying, "This conquest is becoming a fairy tale. If those who write the reports imagine," he wrote, "that they are believed by those who read them, they are much mistaken. Less substance is being revealed every day." Still, who knew? If the stories had never been proved, neither had they been disproved. The royal city of Santa Fe had its being at the very center of an immense wilderness, and any Spaniard knew from the experience of his own countrymen in the Indies during the past hundred years that any wilderness might contain anything, even to great wealth. . . .

The young notary gravely bowed his head before this reference to a dream that was as strong as faith. The governor descended to practical affairs, saying that he had arranged for the notary to be domiciled in a small but adequate room in the house of the royal constable of Santa Fe, who had a wife, two grown sons on duty with the garrison company, and a daughter who though recently come of age was unmarried owing to the discouraging fact that for several years past no new recruitments had been sent to Santa Fe by the Crown, despite great needs as repeatedly set forth in dispatches originating in this palace.

iv.

Because he was someone new to talk to, the royal notary found himself a success in Santa Fe. His landlord, the royal constable, a short, heavy man with an air of puzzled curiosity like that of a gray bear, spent hours trying to dispel the young man's bewilderment over circumstances in the northern capital. He went about this by describing how much better affairs were here than they had been in New Mexico's earlier capitals—San Juan de los Caballeros, and San Gabriel, on opposite banks of the Rio Grande north of Santa Fe. He knew. He had come with Oñate, the first captain general, in 1598, and he had endured all events of the colony since.

He told about the profitless explorations of Oñate to the east and west, and the disappointment of many of the settlers who, remarked the captain general, were enraged "at not finding bars of silver on the ground right away." From the very beginning, hunger and poverty prevailed. The constable was reminded of an epigram by the Count of Monterrey, an early viceroy, who said, "In the Indies no one is content with only food and clothing." He sighed. That was like Spaniards, he must admit. But, even so, it was hard to come to find fortune and to find—corn. "Here corn is God," remarked a friar at San Gabriel, and added, "Any Spaniard who gets his fill of tortillas here feels as if he has obtained a grant of nobility."

The constable recalled two years of terrible drought in 1600 and 1601. Someone said a year's cycle there was like "eight months of hell and four months of winter." The only people who had any food stored up were the town Indians. Colonists asked for it and, when the Indians objected, took it anyway, even though it was the seed corn that was taken. They were all eating the very future. The notary would not be able to imagine how nearly the colony was abandoned—in fact, a large party of settlers did run away home to New Spain while the captain general was off on one of his footless treasure hunts. There were wars with Indian towns, and Oñate was hated by half his kingdom, and a spokesman for many of the Spaniards said they were "all depressed, cowed, frightened, expecting death at any moment." The constable was one who stood by the captain general, thinking he was doing the best he could under poor opportunities.

Neither the King nor the viceroy sent any relief, and one day a paper came by courier deposing Oñate. As it came from the King's viceroy, and spoke for the Crown, the disgraced captain general had to accept it. He placed the royal order upon his head to signify that he came under it and would obey. Presently there was a new governor who arrived with orders to remove the capital from the Rio Grande to a proper new site. In 1610—ten years ago—Santa Fe was founded on the rubble of abandoned Indian settlements. Everything had to be built. This meant that all were busy, and in that resided a measure of content. The royal provisions for the placement, layout, and facilities of a colonial city were scrupulously fulfilled. Heads of families were granted land for house and field which, after four years of continuous occupancy, would become wholly their property. If the royal notary should ever undertake to found a family, he would be eligible for such property ownership.

It was a matter to which the young civil servant had given thought. When he had been sent out of Mexico City he had received no indication of how long he must serve in exile before returning for greater official preferments. Now and then he wondered if after all the Philippines might not have been a better choice. But there was that about his work in the clay palace which he found satisfying. What was it. Was it that he was left alone at his tasks, where before, in Madrid and in the viceregal city, he had been one of a swarm of clerks, all closely supervised? Perhaps it was that as a son of a noble gentleman he used to burn with secret chagrin at how little he could afford to maintain a public state suitable to his heredity, and now, in this little mountain city where nobody had lights after dark, there was little object in putting on airs. Others in the colony were the sons and daughters "of somebody," and yet they seemed content here merely to adore God, love their families, face danger, and breathe the crystalline air. The royal constable also was an hidalgo, and his daughter, so lately a child, commanded the graces and manners of ladyship.

She was sixteen years old. Her small, delicate head was full of memories of this new land at its hardest, for she had been born in the river capital of San Gabriel. She was six years old when the colony moved to found Santa Fe. The young notary sometimes gazed at her in wonderment. She had never seen Madrid, or even the City of Mexico, and yet, when on feast days she appeared in the heavy silks and velvets of state dresses made over from magnificent clothing brought here long ago by her mother, she was a proud little figure, enclosed in a miniature formality that made him kindle secretly with sweetness and amusement. He was permitted to see her when all the family assembled for occasions and kindly invited him to join them. Sometimes he knelt and stood beside her at mass in the *jacal* church. When she bent her head and shut her eyes and tightened her folded hands in piety, he watched her from the corner of his sight and, as her lips moved in framing words of prayer, he could imagine how they might shape other words that increasingly he longed to hear her say to him. What if some day she should be a wife, and give children to the world—his wife, and his children? His heart grew in him at the thought of joy and of sorrow such as came to all in time. He would share both with her and save her from danger.

Lying awake one night at the end of the house in his small earthen room farthest from hers, his serious and thronging hopes yielded up a grandiose notion upon which he dwelled with pleasure. If he was Spain, she was the Indies. If he married her, he would be marrying the New World. It gave him satisfaction to have thought of such an idea, in which his own passion and the passion of his fatherland seemed to have common identity.

After a few days of memorizing what he would say, he asked the royal constable to receive him alone in order to permit him to make a certain declaration.

v.

Late in the winter of 1621 messengers came up to Santa Fe from the pueblo of Santo Domingo on the Galisteo Creek to say that a party of mounted Indians from the plains were pillaging and threatening all in the neighborhood. Help from the capital was needed. The governor promptly called a war council at the palace. A mounted squad was chosen to ride down the high plateaus to find the raiders. Among those going were the constable's two sons and his son-in-law, the royal notary.

They prepared carefully for the task, cleaning and oiling

their harquebuses, and sharpening their bladed weapons, and choosing their best horses on which they strapped padded cloth armor. The notary shook out his own suit of armor. He found that it fitted him more closely than he remembered. The comforts of married life had added to his weight, despite the hard bodily work he was still doing to build his house. Already he owned two rooms. In one of these he slept with his wife and their son, who was four months old. In the other his wife cooked and served meals, some of which they shared with invited guests when enough food had been saved up for occasions. In less than four years the property he had been granted would be his in perpetuity. If his wife was no stranger to the Kingdom of New Mexico, neither was his infant son. The notary found gratification in this.

The pursuit squad was to march early in the morning. Late in the afternoon before, he went to his office in the palace where he kept his feather pens, ink, and paper. Sitting at his desk he looked out of his deep window at the broad bare spaces of the plaza before the palace. There he projected many things to remember out of the past and many others to imagine for the future. Presently, as the daylight failed and before it should be altogether gone, he stirred himself and took up a pen. With it he wrote something on a page like limp cloth. It was the full name and address of his father in Zalamea de la Serena in Estremadura, who, so far as he knew, was still living. When the writing was dry, he folded the page and took it home. There, without comment, he handed it to his wife. She opened it, read what was written, and then looked at him, seeing with him one of the possibilities to which he had given long thought at the palace. Like a woman suddenly much older she bowed her head in the face of a duty that might need to be done.

Through a light stinging snow just after dawn the next day the squad rode away from the palace. All Santa Fe assembled to watch them go. The governor's Franciscan chaplain blessed the soldiers, all of whom had made their confessions, attended mass, and received the Holy Eucharist. A sharp sense of community passed through those who departed and those who stayed. The snow blew like curtains, now showing, now hiding, the mountains above Santa Fe. Soon the clang and creak of weapons and leather, the cupped walk of hooves on frozen ground were lost beyond thickened white air.

vi.

In four days the column returned, bringing a victory. The enemy was engaged on a plain to the east and, after a close encounter, was driven off. Many of the raiders were killed, and one soldier. He was the royal notary. He fell with an arrow deep in his side, and died of his wound the day after the battle. His body was brought to the capital by his brothers-in-law, and after a solemn requiem mass was buried in the floor of the parish church. There was a sense that, if his life had been brief, yet it was complete, in the terms of his place and time. The church bell—it was bell song above all other attributes that made Santa Fe a Spanish city —the bell tolled for him in the thin mountain air which he had breathed at times with conscious well-being. His exile was ended, for he was now in honor a part of the land where he had been sent to redeem himself.

II

The Father President: 1635

i.

WHENEVER the old father president of all the Franciscans and their missions in New Mexico thought of the idea of "spring," he did not think of a time of year, but of a time in his life—his youth. Newly ordained as a friar in Spain, he had come to the City of Mexico, and then to Santa Fe in 1635 as a missioner. If he then saw the country as dry, stony, and vacant, he bore within him all the green and flowering certainties of growth, the seeds of a new life that he would plant in the desert wastes of the Indian soul, to the honor and glory of the two majesties that governed him. These were his Divine Lord in Heaven and his royal lord King Philip IV of Spain. In his enthusiasm and inexperience the young friar believed that these two majesties were by nature indivisible. He set out to serve them with his whole being, adoring the One and revering the other.

If his convictions which he held so strongly gave him great firmness of character, he was saved from hardness of mind by a vein of comic irony that ran through his temperament and made him a good companion, whether to Spaniard or Indian. He was one of those whose views were often quoted by others to win arguments, and whose drolleries were repeated by less original men who did not always mention their source. Any reminder of him brought up his image.

He was of medium height, stockily built, quick and darting in movement, and, when still, quivering in fixed alertness like a jack rabbit. His hair was prematurely iron gray. Wiry black eyebrows curved upward above his brilliant gray eyes. Through his stubby pepper and salt mustache and beard gleamed his prominent upper teeth. Always showing, they seemed to give extra wit or force to the notions he was never at a loss to make articulate. The voluminous blue-gray cloth of his Franciscan habit was always awry, twisted against itself by the energy of his limbs. When he walked his rapid steps caused a bobbing motion. He could always be picked out of a procession, for he moved like nobody else. He spoke, read, and wrote Spanish, Latin, and Italian, and he could read and write French and German, and it would not be long before he could talk to Indians in their own tongue. He seemed to know things without learning them, which made some of his religious brothers envy even as they admired him.

When he felt their envy he sobered his humor and displayed a begging interest in their concerns, that they might show their own best selves, which, he believed, all men deserved to do, under the dignity which God had put into human nature.

It was in such spirit that he approached his Indians, in the springtime of his faith and work.

ii.

His duty in 1635 took him first to the mission and pueblo of El Agua de Santo Domingo, on the Galisteo Creek a few leagues east of the Rio Grande del Norte, which was the ecclesiastical capital of the kingdom of New Mexico. There he saw a large terraced city of clay rooms, clustered rather like cells in a great hive, to which at one end was attached the recently built mission church with its convent, its holy burying ground, and its animal corrals.

When he asked why the headquarters of the religious province was not at Santa Fe, where the Crown's governor had his seat, he was told by the then father president that the more distance that separated the two authorities, the better.

No, how could this be? wondered the new missioner. All of life on earth was made in the image of Cross and Crown combined, the two majesties upon which mankind depended. They must not contend in strife.

Nevertheless, stated his superior, no priest could get along with any governor.

To the young man this sounded like simple bad temper based, probably, on too many years of troubled labor in a harsh land. His own experience would surely be different. He was aware that he had a gift for dealing with people. With a smile of affectionate respect he concealed his confidence from his embittered old superior, and listened with suppressed eagerness to his assignment. He was to go as pastor to an unconverted pueblo near the Rio Grande upriver. In a few days he left for Santa Fe in the company of a party of Christian Indians who took a cargo of corn and beans to be delivered as a portion of their annual tribute to the royal governor. There through the pastor of Santa Fe the missioner was to apply for an escort of soldiers to protect him against war parties of plains Indians on his march to his new parish.

If he expected a squad to be turned out for him offhand, he was mistaken. The pastor made application on his behalf at the palace for his soldiery, but nothing happened. When the young friar made inquiries, he was told to moderate his impatience until his request could be acted upon one way or another. Not quite concealing his surprise that there should be any question about his needs, and that the petition of a holy friar should be treated as a nuisance, he gave the interim to gathering an impression of the royal city.

Its recent history, he thought, was best reflected in its churches. In the first years of the colony, people had attended mass either in Saint Michael's chapel across the creek, or in the old parish church which was like a granary of upright posts and brush covering. But as the population grew, so did the need for a larger and more solidly built parish church. In 1627 this was built of adobes on the same site as the old one on the plaza. Now in 1635 Santa Fe counted 250 heads of families, of whom 100 were soldiers. With their kinfolk and servants they made a population of almost a thousand.

"The most important Spanish women" devoted themselves to the housekeeping of the parish church. They swept the clay floor, washed and stretched the altar linens, and gave special attention to the propriety of their greatest treasure. This was a statue of our Lady of the Holy Rosary, clothed in silk and rayed with a gilded glory about her head. She had come from Spain, like any other colonist, and in the shelter of those clay walls she spoke not only of Heaven but of the home kingdom, for her style was European. She was small, scarcely a yard tall, but her little oval face gleamed with a perfect complexion in polished bisque. Through her fixed dark eyes shone a message of innocence and love that would never change. Her presence seemed to uplift the world's life and make it visible for those who came to find the answer to all things in her rude chapel of dried mud. She had power. The resident pastor told the newcomer how the principal captains of an Apache nation, having heard of her from missionaries, came to Santa Fe to see her, and were at once converted, kissing her feet and saying proper words.

"Yes," remarked the new missioner, the establishment seemed complete, and he praised the ingenuity with which out of the humblest native materials all elements of the church had been contrived. "I shall make drawings and measurements here."

"Drawings?" asked the pastor.

"Yes, to guide me as I build my own church at my pueblo."

"Yes," said the pastor, "well, in any case, you will not have the benefit of a bishop's approval of your constructions, as we have no bishop nearer to us than five hundred leagues."

It was true, even though the Crown had been asked thirty years ago by Governor Oñate at San Juan to appoint a bishop for New Mexico. The petition had been renewed since, but without avail. Heaven only knew when it might be approved, sighed the pastor. It was possible, in his view, that recent governors had secretly opposed the appointment of a bishop, who might exert his power against them.

Again the missioner was struck by the hint of strife between the two majesties of Cross and Crown, and in the following weeks he came to think of himself as a victim of such contention, as his request for an armed escort received no attention. At last, having exhausted the resources of Santa Fe and his own eager patience, he one day filled a haversack with food and set out alone on foot for his new parish.

He was equipped with a conjectural map of his way drawn by the pastor of Santa Fe, who, having spoken of real and well-known hazards, let him go with a spoken blessing and one even more fervently made in the silence of his envious heart. What he envied were the confidence, the morninglike vitality, and the plain acceptance of the possibility of martyrdom that animated the younger man.

iii.

After several days of walking alone the young missioner came to a side valley with a shallow creekbed. He followed it rising upstream amid flattened hills of now rosy, now white earth. Late one afternoon he saw a flat hilltop stained by an ink-dark cloud shadow; and then the shadow was drawn aside by wind aloft, and he saw the pueblo on the hill's rim, and he nodded as if in recognition and hurried forward, thinking what a pleasure it would be to find other beings to talk to.

But when he stood near enough to see his people, there was nobody to be seen. The pueblo was inscrutable, without human sign. Slowly he went toward it, searching the rooftops where the entrances were, watching for a quiver along any of the tall poled ladders that stood up out of the interiors. Nothing stirred. He sank slowly to his knees, and then sat on his heels, rubbing his hands on his thighs. He was hungrily disappointed.

And then, suddenly, from behind a corner of the hive came a naked child in a tumbling run. It was a small girl. After her raced a thin gray dog. On seeing him they both stopped dead and stared. He sat still. They came a few steps nearer, and the dog began to snarl. The missioner put out his arms toward the two young animals. He said nothing, but smiled with his eyes brilliantly open.

Against their will, it seemed, the girl and the dog came to him. He picked up the child in his arms and spoke to her gently, in her very ear. The dog earnestly sniffed all about him, and then set its paw on his arm, and he patted it on the head. When next he looked toward the pueblo he saw the roof lines edged with men and women and other children, regarding him in silence. Bearing their child forward in his arms, he rose and went to them, and, coming down from their lofts, they received him impassively.

That night when he was to be fed a certain family asked him to their roof. He watched them prepare a dish. The ingredients were sand, corn meal, and two small field mice which they minced, fur and all. They then moistened the whole for stewing with the unmistakable contents of a night pot. As it cooked he thought of what he must do, and when it was placed before him as an act of deliberate offense, he threw back his sleeves, took up his stew, and ate it, nodding pleasantly.

For he thought that he must either eat it now and have done with it for good, or eat the meaning of such challenging hostility every day in many other ways, for as long as he should remain—and he intended to remain.

The Indians asked him in gestures how he could eat such filth, and he replied that for "a good appetite there is no bad bread." They gazed at him. A child trusted him, and a dog, and he did not sicken at eating ordure. He had passed certain tests, then, and beyond these, he could smile into their eyes with a perfect humanity unafraid. He remembered, even then, how earlier Franciscans had been struck to death, and how "Indians crushed the heads of three of these and ate them as fricassée, as it was said."

He asked where he might sleep, and was taken to the deepest cell of the hive. They pulled away his ladder and left him alone. During the night drums rumbled softly, and discussions were held, but he heard only the first sounds of such fateful mutterings. If they came to look at him in the night, he did not know it. In the morning he called for his ladder, and they brought it, lowering it to him. He thanked them, and came up, and symbolically embraced them all in a gesture of wide-flung arms. He then asked them to do as he did, and knelt down on the roof.

"Kneel with me," he said several times, smiling and blinking both eyes, until one by one they did so. Something shone out of him, some trapped, yet freed, sunlight. "Now," he said, and made the sign of the cross upon himself, slowly showing them how, until their right hands moved from brow to heart, and from shoulder to shoulder. His delight at their agreement was so joyful that they felt like creators of a fine spirit. That was something to which they could give respect. None of this came to him as a surprise, for he knew that the grace of God must work; but he admitted that he was gratified. For his breakfast then he was given long strips of dried melon, and shreds of dried meat heated in smoke that gave savor, and scorching hot thin cakes of corn meal. Again they watched him eat, and when he sighed heavenwards at such good fare, they hung their heads to conceal their satisfaction.

The only essential thing left for him to do, then, was to convince them that he wanted nothing of them but their souls, and those not for himself, but for the one God from Whom they came. Accordingly, his next acts were acts of work, in which he labored as hard as they.

iv.

After the first exasperating yet comic weeks of learning to communicate with each other, the missioner and his people found time flying. No day seemed long enough to enclose all the tasks they met.

The hardest of these was to teach, on the one hand, and on the other, to listen. How should he manage? Perhaps if he said that God was the whole sky and all the earth, then Jesus Christ His Son was like a star, the brightest of all, among the stars of heaven, and among men, like any man, but the best of them. And then it would be necessary to modify all that, and remove misunderstanding, for his pupils too easily decided that Jesus was not *like* a star, but *was* a star, at the same time that He was *like* a man, but *was not* a man. . . .

It was easier to work at making adobes, bricks out of earth, with which to make a church. For months the long piled rows of these grew till there seemed to be enough. Then with a party of men the missioner went to Santa Fe and Santo Domingo to bring back tools, and instruments of measurements, and sacred vessels, and a set of vestments, and holy oil and wine, and candles, and a missal, and a crucifix, and a bell for his bell tower. Next they went to the mountains thirty miles away for timber large enough to support a roof. He showed them with his drawings of the Santa Fe church how these would look when placed, and, after many more months, there they were, high overhead, and for the first time his drawings had meaning for the builders.

His daily lessons were many, and they understood how everything else they worked at was tied in meaning to the making and use of their church. He held up a piece of Indian pottery and then indicated the mission chapel, and said that together they were all shaping with clay a new vessel. The gesture delighted them, and gave him an idea for a happy detail. Choosing the best potters from among the women he asked them to go within the church and paint the walls with designs like those on their pots— corn leaves, birds, lightning, clouds, all touched alive with the repeated symbol of the cross, with which they were now familiar.

He thought the church looked like a coffin, narrow at the head, wider at the elbows, and slim again at the foot. But this was his private fancy, and when he was ready for his first mass, and the fresh clay room was decked with boughs of pine and starred with the still flames of candles, he knew it was a true container of life, and he thought his people knew it too.

The jobs never seemed to end. He worked fields with the Indians, planting and irrigating. He procured a few sheep, a small herd of cattle, some horses, and taught their care and breeding. He trained a group of children to sing —in Latin—and presently had a choir for the responses in the sung mass. When the children showed him how to imitate the songs of birds by blowing through hollow straws into little bowls of water, he let them make bird song as an act of worship during the Consecration at the mass. He appointed a sacristan who learned to ring the tower bell for all occasions. Spain rang out over the valley, and New Spain came to pray, to study, to wonder. All was new, all was creative. It was a season of budding and promise. It was his springtime.

During his years of residence with the Indians, he often reviewed notions about them long debated by Spaniards. For more than a century the question had been asked,

"What is an Indian?" Was he a man? An animal? An intermediate species? A natural slave, such as Aristotle described? Was he capable of the faculty of reason? Such questions were argued for generations in courts of law and before ecclesiastical tribunals.

There were two sets of answers, as the missioner knew. One set, believed by the colonial conquerors and landowners and soldiers and governors, concluded that the Indian was a miserable creature, inferior by nature and degenerate in his ignorance, who existed only to serve his Spanish superiors. He could not read or write, he possessed no sense of property and did not even mine for gold, and his idolatries were obscene. He was a beast of burden and a source of work, that was all. Let him be used, therefore, to the advantage of his masters.

But the Crown, the law courts, and the Church held an opposite view. The Indian, they said, could be lifted up. What had Pope Paul III stated in his bull *Sublimis Deus* in 1537? With grand compassion he enunciated the doctrine that "the sublime God so loved the human race that . . . all are capable of receiving the doctrines of the faith. . . ." The Indians were truly men, elaborated the pontiff; they were not only able to understand the Catholic faith, but even desired exceedingly to receive it. The Pope commanded that "the said Indians and all other people who may later be discovered by Christians are by no means to be deprived of their liberty or the possession of their property, even though they be outside the faith of Jesus Christ; and that they may and should, freely and legitimately, enjoy their liberty and the possession of their property; nor should they be in any way enslaved; should the contrary happen it shall be null and void and of no effect. . . . The said Indians," concluded His Holiness, "and other peoples should be converted to the faith of Jesus Christ by preaching the word of God and by the example of good and holy living." It was under these terms that the missioner lived with his people.

Knowing them well, he became devoted to them. They

were peaceable. They governed themselves under an order
that seemed to be theirs by natural law. They cherished
their children and respected their old people. He considered them "the best infidel people" he knew. Yet since
to his satisfaction they were human beings, they were of
course capable of great error, and to this he did not shut
his eyes, but labored to bring them to goodness through
penitence and hope of salvation. He learned much about
their pagan practices, and saw that at the base of their
worship lay not love but fear. All objects and acts in
nature were propitiated out of fear by forms of worship
that must be allied to despair, for how could a tree, a stone, a
cloud, the sun, the moon, a clutch of turkey feathers, answer
prayer? He caught his breath in shame at some of the acts
he saw performed when the Indians danced in community
to call forth the powers of generation, whether out of the
sky and earth in costumed imitation of the acts of the
weather, or out of human loins in public, naked repetitions
of acts of lust.

It took him years to do so, but in the end he persuaded
them to desist from their seasonal enactments of dance
worship. Their fear was even greater, at first, for they
feared that if they ceased dancing for rain and corn, no
rain or corn would come. But when after some years they
saw that corn and rain returned after all under the laws
of Divine Providence, they abided under their new faith
and lived with ther pastor at peace. They saw that he asked
no more of them than of himself. They marveled. Was he
really a Spaniard? They touched him in the simplicity of
their uses of Christianity. Sometimes when they came to
confession he saw them carrying bits of string made from
yucca fiber with knots tied every so often. When he asked
what the knots were for, they told him that these represented
sins which they had made note of. "Of such was the Kingdom of Heaven. . . ."

v.

But if they were like children, obedient when led with
love, like children they were credulous only so long as

there was but one thing—not a choice of things—to believe.

It was just here, in this trait of the Indians, that the quarrel between the two majesties of Cross and Crown found its opportunity to erupt. For, as the missioner had done, so too had many other Franciscan friars done. Under their teachings the Indians were finding their way toward individual dignity. With the sense of that human attribute came a sense of justice—and injustice.

What the missioner taught would inevitably lead Indians to resist persecution by the Spanish colonists. If the civil majesty was to retain its sense of irresponsible privilege, then governors, captains, landowners must work their utmost to undo the work of the priesthood—not in matters of Christian dogma and faith, for to these they were bound like any men aware of the terrible stakes of heaven or hell, but in the simple, practical issue of fixing the Indian's allegiance. Since the Indian, despite papal pronouncements and crown laws, seemed to the lay colonists more animal than man, more beast of burden than vessel of soul, then why hesitate over questions of the Indian's salvation? The sooner he was returned to the unprivileged state in which he had been discovered, the better. If the friars chose to protect him, then so much the worse for the friars. What were they, after all; were they Spaniards, loyal to their own kind? or were they renegade servants of the Crown, more devoted to their apelike charges than to the conquerors?

The Spanish society of Santa Fe and all the kingdom was riven down the center by the opposed points of view of the two majesties—for the friars responded with wrathful vigor to the persecution of their pueblo peoples. In doing so they were furiously sustained by their conviction of carrying out divine law, with charity and mercy for the oppressed, in the face of those who made their own expedient policy to assure themselves a continuation of the earthly gains—the wretched, meager gains—to be wrung out of the New Mexican town Indians, through labor and tribute. It was war between Cross and Crown.

One day, after many years of work at his pueblo, the missioner was on his way back from a week at Santo Domingo where he had been summoned for certain fateful discussions with the father president. He traveled on a burro. He was now wholly white-bearded. His eye was as darting and compelling as ever, and his mind as full of humors and fancies; but he sometimes wondered what had become of the fluent expounder in Latin, Spanish, and Italian, the scholar of French and German, who had once inhabited him. If he still acted with as much energy as ever, perhaps now his powers were less scattered, perhaps now expressed through a narrower and deeper purpose.

This, he thought, was just as well, for at Santo Domingo he had just been vested with new work which would take all he could summon of hard purpose and will. In succession to his superior who was retiring for reasons of poor health and an incapacitating embitterment, he was about to assume the office of father president of the Franciscan province of New Mexico. As such he would be plunged into the very center of the struggle against the Crown governors and their followers who in exploiting the Indians were engaged too in attacking the friars. He was now going home to his pueblo to say good-by.

As he turned into his familiar and beloved valley he passed a mounted party of soldiers. They saluted him respectfully, asked his blessing, and rode on to Santa Fe with an air of accomplishment.

As he approached the pueblo he heard drums and singing voices, the beating cadences of the old massed dances, with all their terrible splendors and indulgence of outrage. His heart turned over. He hurried forward and soon he saw his children, most of them painted, feathered, quivering with strapped boughs of green pine, others capering naked and wild with shameful joy.

What had his years of hope come to?

He went to his small cell in the earthen cloister beside his church and knelt down to pray until at sundown the dancers ceased their pounding of the land and went to the creek to wash off their pigments and to cast away their branches. Then he went among them and asked why they had done that day's deed, and they told him that soldiers came from Santa Fe bringing orders from the governor which told them to resume their forbidden dances as they had longed to do for years. There was nothing wrong with the dances, said the soldiers. Moreover, if Indians did not want to sing at High Mass, they need not do so; and if they did not want to labor in the fields in order to fill the mission granary, they need not do that either.

Their lord was the governor, not the missioner. Let them forget that, said the soldiers, and see what would befall them. The soldiers had departed, taking all the grain their saddle bags could hold.

In such a homecoming the new father president found the measure of the enemy he must fight. He saw that he must no longer fight the war through a single battle in his old outlying field, but must lose no time in returning to Santo Domingo to fight it everywhere in the kingdom, with all the power of his new and heavy office.

When he turned to go early in the following morning, he left behind him all his sense of the inner springtime that had sustained him for so long. Another force arose in him to give him strength. It was cold rage, like the drive of winter.

vi.

Now by his new purpose the scholar in him was called alive again, after more than thirty years of hard physical labor at his mission outpost. He soon found again the exhilarating faculty of ripping across a page with his glance and grasping everything written there. Working in his cabinet at Santo Domingo he read copies of all the accumulated records left by his predecessors. He was appalled by the chronicle of misprision that came to light. Even under the first governor official abuses were committed, and had been continued without cease.

Such deeds as these were recorded against the governors

and their kind: when Indians concealed their small stock of corn in secret rooms, a governor had the walls torn down, and when an Indian protested, the governor himself knocked him off a roof, killing him; chieftains were tortured till they revealed where their little stores were hidden; Spaniards robbed Indians of everything in their houses until they ran away to the mountains, where they were beyond reach of conversion and persecution both, saying if Spaniards who were Christians caused so much harm and violence, "why should they become Christians?"

Spanish soldiers mistreated Indian women and "violated them often along the roads." In winter when all people were cold, soldiers for their own use pulled the blankets off the very backs of Indians, and the Indians, "finding themselves naked and miserable"—the father president exclaimed with anger as he read—"embraced their children tightly in their arms to warm and protect them, without making any resistance to the offenses done them, for they are an humble people, and in virtue and morality the best behaved thus far discovered." The father president nodded in homesick recognition, and read on.

A governor once fired with his horseman's wheel-lock pistol at a friar who had chided him for abusing Indians, missed his aim, and hit another friar and a civilian. A governor denied the highway to friars who wanted to send sheep, raised in their mission, to Mexico to be sold in order to purchase "ornaments, decorations for the church, and other necessities," and gave as his reason that "churches with decorations and costly ornaments were not necessary," and that "a few huts of straw and some cloth ornaments . . . were ample." A governor sent Indians to New Spain to be sold as slaves. Spanish landholders were permitted to move into Indian towns without the consent of the Indians. Governors, against royal edict, trafficked in the livestock trade, and sent Indians south to New Spain as herders with small chance that they would ever be able to return home. When a governor was murdered by a colonist with whose wife he had committed adultery, the friars were accused of complicity in the murder. Again and again governors set the Indians against the friars by authorizing them to practice their pagan idolatries. And more. And more.

 ˙ Through the years the father president wrote and wrote to his religious superiors and to the viceroy in the City of Mexico, describing scandal upon scandal. Driven by the vehemence of his thoughts he rode his chair like a horseman, while his pen clawed its furious way through his reports of outrages he had seen or heard of.

Thus, "from the most petty to the most damnable harassment, those native peoples and the sons of Saint Francis are persecuted without cease by the very powers who should be their protection," declared the father president, "and I state so for all who may read."

He took pleasure in making that remark, for he knew that more often than not his letters were opened and read by the lord in the palace, who had copies taken upon which to base later reprisals. The governor did not quite dare to destroy the father president's reports, but he usually took the opportunity to send by the same dispatch bag a report and counterattack of his own, attempting to invalidate dispatches from Santo Domingo. This was known to the father president who, for his part, had his friends in strategic positions whose task it was to open and copy the governor's papers and deliver the copies to him.

His unending stream of damning reports was one weapon of the father president in his war with the crown authority. His other weapon was more terrible, and each time before putting it to use he weighed the consequences with a shaken heart. It was the instrument of excommunication, by which he denied the sacraments to those officials and individuals whom he judged guilty of rejecting by their behavior the teaching and example of Jesus Christ. He knew what anguish such condemnation must cost those Spaniards upon whom he visited it. He was ready for the cries of misery that went up. They wrote about him to the viceroy, begging for relief and restoration to the grace of the sacraments and the mass through the recall of the father president and the appointment of some more amenable priest to succeed him. He withstood their appeals and required proof of reform before he would lift his bans, copies of which were posted on church doors throughout the kingdom. There for all to see would be hung the names of those who were forbidden to enter and seek salvation in Almighty God.

As the century drew into the 1670's, the father president saw signs of demoralization increasing all about him in the colonial kingdom. It was strange—as resources fell away, and the spirit of harmony seemed destroyed forever, and the land showed every hostility of climate and temper, the colonial population actually increased, until there were twenty-five hundred Spaniards living in Santa Fe and on their estate farms along the Great River. To see families so scattered was regrettable, for they were open to Indian raids, and, furthermore, it was the policy of the Crown that settlers should remain together and strengthen by their coherence the established capital at Santa Fe. But Spaniards were individualists, as the father president knew only too well, and persisted in living as far from one another as possible. How then could there be a real community of feeling and work and faith? All sorts of evil absurdities seemed to go through the society like shudders. In Santa Fe there were sorcerers and spell-casters. News came to the father president of how some of these were actually Indians, to whom Spaniards went for guidance, prophecy, and love spells. What a wretched spectacle—the superstitious natives governing the souls of abandoned Spaniards!

How hideous, thought the father president, to see some woman with a hopeless, love-stricken look in her face go to pay a secret visit in some crumbled patio—the walls of the palace itself were in very poor repair—a secret visit to an Indian witch so that he might swindle her with consoling lies wrapped about with some apparatus of abracadabra. And how ominous for the future, to see Indian doctors gaining such power, not only among misguided Spanish people, but among their own, through bad examples set by Spaniards.

For he saw plainly that the effect upon the Indians of the quarrels between the two great Spanish forms of life would be to destroy the Indain confidence in either. Once that happened, who knew what the result might be? In a hungry kingdom, with fewer than three thousand Spaniards who had lost their prestige, embedded in a wilderness really owned by more than thirty thousand natives, what could come but tragedy if the Indian ever seized the power that had been taken from him and attacked the faith that had been mocked in his face? To the father president it was like confirmation from the most august source when a certain event took place in Santa Fe in 1675, of which he received an immediate report.

A young daughter, hardly more than a child, of one of the Spanish residents was dying. All hope had been given up for her recovery. One day she was transformed by a vision that appeared to her. It was the Blessed Mother of God, who said to her that she must rise and be well again, for there was work for her to do. "My child," said the vision, "go and tell everyone that the kingdom will soon be destroyed because of the lack of reverence shown to my priests. . . ." The girl rose in full recovery and told what she had seen and heard. The father president came swiftly from Santo Domingo to interview her and test her story. He was convinced that she told the truth. He confronted the governor with his opinion. The news spread. Remorse swept the colony. A solemn mass was sung, and the governor ordered that all attacks upon the clergy must cease.

Further, he sent soldiers to all pueblos to arrest Indian medicine doctors, and to order all pagan dances and practices discontinued. The Indian doctors were brought to Santa Fe, imprisoned, and tried on charges of witchcraft. Three were hanged—"hanged," reported the father president sardonically, "for practicing that which the governors had previously ordered them, against the teachings of our fathers, to commit."

After this order, seventy Indians came from the river pueblos to protest, for, having been robbed of their Christianity, what had they left to cling to but their own animal rituals? They demanded the release of the surviving prisoners, which was granted to them. Among those who arranged for the release was an energetic Indian named Popé. There was reason to think he was a troublemaker. The Indians had put fear into the kingdom.

How much longer, wondered the father president, could the kingdom survive? Its needs were so many and so great —a rebirth of Christian faith, a supply of arms, and food, and a new complement of soldiery to protect the settlers, and a general sense of stronger support by and relation to the Crown. . . . He had written and written, banned and banned, yet the war was far from won. While he had strength, he must make one last effort to convince the higher authorities of how matters stood in the King's farthest colony. After forty years in New Mexico, he must hurry to Mexico City to tell his story in person.

vii.

In late life his skin was tightly leathered over the bones of his skull, modeling the wit of the death's-head that lay in hiding under his face and seemed like a hilarious confession of what people had always thought of him, especially in his young days. Behind that grin was something else, something that could afford to smile for its great righteousness. It was the power of one who intended to battle to the end for what he believed in, to which anyone or anything must be sacrificed.

On his journey southward the sense of hurry was only in his mind, for the journey must take many months, no matter how greatly he was animated by his own urgency. Once arrived in the City of Mexico, he encountered a grand indifference to the report he made, over and over, before one official after another, while files were consulted, and royal precedents were exhumed, and barren realities were exposed to the softening luxury of debate over policy. Try as he would, he could not make the viceroy's government really see the condition of the northern kingdom.

His last recourse was the Council of the Indies at Madrid.

Sending word back to Santo Domingo that his leave must extend itself for the best of reasons, he sailed for Spain. In Madrid he thumped on one after another of leather doors studded with brass nails and embossed with royal quarterings. In each office he was referred to another, or advised to submit a written statement, or asked to wait while the archives of the Indies were searched for the earlier reports he claimed to have written about the conditions he desired to discuss.

After almost two years of conscientious procrastination, the government heard his case in council, and at its conclusion asked him to read and certify the minutes made of their questions and his answers. This he did. That was all. He was then dismissed. Before he could leave Madrid on his return journey to his doomed kingdom, new duties were found for him in Spain by his Franciscan order. There were rumors that he might be consecrated a bishop. Let him remain to attend what might be decided for him.

It seemed to him the ultimate irony now as he was distracted by a new turn of his personal fate, when Santa Fe with its kingdom seemed so far away, its passions so reduced in gesture and hazed by forgetfulness, that in the end he could no longer feel them, but only recall them.

Once again the royal city of Santa Fe was victim of time and distance in the world, and he with it.

The father president could only pray for those whom he had left behind, and remember some of the sweets of that life—on the sky, a line of mountains rising and falling like the written melody of plain song; his Indian people at their best; the patient Spanish mothers who endured apart the strife of their husbands and sons; the world of the children so full of a private happiness; in the lost pueblo of his springtime a star that used to appear just above a certain one of his blossoming fruit trees as twilight deepened away.

III

The Bannerman: 1680

i.

IN THE ROSTER of the garrison of Santa Fe he was described in 1680.

". . . The bannerman [flag bearer] to the governor and captain general passed muster with his person, a sword, a dagger, a pair of horseman's flintlock pistols, twelve gentle horses, leather jacket and shield, and leather harness for carrying the royal standard; he having as distinguishing marks a tall and slender stature, long face, somewhat handsome, the scar of an arrow wound in the left—correction, right—side of his chin, thick eyebrows, pale blue eyes, fair complexion, broad shoulders, and is twenty-six years of age, married, with two children."

He read all that soon after it was written down, and for the first time owned an idea of himself which lifted in him a secret vanity. He hoped his little son, nine years old, would grow up to resemble him. He hoped the boy would find a career in a better place than this far kingdom where there seemed so few opportunities for a man of worth.

In the summer of 1680 Santa Fe was dry and hungry and poorly guarded. Soldiers rode out every day on the royal highway looking to the south for sight of the supply train, so long overdue, that must bring new troops, new cavalry horses, new weapons, new saddlery, and stores of food. In late July no sign had yet been seen of it. What if it should never come? The question reflected the sense of uncertainty that hung over the royal city and the whole colony with—so it seemed to the governor's bannerman—with the charged stillness before storm.

Yet a stillness not unbroken, for like thunder approaching from behind hills in summer heat came disturbing information out of Indian towns. The bannerman heard it discussed in palace councils.

Pagan dances were being performed in secret, though officially proscribed. Apache delegations were seen now and then in the pueblo towns of their traditional hereditary enemies, now not on errands of robbery but seemingly of friendship. The bannerman had fought Apaches, and knew that their friendship was more ominous than their enmity, of which he bore a sign on his chin. When soldiers went to pueblos to collect seasonal tribute for the governor and his people, the Indians as usual declared that there was nothing to give—such a statement as they made every year, but now with this difference, that it was true, and with this further difference, that they added in a spirit of empowered calm the statement that it was the turn of the Spaniards to yield up corn, beans, and cotton to the hungry children of the sun, as they called themselves. Almost everywhere Indians had quietly absented themselves from church. Perhaps all such behavior represented no more than the apathy of the dispossessed and hopeless.

Perhaps not.

The governor could take no chances. He resolved to anticipate the train, and, if it should never come, even so he would be ready with the most important of the supplies that it promised to bring. This was a recruitment of horses for the garrison. If none were obtained before winter, then, with his present exhausted and depleted bands, he would be unable as captain general to order troops out on protective or punitive missions throughout the kingdom.

With his council he reviewed the possibilities, and, as the bannerman agreed, came to the only realistic conclusion, which was that a purchase of fresh horses must be made from the Yuta Indians north of Taos—the only horse Indians with whom the kingdom was at peace.

A question was raised—was it known that the Yuta people had horses to sell? If not, what a waste, what a risk, to send an expedition all that way out of sight and knowledge just to encounter disappointment!

The governor explained that it was his plan to send a scouting party—perhaps just one man—to make inquiries of the Yutas, and report back to Santa Fe whether a purchase was in fact possible, and at what price. All that remained was to designate the scout.

Though not a member of the council, the governor's bannerman usually accompanied his chief in all official gatherings, whether with banner or without; and now he asked permission to propose himself for the duty of riding out to the Yuta country for the purpose discussed. He would be glad to go just now, for his wife desired to pay a visit to her brother, who occupied one of the small farms near the pueblos of Taos. She had not seen her brother for four years, as the journey of seventy-five miles, much of it in the awesome canyon of the Rio Grande del Norte, was so arduous. He would like to bring his wife, daughter, and son to Taos, and, there leaving the females, he would take his boy with him north to the Yutas. It would be splendid experience for the son, and good company for the father. They would take spare horses with them. On the return journey, he would pause at Taos to greet his brother-in-law, perhaps to spend the night, and then return swiftly to Santa Fe, bringing home his wife and children. In further elucidation of his request, the bannerman reminded the governor that for the next two weeks no official ceremonies were scheduled; the royal standard would not be unsheathed; the bannerman would be missing no duties if he went away.

After a brief discussion—he was to leave early the next day, and return with all reasonable dispatch—his request for the assignment was approved. His orders were drawn up, signed, witnessed, and dated the second day of August, 1680.

ii.

Ten days later, on Monday, August 12, he rode homeward out of the Yuta country above Taos with a feeling of satisfaction. His powers of courage and persuasion had never, he believed, shown themselves to better advantage. He was able to carry news to Santa Fe that all wanted to hear. In September the Yutas would drive a band of 100 horses to the capital, and would accept in return a nicely adjusted account of small folding knives with steel cases inlaid in ivory, a certain number of pounds of gold and silver bullion lace that would in the meantime have to be unsewed from Spanish garments in private possession, a quantity of selected seeds of edible vegetables, six hens and a cock, a measurement of powdered chocolate in bulk, and however many cotton blankets would be needed to reach the total payment—these blankets to be procured by levy upon Pueblo Indians.

The bannerman was particularly pleased that he had

settled the negotiations without yielding to repeated Yuta requests for firearms and ammunition as part of the purchase price. He replied again and again that the munitions of the kingdom belonged to the King of Spain, and no one else had authority to dispose of them.

The Yutas observed that many Pueblo Indians owned Spanish weapons—the harquebus, the horseman's pistol.

Yes, admitted the bannerman, but these had been obtained by theft or capture, not by grant. In all politeness—for he knew that the best of manners alone would succeed in peaceable dealings with those people—he could not approve further acquisition of firearms by Indians.

But were not the Yuta people at peace with the Spaniards? Did he not think it safe to grant them arms?

He smiled away the truth, and replied that the issue was otherwise, as he had stated, and furthermore, the Pueblos too were at peace with the Spaniards, and yet they had never been given the royal arms. At this a long silence descended, until he asked why.

Then at last a Yuta councilman answered him with another queston. Did he think, then, that the Pueblos actually were at peace with the Crown?

But mystery was an ordinary part of the Indian nature, and the bannerman and his companionable little son were untroubled as they rode through aisles of towering sunflowers down toward Taos. They crossed an immense plain to the southward through which the Great River cut a black gorge. When cloud shadows sailed on that plain, said the bannerman to his son, you could not tell which was cloud shadow and which was the distant cut of the gorge—they looked just the same. The boy peered to the west to see. There was nothing about the country that his father did not know. He nodded and looked at the bannerman, showing in his small brown face much of this confidence. Deeply pleased by his son's opinion, the bannerman scowled, at which the boy joined him in the game of soldierly fierceness, and squared himself in his own small saddle, and rode staring straight ahead like a pygmy conqueror.

They both saw an approaching figure at the same moment.

It was an Indian horseman rocking toward them at a long-distance canter. When he saw them he came down to a walk, and they approached one another in caution. But he was a naked Yuta with his bow slung, and they stopped to speak. The Yuta had no Spanish, but the bannerman, as he had happily proved in the north, could do well enough with signs. He had long known that, when men really wanted to communicate with one another, they could do so, given enough patience and purpose.

Be careful, said the Yuta in his own way.

Of what?

Of everything to the south, said the Yuta, making spacious movements in the air. In them the bannerman—even the boy—read terrible news.

In every pueblo the Indians had burst forth in war upon the Spanish priests and residents. The Spanish farms downriver were under attack. Santa Fe was to be destroyed. At Taos the colonial farms were besieged, the pueblo church was burning, and Spanish soldiers and priests and boys were being killed, and Spanish women and girls were being taken as slaves. The bannerman thought of his family at Taos. His belly went cold.

When had it started? he asked.

Yesterday. The Yuta had seen the revolt in Taos yesterday, and was hurrying to his own people to tell them what he knew. He swept his arm toward the north to say that the bannerman and his son would do well to return northward with him, for they would surely be lost if they went on into the Spanish kingdom. Not a Spaniard was to be spared, he said, for a Taos Indian had told him so.

Holy Mother of God, was the uprising then the result of a general plan?

Oh, yes, the Yutas had heard of it some time ago, and wondered at the simplicity of the Spaniards in not seeing signs of war under the false calm over the land.

The bannerman stripped off his long gloves with their

tarnished silver embroidery and threw them to the Yuta in thanks, and crying out to his boy, spurred forward toward Taos. In utmost hurry, they could not reach there till tomorrow. Oh, Holy Mother of God, he prayed, let us not be too late. Most Merciful Mother, show us mercy.

In the next noon he and his son came cautiously down through tall corn in fields north of the pueblos of Taos. Smoke stood alive in the air above ruins of the mission with its church and cloister. The colonial farms were to the west. The farm of his brother-in-law lay farthest from the pueblo. The bannerman led his son and their two spare horses around to it by a devious path. A shadow lay over the house—but no, not a shadow, the black that he saw was dead fire, the mark of smoke on adobes, the crow-feather satin of charred timber. All was quiet. He dismounted, commanding the boy to keep the horses and not approach. Then he entered the house of his brother-in-law and came upon the only mercy he could now hope for.

No captives had been taken.

His wife and small daughter lay on the packed earth floor before him. His wife gazed up at him with a tender look of pity and horror held in her eyes, as she had never gazed at him before. Her lips were fixed in the shape of the word "no." Near to her side his daughter lay like a child at play rigidly pretending to sleep. He could fancy her eyelids quivering. Both were dead. A little farther off were the bodies of his brother-in-law and all his people. They had defended the farm to death. The bannerman knelt down and covered his eyes. He tasted the scent of greasy smoke.

A thin, treble cry came from outside. It was the boy, calling him. Still with his eyes half covered he ran out of the house, given power by the urgency in his son's voice. Indians were coming on foot from the near pueblo to see who paused and dismounted at this wreck of a Spanish world. Taking his mount in a leap, the bannerman kicked his son's horse in the flank, and spurred his own, and they

rode wildly away from the other half of their family forever.

iii.

On Friday, three days later, they came with caution
through juniper bushes on the crest of a hill overlooking
Santa Fe from the north, and saw at once that their hopes
of joining the garrison were empty. The royal city was
spread out before them like a map whose structures and
contours cast shadows. From across the creek of Santa Fe
and from the ravines opening out of all the hills that circled
the capital north and east moved an array of sparkling
figures, jagged with feathers and lances like bristles, and
dark like the scrubby evergreens that clung everywhere to
the land. It was a force of twenty-five hundred Indians,
converging on the plaza. They went through every street
and around every house, choking all exits from the city.
They swarmed on rooftops making their death music. As
the loose lines at the rear closed into the streets and alleys,
those already there were thrust forward into the clear
space of the plaza, and suddenly they flowed forward like
a stain spreading on a map and surrounded the palace.
There on the roof edges were rows of men-at-arms. In the
main gateway to the south stood the pair of brass cannon
that were the garrison's pride. They were fired now, and
the bannerman and his son lifted their heads with excitement to see the battle joined. They saw small round clouds
of gunpowder smoke bloom in the air, and then break, and
drift into nothing, and then they heard distant sounds of
firearms like the breaking of pottery, as shots were exchanged between palace and plaza.

But not all Indians were before the palace. The boy
pulled his father's arm to make him look—there, by the
irrigation ditch that brought a silver line of water to run
to the palace wall and under and within, there worked a
band of Indians with square Spanish shovels. They were
breaking the ditch walls. In a moment the sun ran over the

ground with spreading water. The garrison was condemned
to thirst with this loss of their water supply. Soldiers broke
forth from the fortress to attack the Indians at the ditch
and were driven back. A heavy Indian guard remained
on the water line.

Now a clustering swarm of attackers clung about the
doors, the bases, of the parish church on the plaza. They
piled brush and dry weeds against woodwork. The bannerman and his son watched for the first wing of flame that
would fly up the walls, and when it came, releasing heavy
black smoke, they crossed themselves at the sorrowful profanation they witnessed. Even as the fire took hold, Indians
danced in and out of the church bringing sacred ornaments
and furniture and vessels, which they threw on the exterior
fires. Smoke searched for air and burst out of the high
windows, and began to thread its way through cracks in the
roof. Soon the whole church was like a monster in distress,
sucking great draughts into its maw and spewing them
forth through all its eyes and members. Houses nearby
were set to burning, and then others across the town, and
finally a line of Indians ran under the very shadow of
the palace to the little chapel at the end, bringing brush
and brands to its holy walls. But before these could be
set, soldiers came down off their parapets and attacked,
driving the Indians away. It was a task they had to repeat
all afternoon, as the enemy came again and again to destroy
the chapel. The watchers in the juniper clumps above the
city could only grip their hands and pray damnation on the
rebels.

When night came the palace was still secure, but all
through the dark in every quarter of Santa Fe the fires of
ruin were kept alight by little figures that sent wandlike
shadows sweeping over the ground. The wind brought a
ragged chorus over the hill all night long—voices of the
destroyers crying with the appetites and threats of the
wolf, the fox, the dog, the coyote, the eagle, and man.

On his hilltop the bannerman's son felt like a soldier
despite his nine years of age. His father, married at sixteen,

had begotten him while a soldier of the garrison on active duty. The child now bore within himself the seeds, too early, of the knowledge of death. He was too tired and hungry to cry for his mother and sister, even though he knew what had befallen them. When his father whispered that they would crawl, now, down the hillside toward the city in an effort to reach the palace wall, he was ready. They tethered their horses in a clump and started forward. But soon they saw below them that the general firelight was augmented by little campfires of scattered Indians. They would never be able to break through the great crescent of the enemy that enfolded the city in its wakeful arms. They returned to their hill. The boy fell asleep against his father's long leg.

The bannerman laid his hand over the small bony shoulder that breathed on his booted flesh, and resolved to take no more risks. If it was his official duty to reach the garrison and join the defense, he must yet protect above all the last life of his own blood. He watched all night and with dawn—for he was not a quick-minded man—he achieved the thought that what he most wanted now in the world was to quit this miserable kingdom and bring his son to safety in the provinces to the south, perhaps in the City of Mexico itself, which none of his family had ever seen.

Before the sun rose that morning, the attackers returned to the palace, fighting with stones, firearms, lances, and arrows. All morning they directed their fury toward the two brass fieldpieces. From the palace roofs the garrison— there were, as the bannerman knew, only a hundred men-at-arms among the whole population gathered within—drove off again and again with brave volleys the surges thrown forward by the Indians. The church on the plaza was still burning. In the afternoon the bannerman thought he recognized the governor on the palace, directing a sortie below to make another effort to regain the broken ditch. It was defeated, and, with it, the bannerman could realize the thirst that took the men and women, the children and animals, in the besieged royal house. His own canteens were empty of water, his saddlebags of food.

Under nightfall more fires sprang alive over the royal city, until "the whole villa became a torch," as he later said. Again the Indians sang, now in a wild mockery of the Latin mass. Even if the palace did not fall, the two soldiers on the hill could see no way to reach it; and if it fell, they must not linger nearby to be found and destroyed along with all its people. Under the darkness pungent with drifting smoke and mountain airs bearing the cool breath of pine forest, they felt their way at a walk far to the south around the royal city, and, once free of the battleground, rode as fast as starlight permitted until they dropped below Santa Fe plain near the bottoms of the Great River. Then they lost the halo of fire in the sky above the burning city. They watered at the river, and rested until daylight on that Sunday, and when they resumed their travel they avoided the cart ruts and hoof trails of the royal highway, hurrying southwards.

The country seemed deserted. When they saw a pueblo in the distance they rode widely by it, even though all able-bodied Indian men must be absent to fight the battle at Santa Fe. When they saw a Spanish farm they stared for smoke, and saw none, and knew it must be as empty as the farm near Taos, and for the same reason. But Indians might still be about it, and so they passed it by. They ate pods off cactus plants, and caught a turtle at the river, and made a stew, and several times they caught fish, giving thanks to Saint Raphael the Archangel for once again protecting travelers and providing them with fish like that with which he helped the young Tobias to heal the blindness of his father.

Not until they had traveled forty leagues throughout several days did they meet anyone, and then, coming to the great hacienda of Las Barrancas in the downriver district, they found a large and disorganized party of colonists who had escaped with a few wagons from their farms, and were now working to form a company that could make a fast and defended retreat out of the kingdom. The bannerman told them what he had seen, and then heard what they could tell.

iv.

They were astonished to hear that the garrison at Santa Fe was still fighting so lately as last Saturday, for the report had been that, except for the present company gathered at Las Barrancas, every Spaniard in the kingdom was dead. All settlements north of Sandía pueblo were supposed to be wiped out. The bannerman shrugged. He could not actually say so, for he had not been able to wait and see, but he thought there was a chance that the governor and the garrison might still be fighting—provided they had managed to recapture the ditch.

He had an uneasy thought.

Should he not raise a platoon here among these escaping colonists and march northward to raise the siege of Santa Fe? He looked about him. Nowhere did he see a sign of such a qualm in anyone else. Men were burying their plowshares and other heavy objects in order to lighten their carts for a swifter escape out of the terrorized land. The spectacle gave him a thrust of anger. Yet he could not say why, for he was as eager as they to run away. God knew he refused to stay a day longer than necessary in that place which had cost him everything—everything but his son, for whom henceforth he must live, at whatever cost to anything or anyone else.

He had to tell his doleful story many times, as one after another Spaniard in the encampment heard of it and asked him to repeat it. And when he had done so, they told him what they had left behind, and what they had seen on their flight down through the river bosks. In house after house, the same kind of piteous abomination as he had fled from in the farmhouse at Taos—whole families murdered, the bodies left often naked and unnamably defiled; burned buildings; wrecked furnishings; empty corrals; ruined churches and the corpses of Franciscan priests; at

Sandía, in the smoldering church, a sight out of hell, for there were found the holy figures thrown down and covered with human excrement, and two chalices buried in excrement inside a wooden chest, and a crucifix which had been whipped by the Indians until all its flesh color and varnish were worn away, and again, on the altar stone, a deposit of excrement and a statue of Saint Francis with its arms chopped off—such marks of crazy hatred as only the Devil himself could inspire.

How could there be any hope of peace or mercy amid creatures capable of committing all such acts? Why should any Spaniard remain in the kingdom? The government was destroyed, the capital was lost, by now the governor and all his company were surely dead. It was time to go. They moved down the river under the command of the lieutenant general of the kingdom, who had escaped from his middle valley farm. So far as they knew, he held the last duly constituted authority of the government. If he approved their going, then they were acting legally.

And yet the bannerman could not quiet his sense of duty. Must no one try to discover how matters stood at Santa Fe? And then he would look at his boy, and he would harden in his other resolve and hurry ahead in his thoughts.

But yet another image would trouble him—the image of the big stiff square of yellow watered silk, fringed in gold and silver, on one face bearing in its quartered field the scarlet castles and lions of royal Spain, on the other an embroidered likeness of Our Lady of Remedies—the banner of which he was the official custodian and bearer. It had come up the river with Governor de Oñate in 1598. Where was it now? If the palace had fallen, did the enemy find it rolled up in its leather case, standing in a corner of the governor's private chapel, from which the bannerman so often had taken it for ceremonies? It was, after the governor's signature, the most direct expression at Santa Fe of the very Crown itself. How could it be abandoned to anyone at all, so long as its official bearer was alive? The bannerman looked at his fingers, large yet adroit. He alone, so greatly did he love his royal silks, only he worked with needle and thread to keep the embroidery thick and fresh, the fringes even and properly knotted, the tassels on their long cords free of raveled ends. When he rode wearing his leather harness in which to pole the banner, the wind sometimes was strong against him, and then it was his pride to make his arm into an angle of steel, so that the banner staff never gave an inch, even though the great weight of the silk now stood straight out or again whipped against itself making a whispery shriek.

And then he remembered Santa Fe burning, and the death music in the streets, and he said his flag was lost, and he marched southward like the others, making haste, like them, against his own guilt. Never, said the bannerman to himself, he would never return to the northern kingdom, even if "they should kill him for it."

v.

But one evening when the lieutenant general's division was encamped at the foot of Fray Cristóbal mountain by the Great River, a small party of horesmen overtook them with astonishing news. The governor was alive—they came from him—and, though twice wounded in the siege of Santa Fe, he was well, and in command of a division consisting of a thousand men, women, and children and the few sheep, horses, and cattle they could save. They were moving down the river in misery, "defeated and robbed," as one horseman said, "on foot, fighting and dying of hunger." They needed help. The governor had sent these messengers to the south to find the escaping colonists of the middle valley. He sent orders that they must "come to his aid with some provisions and beasts." He was moving slowly because of the great weariness of the people, all marching on foot, and a mounted squad could reach him in two days. Meanwhile, his command was that the remainder of the population must await his coming so that all could join together and make greater strength in case

of Indian attack, or, indeed, in case of a campaign to reconquer the kingdom for themselves.

Reconquer? Now? In this piteous condition? The colonists thought not. But they obeyed the command of the
lieutenant general to remain encamped until the governor's
division should come down to them. The lieutenant general
prepared to go north to the rescue. He gave no orders to
anyone to accompany him, but called for volunteers. Only
a few men responded. Everyone else was still facing south
in mind.

The bannerman grew sick of himself as he watched the
volunteer squad prepare for their duty. Once they undertook it, their work filled them with self-forgetful energy.
He looked at the others—those who made no move to
help. They were anxious over their possessions, and quar-
reled among themselves about the size of the rations issued
to them, and in their hunger many tried to hoard food in
secret. Who was he, the bannerman? To which group
must he belong? He knew well enough. He was a member
of the governor's personal staff. The army had described
him in happier days—"tall and slender stature, long face,
somewhat handsome . . . arrow wound . . . broad shoulders . . . the bannerman to the governor and captain general. . . ." When the rescue squad rode away, he bitterly
watched them go, telling himself that it was for his son's
sake that he remained behind.

And then something reminded him that one day he must
die, and leave his son in any case, and the decision he had
tried so hard to make came free at last in his troubled
mind.

He went to friends in the camp and asked that they take
his son, guard him, help him, and, if need be, raise him
to manhood. They agreed, leaving the bannerman free to
ride out after the northbound column. Severely then he
went to his boy and told him what they must do, the
father and the son. For the first time they must now be
separated, since there was great danger waiting along with
duty in the north where the father must go, while safety of

a sort, and a promise for the future, lay to the south, where the child deserved to be. They must say good-by to one another, for a little while, anyway. Would his son be a good son, and obey the kind people in whose care he was giving him, and remember his prayers, and help with work to be done?

No. The boy would not do any or all such things. He clung to his father.

The bannerman shook him with anger. He must obey; there was no other way in which the father could do his duty.

The boy's face was wet with tears and puffy with rage. Yes, he said, choking, there was a way.

And what was that? asked the father in loving fury.

He would go too, replied the son, for he also was a soldier and a good one, as he had proved in the long journey to the Yutas and back.

Most Holy Mother of God, said the bannerman in silence, bowing his bearded head to his son's quivering shoulder. By the rough, brief bear hug of his father, the boy knew he was safe. Soon they were mounted and riding out to overtake the rescuers. Glancing sidewise at his companion, the bannerman had reason to hope that his son was growing up to resemble him.

vi.

In due course they came to the governor's division. The royal standard was nowhere to be seen, though it should be flying at the head of the march beside the governor. If the bannerman was shocked at this, he was also pleased that no other officer had his silks. He made inquiries, and was told that the banner was packed in its scabbard in one of the carts. He went in search of it, while again those who met after the catastrophe exchanged news.

Santa Fe had been warned on August 9 that the revolt was in train, and on the next day the outlying pueblos had risen, slain their missioners, and wrecked their churches. On Sunday the eleventh the terror was sweeping the river estates. Residents in the middle valley of the kingdom turned to escape southward, while those in the north hurried to Santa Fe to take refuge in the palace. The reports they brought were by then familiar in their horror.

On Tuesday the thirteenth of August—the very day when the bannerman had returned to Taos to find what he had found—the Indians came bristling through the cornfields of Analco by Saint Michael's church across Santa Fe creek to make the first attack on the palace. In the palace were gathered over a thousand people. The governor had sent word southward, asking for help from the residents of the downriver valley. None came. Instead, the enemy was reinforced by Apache warriors.

The siege lasted all week, and, as the bannerman knew, must have been lost by thirst, until, as he did not know before, the garrison in a last great effort came out in force on Sunday the eighteenth of August and fought with such power that the Indians were thrown back. Hundreds of them were killed. Forty-seven were captured and questioned. They told the worst—by order of the heathen gods who had been outraged for so long, the whole Indian kingdom had revolted, under pledge to kill every male Spaniard. No Spaniard, said the prisoners, was left between Taos and Isleta except for those so nearly destroyed at Santa Fe, and those others who had escaped southward.

What else did the prisoners know?

That was all, they indicated. They were forthwith executed.

Then, with the capital wholly in ruins, and the surviving kingdom divided, the governor with his council resolved to abandon Santa Fe and go to overtake those already in retreat. Reunited, they must recover from their shocking sorrows, make a stand at some suitable place, and eventually, none could say when, turn again to reconquer the lost kingdom.

The governor brought his people out of Santa Fe on August 24, with two carts, three hundred animals of burden, and for food a few sheep and goats. On their way down the river they were watched day and night by Indians on the mesas who talked to one another with smoke. Nobody else knew what the messages said, but, though the Indians watched, they did not attack. The strain, as the bannerman could understand, was most trying.

Presently he found a cart heavily loaded whose canvas cover was lifted at one end by a long object. It was the leather scabbard he sought. He pulled it out and unbuckled its straps, and revealed to the daylight once again the royal colors of Santa Fe. When next the column moved forward the silken standard was free to the air where the bannerman and his son marched beside the governor. From this act the form, the official style, of the kingdom took its first measure of restoration, even as the retreat southward went on through the simmering days of late summer.

At last, coming to the Great River, they met the summer's supply train on its way to Santa Fe.

vii.

The kingdom, united again, took its stand for the next many years at the north pass, called El Paso del Norte, where the Great River separated New Mexico from the next southerly province of New Biscay. Those residents who still hoped to escape further southward were prevented by viceregal edict, though many did contrive to slip away. Those who remained lived in miserable huts of wattle and mud, strung along the river in several villages.

More than once the governor was urged by the crown offices at Mexico City to reconquer the lost kingdom. He was powerless to do without substantial reinforcements, which were not sent. In 1681 a penetration in reconnaissance to the north was mounted, and among the armed company who went were the bannerman and his soldier son. It was a hard winter march lasting several months, full of disappointment, hardship, and grief for the ruins it revealed and the memories they revived. The expedition did not reach Santa Fe, where, according to what they heard, Indians were living in the palace, which they had converted into a pueblo. There, with every profanation, reigned as governor the Indian doctor named Popé, who was identified as the master planner of the rebellion. The rest of the city was grown with weeds and charred with long-dead fire. The expedition returned to El Paso and once again the north was lost in distance and memory.

As an act of probity and good sense the bannerman married again, receiving the matrimonial sacrament in the mission church of Our Lady of Guadalupe at El Paso. His wife was a widow of the revolt, much older than he. He thought of her as a fine woman. His love, that had come to him at sixteen, was long since over in the ashes of Taos.

Presently a new governor came to replace the victim of the revolt, and under his command a few government houses were built by the river. His commission included instructions to make ready for a reconquest of the north, but again the colony was left without reinforcements to make the campaign possible.

The new governor sent explorers to the east, in the country of the Tejas Indians, with at least one curious result. They brought back a flag which the Indians had given them. It had come from the seacoast of the great bay of Mexico. The bannerman inspected it. It was made of white silk embroidered with three blue crosses: a French flag, without doubt, the governor decided. Were the French making ready to enter the Spanish lands north of New Spain? It was another reason, perhaps the most urgent one, to reconquer the northern kingdom.

But until the Crown moved to furnish men, arms, and supplies, the exiled colony could only wait, the bannerman's family along with the rest. Life was made of waiting. Time itself seemed the stuff of patience. On occasion the bannerman inspected his royal flag and set to work with his needle and thread to keep all in order. He came to remember Santa Fe as a fine city, the largest he had ever seen, its palace the grandest building. He mused through recollections of guard mount in the plaza before the palace, and parades and processions on feast days, with the banner always in his grasp as he had marched beside the governor. A splendid life, it was one that he longed to recover.

Now and then as his son grew with the years and began to show a man's stout arms and hands, he took him to a clear place and gave him lessons in the manual of the banner. Some day the royal colors would have to stand forth again in the royal city, and someone would have to carry and guard them, in all their meaning, the yellow silken faces quartered on one side with scarlet castles and lions and blazoned on the other with the glory of the most Holy Mother of God.

IV

The Alderman: 1691

i.

LIVING IN EXILE along the right bank of the Rio Grande at El Paso, the people of Santa Fe in 1691 maintained the forms of their society, however miserable their circumstances. If the day would come when under some new governor they must return to their own city in the north, then there could be small purpose or satisfaction in making a permanent capital here by the dusty river. Many—perhaps most—of the families wanted to retreat forever from New Mexico, where they had known such horror and loss. It was a desire which the government refused to entertain. The governor held his little garrison and the garrison held the population and the population waited as they had waited now throughout eleven years for some new energy to come alive in their midst to change their conditions of life.

These were harder than any they had ever known before. Their dwellings were poor things made of withes and clay, mere diagrams of shelter against the sand storms of spring which scoured the breath out of their mouths, and the bearing heat of desert summer, and winter storms that cried out of the north.

Their memories were hard to live with, and their wonderings about the fate of beloved men, women, and children who might yet be alive in bondage under the Indian masters of New Mexico. Beyond these concerns remained those that dealt with property. To an intensely practical people it was worrisome to know so little about the possessions, the lands that had been left behind in the north. Records and documents had been lost in the abandonment of the kingdom. Even an alderman of the City Council of Santa Fe might have reason to wonder about the eventual recovery of his deeded lands in the capital.

A certain alderman enjoyed an advantage over his fellow exiles which gave him social prestige and the respect owed to wisdom. He could not only read, he could write. He had belonged to the Kingdom of New Mexico for many years, but, before taking up his residence at Santa Fe, he had seen the world, studying for two years in the University of Mexico City, where he had taken the degree of *bachiller,* bachelor of arts. He never signed his name without adding to it this distinction. He was variously addressed as alderman or bachelor or sergeant—for he was also a member of the New Mexican cavalry, whose troopers were known as leatherjackets, after their quilted leather armor. Having seen the world, the alderman was better able than most of his associates to judge the miseries of the colony.

Of all his feelings the harshest were directed toward the present governor. The alderman was a born subordinate, which meant that he could be highly critical of his superiors, even while he paid them the formal respect due to their offices. When along with the rest of the colony he heard that a new governor was soon to arrive in February, 1691, he was interested for many reasons.

In the first place, the colony needed leadership, a sense

of purpose, beyond the wretched duty of merely living from day to day. Again, if the lost kingdom was to be recovered, it was plain that a new man must recover it. Further, if the affairs of the kingdom were ever to be restored, they must be revived with a certain style. And, finally, the alderman wondered how he would fare as a man of property under the new governor, in whose power lay the disposal of all lands that might be recovered from the Indians in the north. The alderman owned a fine large lot in Santa Fe in addition to the small plot near the plaza where his house stood. It must stand there now—that house—with only charred walls, for the roof with its beams had gone up in smoke during the night when the city had been put to the torch by the rebels. He had seen it from his place of refuge in the palace.

ii.

During the afternoon of February 22, 1691, the leather-jackets were drawn up in mounted formation at El Paso. The alderman was in his place. He was a small man who looked larger when mounted. His helmet gave dignity to his head, which when bared showed a close cap of black hair. His eyes were narrow and speculative, and his mouth was habitually open, showing large front teeth and an expression of doubt, not of himself but of others. He wore his mustache and beard cropped short. If as a man of ability he was respected but not liked, this was because he liked so few people himself. Now with the rest of the cavalry he was waiting in formation to receive and escort the new governor and captain general of New Mexico to the government houses that stood, a small huddle of unfinished earthen buildings, in an open plaza near the river.

In that land the first sign of news from far away was dust. Dust rose far down the plain and showed against the dark blue of mountains in winter afternoon. The cavalcade was approaching. The alderman knew excitement, compounded equally of skepticism and hope. Soon there were salutes from firearms, trumpets, and drums.

The old governor rode forward to greet the new. Both dismounted to embrace.

The march was resumed, the cavalry turned in escort toward the river plaza, and the troopers could look ahead and see their new commander in chief against the yellowing sky. The alderman knew his name from having read it on documents brought weeks ago by courier. His name was Don Diego de Vargas Zapata Luján Ponce de León. It was the name of a great lord, and the alderman was uplifted to observe that Don Diego de Vargas bore himself both mounted and dismounted with an air of thoughtless confidence that had a certain grandeur to it. It made a soldier feel that the first thing he wanted to do was fulfill his commander's excellent opinion of him. In this very first impression, the alderman felt that the new captain general was bringing a great gift to his exiled people—the future.

iii.

Soon the alderman knew that the captain general had come north from Mexico City with three objectives. The first of these was to put down scattered Indian revolts in those provinces of New Spain that lay along a line that marked the southern reach of New Mexico. The second was to reconquer the New Mexican kingdom. The third was to investigate rumors of rich deposits of quicksilver in the mountains of western New Mexico in a range called the Sierra Azul. All three of these missions had some relation to a larger purpose; for the French from North America had been intruding in Spanish lands on the Gulf of Mexico, and it was vital to Spanish crown policy that all foreigners be kept out of Spain's vaguely defined territories. Outlands in upheaval through Indian revolt would be far easier for the French to attack than peaceable provinces ruled by a strong governor.

The alderman had the tyrannical vanity of the obscure man, which grew naturally from his acid pride as a Spaniard. Threadbare, soured, hopeless, dispossessed, often hungry, he stood as an image of the whole exiled colony. It was almost as an act of piety that he turned to the new governor. To conquer provinces and find mercury and obstruct the French—these were large and noble duties and he had no doubt that the captain general could fulfill them. But closer to the alderman's interest rested two others. These were the recovery of his real estate at Santa Fe and the restoration of his pride as an officer of a government once more established in its own palace at the northern capital. As was often the case in human affairs, the selfish and the ideal were mingled in the alderman's will. When he asked himself the question, "My lands—will I get them back?" he answered it, for the present, with the knowledge he had been able to gain of the captain general, who seemed like an official embodiment of the established order. If in truth he was, then the future looked promising.

Don Diego de Vargas looked younger than his years. He was in his forties. His hair was dark, and worn long over his shoulders, spread on wide lace collars. He kept his mustaches and beard narrowly trimmed. In his pale, long face his eyes were large and dark. There was little occasion at the temporary capital to appear in court dress, and accordingly he wore a soldier's attire—hip boots, body armor, velvet doublet, and sidearms. As a young man he had served with the Spanish forces in the kingdoms of Naples and Italy, and in 1672 he came, like many another young lord, to the New World, to make a career befitting his noble inheritance.

Scraps of information dropped at various times were fitted together to give the alderman a satisfactory view of his commander's circumstances in the world. In Spain the Vargas family owned town palaces and country villas— Madrid and Granada, Torrelunga, Buytrago, Miraflores and Salamanca and Orcaña. His lineage included famous warriors and courtiers. One of these, an ambassador, was also a great lawyer who served as a lay theologian at the Council of Trent. His father wrote twenty volumes of "general information of the period." In his line of uncles he numbered a bishop, and—it was the summit of distinction—on his mother's side he was related to Saint Teresa of Jesus, who was his grandmother's second cousin. In Madrid the Vargas family maintained in the perpetual light of countless candles a certain altar heavy with gold and silver to the glory of the Blessed Mother of God. Power, responsibility, the acts of thought, and the style of sanctity were natural to such a noble line. An alderman, a bachelor of arts, could serve in honor and self-respect the heir of such values.

They were expressed in even the most routine of administrative duties. Like others who attended the captain general's open hearing, the alderman often heard the captain general at his dictation, and was somberly pleased at what he heard.

"The petitioner," the captain general would dictate slowly, holding in his hand a laboriously inscribed paper, "presented the petition of the preceding page, which I ordered my Secretary of Government and War to read to me in his"— the petitioner's—"presence. And having heard and heeded it with the attention which I owe, I order that—" and then would come the decision.

"The attention which I owe"—these were the reassuring words, delivered out of a simple obligation of nobility. In due time, the matter of the Santa Fe property of the alderman came up for consideration. The captain general deliberated, interviewed scores of colonists, heard many descriptions of legal grants now lost to record but not to memory, and presently decreed that those lands held in the north by families before the revolt of 1680 would be restored to them so soon as the kingdom of New Mexico should be regained.

It was a typical act of routine by which the new governor made his people feel that it was only a matter of time, to be taken for granted, until the northern kingdom would be theirs again. With him they came to believe it. Believing it, they knew it would come true. Day by day, in countless small ways, the powers of confidence, pride, and faith were quite thoughtlessly brought alive in them by their new lord.

iv.

A year and a half passed by before the captain general was ready to take the army northward on his mission of reconquest. When in the late summer of 1692 they were ready to march, the alderman was at his post with the leather-jackets. For the next four months he took part in what he knew at the time was a marvel, as great as something to be read about in written histories at the university. With his educated powers, he felt he might be able to write a book about it, but the captain general was already making a written record which was dictated every day to the Secretary of Government and War. Nothing that happened on the great march would be forgotten.

They went up the old road along the Great River of the North. When the river bent away westward to disappear between mountains, they continued northward to cross the desert stretch of the Dead Man's March and ninety miles farther on came again to the river. They passed Indian towns that were deserted. They paused to see what had been wrought at Spanish farms in the valley, and saw tumbled walls and gaping roofs all taken by weeds. As they marched into the center of the kingdom, where the largest Indian cities were, again they found no populations. All must have retreated to gather at Santa Fe. The capital was the heart of the tactical situation, as the soldiers said, both for the enemy and the royal expeditioners.

On September 12 they climbed the escarpment of La Bajada by an old and obscure trail. When after much trouble with the supply carts they reached the top, they were on the Santa Fe plain, looking to the mountains of the Blood of Christ at whose base twenty miles away lay the royal city.

The captain general ordered a halt. A great affair was just ahead, and he gave rest to his men and animals to meet it. He called an assembly and spoke to the troopers. Battle must be waiting for them. Preparing them against the powers of that night, he spoke of duty, and referred to the Two

Majesties of Christ and Crown. A cold night was coming.
The alderman and his fellows shivered with excitement and
chill.

At eleven o'clock in the darkness they moved out again.
Long after midnight they again halted and further orders
came down. The soldiers would make their final approach
to the city at three o'clock in the morning—an hour to be
recognized by certain astronomers in the troop who could
read the stars. Again marching, and again halting, the
soldiers received absolution from their chaplains. It was
ghostly. Last orders told them to withhold their fire until
they saw the captain general draw his sword. As they came
to the open fields before the city, they were to watch for
another signal, and, when it came, they were to face the
palace, and cry out in unison in all their two hundred
voices, "Glory be to the Blessed Sacrament of the Altar!"
After that, their fortunes must unfold moment by moment.
In all possible silence and caution they moved forward
again upon the city of their homes.

Between four and five o'clock they were in position facing
the sleeping city. The governor was foremost in position.
Beside him were his chaplains and his standard bearer.
When all was in readiness, the whispered command came,
and the army shouted out the Gloria.

The night was broken.

In a moment the palace roof was crowded with Indians.
They called out to know who was there, and were answered
by the governor's interpreter who proclaimed that it was
the Spaniards who had come back to take what was theirs.

No, said the Indians, it was their enemies the Pecos and
Apache Indians.

Again the signal for the Gloria was given, the soldiers
cried out their chorus.

The Indians considered in silence for a pause, and then
replied that if those were Spaniards in the dark fields, why
did they not fire an harquebus? The alderman never forgot
the reply to this.

"Be calm," declared the captain general. "I am a Catholic,

and, when the sun rises, you will see the Blessed Virgin on my flag."

Now the Indians demanded that in proof a Spanish trumpet be sounded. At a command, the trumpeter blew a blast, and the drummers beat a long roll. It was enough. The Indians knew. They began to shout defiance, called on their animal gods in imitation, and battle seemed inevitable. The captain general moved his forces into sound positions about the town. When the sun rose, they were ready to storm the walls. But not before the captain general made another effort in peace. He rode forward with his chaplains and his colors and engaged in parlays. At one point, he removed his helmet and went closer alone. He promised amnesty, peace, and absolution. An Indian spokesman came forward on the roof and a long exchange followed. Every moment gained by negotiation was valuable.

Behind him, the captain general knew his supply camp was being set up in the fields. And then came a threat from a new quarter. Bands of Indians from other pueblos were coming down the hills above Santa Fe, and the reinforcement moved the rebels in the city to new defiance. The captain general acted swiftly. He sent squads to hold the newcomers, and ordered the water supply in the palace ditch to be cut off. At this a great commotion rose from the palace. The captain general replied that the water would be restored, and peace given, if the besieged people came down from their walls to render obedience. He gave them an hour to decide, and joined his troops for rations of hot chocolate and biscuits while his two pieces of bronze artillery were placed, and mines of gunpowder were laid by the walls. Presently he returned to the parlay, taking his banner, his rosary, and his cross. He was at ease in his saddle close under the walls, exposed and indifferent to danger, and the grave strength within him at last prevailed.

The Indians, coming down unarmed, opened the way through their barricades. He entered in and embraced the people one by one who came to him. His chaplains blessed them, and the next day celebrated the *Te Deum* in the great patio of the palace. General absolution followed. The royal city was restored to the Two Majesties in peace. When he had opportunity, the alderman went to see his real estate. As he expected, the house, the separate lots were in wretched condition. He shrugged. Everyone would have the same trouble and duty of restoring their ruined property when the whole colony was here at home again. Meanwhile, the captain general and his troops had much yet to do before the families at El Paso could be brought northward.

In the next many weeks, the army made a swift tour of all the pueblos, received submissions, held mass baptisms, and carried everywhere the pledge of peace. True, they heard rumors of treason. At Taos, they were told that in the far western cities of Zuñi, near the mercury mountains, an organized campaign against the returned Spaniards was being formed. The captain general turned at once for the downriver and west. At Jemez there was a while when the Indians seemed irresolute between peace and battle—but the Lord de Vargas walked about among them, pulled off his glove, and shook hands and embraced them, and they ended by kneeling as his children.

Moving on westward, the troops came to Zuñi, and went up the rocky mesas where the Indian dwellings were, and, once again, faced by that suspended decision in the Indian mind, the governor in his gentle assumption of an invincible superiority brought the Zuñi conspirators to make their proper homage. With the rest of the light scouting force, which was all the captain general had kept by him for the westward mission, the alderman sang the *Te Deum*.

After the submission, the Zuñi chieftains produced a trove of objects which they had kept ever since the rebellion. The father president sorted them over for the captain general. He found altar vessels, candlesticks, crucifixes, and several books, among which—a somewhat stirring personal touch—was a copy of the works of the captain general's distant cousin Saint Teresa of Jesus. It had not been very long since her feast day of October 15, when in the *secreta* of her mass the celebrant would have read of *"Bienaventu-*

rada Santa Teresa" and found reference to *"el holocausto interior de su corazón,"* and in that ardent fire, so deeply buried, was something held in common not only by the saint herself and her kinsman the captain general but by all the Spanish people to one or another degree. The sacred treasures were removed to El Paso, where the captain general and his squads arrived five days before Christmas, 1692. They brought with them also a sample of the "vermilion earth" from the Blue Range supposed to contain mercury.

It was an honor for the alderman, in all his capacities, to be selected as one of the couriers to carry the great news of the peaceful reconquest to the viceroy in Mexico City. He took with him also the samples of mercury ore and rode off southward with the escort and the light carts. When he returned many months later, he had much of interest to bring to the captain general.

On hearing the news from the kingdom of New Mexico, the viceregal capital had gone mad with joy. The cathedral was dressed with lights on all its outlines, and all the bells of the city were rung in jubilation. The captain general's report was sent on to the King at Madrid. The viceroy and his council voted commendations which they forwarded to the captain general. There was a sense of triumph, marred by only one disappointment—the vermilion earth had been analyzed, and showed no quicksilver content. Nevertheless, all efforts were to go forward for the consolidation of the victory, with the return of the colony to the northernmost capital.

Accordingly, in the following October, with military reinforcements that brought the professional troops up to a count of one hundred, the train moved out from the temporary capital where they had spent thirteen years. The kingdom was to be resettled by seventy families, accompanied by eighteen Franciscan friars and many Indian allies and servants. They took eighteen freight wagons and three cannon in carts, and a thousand mules, two thousand horses, and nine hundred cattle. Many of the company were returning to repossess their property; others to assume newly granted sites of land in reward for their good work as soldiers of last year's expedition.

By December 16, 1693, after a hard journey during which thirty women and children died along the Dead Man's March, the company was once again in Santa Fe. Their feelings—the alderman shared them—were somewhat discouraged, for, passing by the Indian cities on their way, they found most of them again defiant, and at Santa Fe, after giving the Indians in the old palace a reasonable time to vacate the city, the Spaniards settled camp outside in what the alderman agreed was "a despicable dwelling place." The Indians delayed for two weeks. During that time, twenty-one Spaniards died of exposure in their snow-covered cantonment, and the Indians threw up new fortifications about the palace. On December 28, the Indians cried out their defiance. The Spaniards could not but sigh over the exasperating task they now had to do all over again. This time the captain general was obliged to act sternly.

He ordered an attack for the following morning. It was his first battle in the kingdom. It was over in a day. By dawn of the thirtieth the Indians were defeated. Seventy of their leaders were executed. The rest retreated down the Great River where they held war councils and sent their word by smoke from mesa to mesa. The kingdom was in a state of civil war. Seeing his people safely into their city, and at work with the first acts of restoration, the captain general took to the field again to subdue the pueblos one by one under cannon, torch, and battering-ram. Now as firm as he had been patient, he took back all the previously converted pueblos and, once they were his, promised them peace under the hands of his most powerful soldiers—the unarmed ones, whom he re-established in the ruined missions which they would rebuild, and in which they would sing again the glory of an all-merciful God—the friars, come back to heal, to teach, and to protect.

The powers of the Two Majesties were back to stay—though not without meeting further endurances, as the alderman, with his governing colleagues, was in a position to know.

v.

From the reigning lord of Santa Fe to the alderman and others of his station to the poorest man, all took comfort from various guarantees of their places in the world. The first of these lay in the promises of Christ, of which they prayed to be worthy. The next resided in their native dignity and formal manners. Another was once again made plain in a paper received from the Count de Galve, viceroy of New Spain, in 1694, which stated "I concede . . . to the children and grandchildren of the conquerors and founders of the Kingdom of New Mexico, all the privileges, exemptions, honors, favors, and other pre-eminences belonging to them, and which are their due, to be preserved in the same manner as for the conquerors and founders, according to that which is disposed by the royal laws . . . to be preserved for them precisely and faithfully. . . ."

In his person and in his style of living the captain general seemed to stand forth as a visible embodiment of proper state. If his palace was built of clay that crumbled and leaked after heavy rains, still, it was the greatest building in the kingdom, no matter how during the Indian occupation it had been altered to the Indian style of living. There he kept his offices and his dwelling, and, when occasion required, there he gratified his people by presiding with appropriate ceremony.

His morion and body armor were chased in the best steel. His shirts—he owned six of them—were of the finest Dutch linen, with shoulder-wide collars "embroidered with the best of lace." He owned four pairs of Genoese stockings, another pair of blue silk tricked with gold, another pair "silver curled," and a yellow pair embroidered in silver. Sometimes he wore a blue brocade suit with gold buttons, and blue velvet trousers—galloned and tied at the knees with ribbon; and again, a white suit with waistcoat and trousers of brown cloth trimmed with ruffles of gold and silver. His waistcoats reached almost to the knees, and were trimmed in Germany-dressed martin skins. He had a dark suit for occasions of mourning. His hats carried plumes and some were faced with ermine. His cloaks were of French broadcloth laced in silver and lined with blue velvet, or of gold cloth lined with serge, or of fine native cloth, plain. For the field he wore leather hip boots and his armor and a leather jacket—one of his was blue—or a jerkin with grosgrain and silk lace. He carried pistols, of which he owned two pairs, in leather holsters, and wore any of a variety of swords, one of which had a "fine" hilt. If he was afoot, he used a tall, gold-headed cane.

The alderman had seen the captain general wearing his jewels—a pair of pearl earrings with eight large emeralds, and two finger rings, one with a rose diamond "checkered and enameled in black," and the other, enameled in black and gold, showing two diamonds.

The captain general was fond of an elbow chair which he owned, and, when he sat at table, it was to use a silver service, most of whose pieces bore his coat of arms. He had long since paid to the King's treasury that fifth part of their value owed to the Crown in taxes. There were thirty small silver dishes, twelve silver porringers, two silver platters, one flat salver of silver, a small silver keg with stopper and chain, a large plain tankard, six silver forks and six teaspoons, three tablespoons, two silver fountains, one large, one small, a large silver waiter, and six candlesticks. Behind his chair, when occasion required, he displayed the silken banners of Saint Anselm and Saint Michael the Archangel, to whom, it seemed, he gave special devotion.

For shaving purposes he had a deep silver bowl, and, for use in his bedroom, a silver basin. His four pairs of bed sheets were matched by embroidered pillowcases. He kept a large piece of fine linen from which handkerchiefs were made, and he owned six pairs of drawers.

His carriage was driven by "two young negro coachmen"

whom he had bought for 660 pesos, and his manservant was a mulatto slave, José de la Cruz, who served him, stated the captain general, "lovingly and willingly." So, it would seem, did the members of the colony, including newcomers who came from Mexico. The city of Santa Fe grew under his administration. Presently he was informed that the water supply for the city was no longer sufficient to "insure the irrigation of the cultivated fields, in order to maintain the families domiciled thereon," as he put it in a state paper. Old settlers, like the alderman, found their farming plots endangered by the requirements of newcomers. The matter was solved, at least temporarily, when the captain general requested Indian holders of two pueblos—San Lázaro and San Cristóbal—to vacate their towns so that Spanish families from the capital might occupy them. The new Spanish community was named Santa Cruz —"the New Town of the Holy Cross of the Mexican Spaniards of the King Our Lord Charles the Second." The proclamation ordering the emigration was "published in the two public plazas of this city in the presence of a large concourse of people in the same and in a loud and intelligible voice by Sebastian Rodríguez, negro drummer." The captain general provided mules and horses for the movement, and he said he would aid the settlers in all things, "assuring them that a ration of beans and corn shall not be wanting, as well as half a fanega of corn to each family for planting which I promise to give them, and also implements, such as picks, shovels, hoes, and axes." He appointed a military and civil government for Santa Cruz, and issued firearms, powder, and ball. At nine o'clock in the morning of April 21, 1695, sixty families took their departure for the new town north of the old capital. The kingdom was putting its roots down deeper. What had the town council written to the viceroy two years before? The alderman remembered. To try to resettle the kingdom without new families would be useless. It "would be like dropping a grain of mustard seed into the sea—" a felicitous expression of which a bachelor of arts, with his training, might be justly proud.

The captain general kept his attention fixed upon the fortunes of his new town, and in the next year went there for an inspection. For one thing, settlers were losing sheep through the poisonous effects of "hairy bastard vetch weed" which grew abundantly near Santa Cruz, and also of "a great deal of sword grass, which also sickens the sheep very much." One farmer lost forty sheep. Further, the new town needed more buildings, and he told them so when he went to visit. It was gratifying to see the farms prospering, thanks to their irrigation ditches, "clean and running," which he had established at his own expense, as he reported to Mexico, and he added that, without expense to the Crown, he had "repaired and made secure" the dam at Santa Cruz. "With sails full, we forge ahead," he wrote.

Forty-four families had come to the colony since the re-settlement. Down the river, the great estate farms were reoccupied. In addition to Santa Cruz, the town of Bernalillo was established. In Santa Fe, the palace and fortress, so greatly reduced by the Indian occupants of thirteen years, had been restored, and, while it was not in any sense a fine building, it had space, dignity, and meaning. The royal army was drilled into a disciplined, effective force of high mobility and spirit. The captain general was a soldier, and his men, like the alderman-sergeant of leatherjackets, tried to match him. Legal records were coming into order after laborious effort. All the new grants and all the old ones newly confirmed by the captain general were in full effect with all the power of the law which a man could ignore or disturb only at his peril. Yet there was much still to accomplish, and the captain general, seeing the end of his term as governor draw near, made a routine application to the Crown for renewal of his tenure. It would take time—a year at least—for the application to be acted upon. Meanwhile, there were yet many problems to meet.

Indian raids fell upon the outlying cities, and, torn between defense and farming, the settlers had not all the time they needed to plant crops and till the fields. The re-occupied pueblos knew internal uneasiness, and the friars sent warnings to Santa Fe that the temper of their people was not encouraging. Winter came and with it hunger, for the storehouses were not as full as they should have been. In the spring of 1696 friars came to the capital from their pueblo missions and conferred at length with the captain general. The alderman heard later what they talked about, for troops were presently ordered out on special duty among the pueblos to be ready for trouble if it came.

It came like a repeated act in nightmare, and the alderman bitterly remembered 1680. For on June 4, 1696, another coordinated rebellion among certain pueblos broke out. Five priests were massacred and twenty-one soldiers. Churches were wrecked once again and profaned with every vileness. The rebels having made their damage retreated to the mountains in defiance. They were not safe there, for the captain general, mustering all the power of his kingdom, moved out for the whole summer and fall on a campaign of still another conquest. He succeeded. He brought his miserable Indian people out of the mountains and took them to their homes and once again received their allegiance, in return for which he gave them again forgiveness, peace, and protection. When it was all done, a soldier heard of the reason why revolt had fallen upon the Spaniards once more. The explanation was brought to the captain general. "The sole cause of the uprising," he heard, "was the fact that a Spaniard had said, while at Cochiti . . . that the governor of New Mexico had determined that in the month of June of the same year all the adult men of that kingdom were to be killed, reserving only the boys."

The alderman was angered by the story. It both confirmed and outraged his opinion of his fellow men. The Spaniard who had made such a statement was obviously a fool and a dangerous one. Further, it was an outrage for anyone who served under the captain general to suspect him of con-templating such cruel folly as a massacre of all Indian men.

The alderman had served under many lords and governors, and he knew to a nicety all the gradations of official worth. He could serve a knave or a hero with the same correctness, for that was his duty and his inheritance. But he would not fail to assess for himself the difference between them. He could not speak of it to anyone else, but he did truly believe that in Captain General de Vargas for the first time in his life he had met greatness—the kind that rested within a man, rather than without in all the gestures and state of trumpets, drum rolls, royal banners, silver salvers held by mulatto pages, and every other ordained form of salute.

It was therefore an embittering shock for the alderman when in January of 1697 a party of travelers drew into Santa Fe from the south under the command of Don Pedro Rodríguez Cubero, who had come with royal patents designating him to succeed the Captain General de Vargas as governor of the kingdom. The captain general's petition for renewal of his office had been sent too late. Along with all the kingdom, the alderman accepted the change with respect. The Crown was greater than any person, and a portion of it belonged to each Spaniard to preserve on high in strength and glory. But that was not to say that the alderman admired Governor Cubero.

The captain general remained at the capital to make himself available for the usual official inquiries and investigations that accompanied any handing over of office. Oddly enough, he was not given an early and easy quittance by Cubero. The spring passed, and the summer, and early autumn, and then, one day, the alderman and all Santa Fe heard that the incredible had come to pass. By order of the new governor the great captain general had been arrested and lodged in the jail cells at the west end of the palace. None could visit him, not even the father president. When men wondered why this had been done, the new governor assembled the Santa Fe city council and obliged them to draw up a bill of complaints against his predecessor. The alderman was sick and sour at the odd changes of fate that could befall a man—even one of the greatest. But as he was a professional subordinate, and subject to the powers of the Crown which now resided legally in the new governor, he must carry out orders as given. He helped to frame the list of charges against the man whom he had served with—was he about to think of the word love? If so, he must let it stand, unaccustomed though he was to such sentiment. The captain general was fined 4,000 pesos and deprived of his possessions and left to meditate in prison, while Governor Cubero, attended by wine jugs, sat and sat in his cabinet at the other end of the palace, and wrote and wrote. Deeds? thought the alderman, acts on behalf of the kingdom? On the contrary, the new governor poured out pages and pages to justify his poor opinion of the colony and the man whom he had punished.

For the alderman a kind of concealing blight fell over the life of the capital during the next few years. He saw but he hardly noted what went on about him. He was most conscious of that presence which was held beyond communication in the palace cells. No relief came for the captain general, no inquiries in the twice-yearly mails. He was lost to sight and, it seemed, even to memory. Now and then his friends dared to protest at his treatment, and as likely as not were turned off in a drunken rage by the governor. Finally, in 1700, the father president of the kingdom could no longer suffer to witness the miscarriage of justice. He went to Mexico to report on the matter. In his company, glad to escape from the gloomy betrayal that he seemed to commit every day, went the alderman as part of the military escort.

Before he left, the alderman took care to look out for his property. His extra fields should not be allowed to go to rack and ruin in his absence. Accordingly, he lent them to a good woman he knew, a Mrs. Duran, to farm for herself. She was industrious, hale, and honest, and he was glad to think that upon his return he would find his land nicely free of weeds and ready for his own touch again in the next year's sowing.

vi.

Upon the alderman's return from the City of Mexico, news broke over Santa Fe. The viceregal commission of inquiry sent orders for the captain general to be released at once from prison. Without posting bail, he was to travel immediately to Mexico where his case would be heard. All this was to be done by command of the King, who had reviewed the Vargas matter in Madrid. Governor Cubero could not but comply, placing the royal orders upon his head for a moment in the formal gesture of submission. The captain general was released and lost no time in departing for the south and justice.

Where was there any justice in Santa Fe? asked the alderman, for he had come home to a painful discovery in his own affairs. During his absence of almost a year, his tenant Mrs. Duran had been removed from his property by order of Governor Cubero. It seemed that a leatherjacket soldier, a certain Salvador Matías de Ribera, had cast an eye over the alderman's garden lots and had taken a liking to them. He went around to the palace and looked up the record of deed, and found that Mrs. Duran had no official authority to use the land, which was registered in the alderman's name. But the alderman was far away, and might never come back. Ribera applied to the governor to have the alderman's title set aside and the lots granted to him. This was done, and, by the time the alderman returned, he found Ribera using the cultivated lots as his own property.

He was quick to protest. Ribera exhibited his official grant, signed by the governor. Both men stood upon their legal rights. The alderman applied to the governor, and was stared out of the room. It was inconceivable that an act of the governor's should be questioned. All subsequent petitions drafted by the alderman in his best bachelor of arts manner were ignored. The alderman's opinion of human nature sank lower. He lost weight, his head shrank down between his shoulders, and his age was suddenly upon him. He looked about his city and instead of seeing the sunlight standing like sword blades on the sunward faces of all things, and the embracing splendor of the mountains in which the capital was mantled, and the patience with which most men and women lived within their duty, he saw only the walls that crumbled in dust when dry and in mud when wet, and the fixity of danger all about which was never relieved, and the stupidity and the power of authority as embodied in the wretch who lolled over his bottles and his inkwells at the palace. The alderman often felt a sudden absence in his breast, a dropping of his heart, and he came to relate this saddening feeling with the thought of the captain general, so shamefully used, in a use to which he, the alderman, had given his educated abilities in drawing up the bill of charges for the governor. *Mea culpa.* He struck his breast, and drily went on about his business.

And then one day in 1703 there came by courier a most extraordinary piece of news. It came first to the governor, who plainly tried to keep it to himself, but the courier also knew what it was and it soon spread through the city of Santa Fe, and people's hearts rang like bells.

The great captain general was coming back.

His case had been completely dismissed. He was cleared of all trumpery charges against him. He was reappointed as governor and captain general of the kingdom, and would leave Mexico in July, to arrive in Santa Fe in early November. But even that was not all. He was returning as an even greater lord than before, for the King in recognition of his great deeds and his unjust sufferings had created him marquis, and he was now known as the Marquis de la Nava Brazinas, with his new coronet added to his blazons.

During the summer of 1703, as during every summer, there were reports of Apache depredations. These were laid before Governor Cubero, like all the others before, upon which he had taken no particular action. But this time he was stirred to announce that he must personally lead troops against the marauders, and he readied an expedition. But it was more than a field campaign, for he packed his possessions and, well before the time when the Marquis was due to appear, Governor Cubero vanished into the spaces of the kingdom on his way south, and was never seen there again.

But his works survived him, and they first shocked and then enraged the captain general when he arrived in November. The palace and government houses of Santa Fe were almost in ruins through official neglect of their upkeep. The defenses of the capital were most dangerously inadequate. The army, which the Marquis had left in such a high state of efficiency and spirit, was now hardly a unit, lazy, riddled by desertions and indifference to duty. Santa Cruz, without military protection, had been abandoned, its houses empty, its fields and ditches overgrown. Even the integrity of legal acts given under the Crown was violated —land grants made by the captain general and his predecessors had been set aside arbitrarily by Cubero.

"Why?" demanded the Marquis of the Santa Fe city council and all its aldermen. "With what intention and malice" had Cubero acted to such ends? He supposed Cubero had set out "to destroy all I had done and leave no memory of it." Well. Let the record be set straight, and let the city council which had once been so free with its charges of malfeasance now be as free with recompense. "It is justice for which I ask," stated the Marquis in his written address to the aldermen.

They met to act at once, and on the following day submitted to the captain general a satisfactory document in triplicate which bore evidence of the gifts of expression exercised by a certain bachelor of arts. The council of aldermen withdrew all the charges dictated against the Marquis by Cubero. Further, they declared that Cubero, "in all the time of his government, was solely occupied in drinking and writing papers with no reason whatever." He imagined "things which he had no business to imagine, ascribing faults and crimes to those who had not committed them, like that which he attributed to the said Lord Marquis." As for the charges made against the Lord Marquis, they stated that "the same were made up, hatched and invented by" Cubero. The aldermen meant to offer the Lord Marquis "entire and full satisfaction." He accepted their paper, leaving to lesser men the corrosive pleasure of bearing a grudge.

So it was not only possible, it was not even difficult for the alderman, in due time, to reopen the matter of his legal claim to the property now held by the soldier Ribera. The outlines of the case were familiar, for it was like many others left behind by Cubero. Still, said the Marquis, "with the attention which I owe," he must call for full investigation. When it was completed, he called before him the petitioners for the land—the one who would recover and the one who would retain—and gave his ruling.

"The property will be returned to you," declared the captain general to the alderman. He then turned to Ribera the leatherjacket, and said, "But you also are a soldier in my forces, and I wish to provide justly for you. Select another site within four months, and apply for it officially. It will be granted to you."

The petitioners accepted the decision.

The alderman thought about the meaning of it for a day or two. His bitterness against Ribera disappeared, for he secretly remembered the captain general as an example of how a man should deal with his fellow men. It was not easy for him to do it, but the alderman went to Ribera and offered to give him half of the property which lately they had disputed. In the legal record of the act, which was accepted by Ribera, the alderman "stated he would make donation to said Salvador Matías of part of the lot, so that he can farm and build a house, to live and enjoy as his own."

When the transaction was approved by the captain general, the new ownership of part of the lot was established one afternoon in the customary and legal way. The justice of the town court took Salvador Matías de Ribera to the property in the presence of well-wishers, friends, and idle onlookers. Among the little crowd was the alderman, who

stood on his own side of the line dividing him from his
new neighbor. The justice took Matías Salvador by the
hand and led him on to his piece of earth. There the justice
"gave voices," and "cast stones, and plucked up grass in
sign of possession, which in the name of the King our
Sovereign was given to him, and received in sign of pro-
prietorship." The justice put his signature to the statement,
and witnesses obliged with theirs. The affair was settled.
The captain general could put it out of mind. It was but
one of dozens of such small matters, that were large to their
principals, with which he must deal.

On December 16, 1703, he ordered the high constable of
Santa Fe to compel a captain of the troop to deliver to a
sergeant one Apache woman in payment of a debt, "within
the term of three days." Whether as chattels or as enemies,
the Apaches took up time and attention. Their power was
wild, and it had consequences often to be mourned.

vii.

On March 27, 1704, the Marquis de la Nava Brazinas in
personal command led a detachment of fifty officers and men
of the Santa Fe company out of the plaza to join Indian
allies at Bernalillo down the river. The alderman was with
the expedition in his capacity as sergeant. Apaches, playing
in and out of the mountains, were striking again and again
at the big farming estates of the central valley. Troops from
the capital were needed to end the peril.

They came into the greening groves of early spring by
the river, and the Marquis sent out scouting parties to find
the enemy. The enemy trail seemed to lead away to the
eastern plains beyond the mountains. The troop movement
had scared them off. The Marquis searched the mountains
nevertheless. The nights were high and cold. One day he
took a chill. The next he was carried back to Bernalillo. A
week later—the alderman was angered by the news—a week
later the Marquis dictated his will to his Secretary of Government and War. During the next day, April 8, 1704, he died.

His soldiers brought him to Santa Fe, where he lay in

state for a little while in the palace. They took him with muffled drums and caparisoned chargers to the military chapel behind the palace, where his requiem mass was sung, and his body was honored with "the title ceremonies and privileges of Castile." He was buried just in front of the altar in the floor of the chapel. He left instructions that, for him, two hundred masses be said, and "for the souls of the poor who died in the conquest of this kingdom," three hundred. After his funeral, the needy of Santa Fe were given, by his order, fifty measures of corn and twelve head of cattle, divided among them.

viii.

In the following year, of course, a new governor appeared —Cuerbo y Valdes, who reigned over and tried to correct much the same life at Santa Fe as that known under his predecessor.

Spaniards liked independence, and tended to scatter their dwellings apart from one another. This was dangerous, for Indians advancing like wildcats through the outskirts could more readily attack. The governor was forced to have a proclamation read after mass one Sunday morning when everyone would hear it which ordered all people owning property near the protected plaza and yet living elsewhere to move in and build on their town lots "at once . . . with the understanding that he who will not cultivate and build them, the said sites and house lots shall be declared as arid and unappropriated royal lands and shall be given and committed to persons who would cultivate and build. . . ." The governor was obliged later to call certain of his people to stay out of Indian pueblos. Three Indian governors had complained that the presence of Spaniards caused "grave damage" among the Indian people.

The alderman watched these and similar events with detachment. Years passed, new governors came and went, and he seemed unable to keep his mind upon the course of history. History belonged to another time—the time of the

Marquis, whom he had loved and wronged, and now mourned. Other men might come and command other events, but a senior alderman, a retired sergeant of leather-jackets, a bachelor of arts with no need for his learning might as well sit in the sunshine and feel warm when he could. A governor in 1708 began to have the palace torn down, and was deterred only by an inquiry from the viceroy. In the same year, Saint Michael's church across the fields above the Santa Fe river was examined for repairs, and the work started—the first since the fire night in 1680. A witch-craft case was heard at the palace. The new governor was an admiral of the King's fleet, and a knight of Santiago, and also a marquis, and, when occasion required, he sent soldiers out after Navajos.

In 1712 the next governor appeared, showing his royal letters patent, which were dated five years before at Madrid, and signed by the King. How far from the world was the high city of Santa Fe—but not as far as an old man dreaming awake in the sun. The alderman was proud in 1712 when the city council met on September 16 to declare that every year thereafter the royal city of Santa Fe would celebrate with a fiesta the reconquest of the kingdom by the captain general and Marquis. The council met in someone's house because heavy rains continuing for three days "as also the recent thunderstorms" had damaged the palace until it leaked.

Still, the public business went on and the palace was re-paired and the justice of the town court kept his records of affairs at law. These dealt with land disputes, and mur-ders, and penalties for living in concubinage, and desertion from the army, and neglect of duty by a horse herder, and mistreatment of wives, and thievery, and settlement of new communities, and the kidnaping of a Spanish boy by Indians, and provisions for travel by Franciscan friars, and regulations for entering and departing the kingdom. In 1715 a Spaniard sold some land to a Pojoaque Indian in exchange for "some quantity of corn, likewise chamois skins, woolen blankets, hens, and a chicken." It was a clear case of cheating an Indian, and the government filed suit to recover the Indian's property for him.

Near the city plaza was a small meadow which the leather-jackets used for grazing their horses. A captain held by grant a field bordering the meadow. The field had a spring. He dammed up the spring to provide a flow to irrigate his plantings. The dam caused the meadow below to become a marsh useless for grazing horses. The meadow was considered common town property. Protests were made. The governor reviewed the matter and, in the end, gave the captain permission to continue with his dam. But people felt this had been done not out of justice but "out of friend-ship," and a later governor agreed, and reversed the finding. The spring was closed, the marsh dried up, the grass grew free, and once again the horses of the garrison grazed in the public meadow.

It was like people to do as they did, thought the alderman wryly, when he thought at all about the events of the day. In 1716 the governor was forced to order the demolishment of certain houses and the uprooting of certain fields because people had so far overbuilt and overextended their property that the four streets entering the plaza of Santa Fe at the corners were almost closed. The Corpus Christi procession this year had to go in and come out of the plaza "by the same place, for being embarrassed all the inlets and outlets." Certainly troops on horseback, flocks, carts, and everything useful for "transportation of commerce of this vicinity" must be accommodated, and the selfishness of certain persons undone.

But to be sure there were men of honor, too, and one who died in 1718 said in his will, "I declare that I owe to Felipe Sais, a resident of Parral, a few pesos, which I agreed to pay with a little Indian girl."

Life profuse and teeming, and none of it carried flavor and meaning to the old alderman, whose taste for private involvement in affairs had gone with the captain general. Most extraordinary, he remembered, how when the captain general appeared, people if they were seated wanted to rise, or if standing, to kneel. The captain general was famous now. In the City of Mexico in 1693 he had already been called "the new Cid," and "this Don Hernando Cortés of these times." He was the last legitimate male of his line. Did not this seem bitterly proper? For who could succeed him truly?

Praying for him at mass, the old alderman knew the captain general for an heroic man. There was no one like him nowadays. Anyone kneeling near the alderman heard him murmur at the *Agnus Dei*, "grant him rest, grant him rest, grant him eternal rest," and heard him strike himself vigorously on the breast three times, and it sounded hollow, like a blow of wood on an old box. With his poor, mortal materials, he gave his tribute to an immortal greatness.

V

The Matriarch: 1710

i.

IT WAS HER VOCATION to be a mother.

She was born in 1710 on a large estate farm which was bordered on the west by the Great River just to the north of Bernalillo. Her parents had many children before her, and before she was three years old she was making play at taking care of two younger brothers. It was not long until the play became earnest, and she was confidently left by her mother to watch over the two little boys a whole day at a time. She soon knew how to impose her authority on them. She had heard her grandmother—lately dead—and her mother shrill out at children with torrents of scolding love, to save them from folly or harm, and she could imitate the devoted screams to perfection, while the small brothers sometimes, terrified by the sound, would burst into tears, or again, oddly unmoved, would merely pause and regard her with eyes like large black pebbles lying in pools of clear, sky-reflecting water.

Further, she could establish her powers over them by another means—she could make little surprises for them to which she would introduce them with gravity, as if to impress them with the importance of earning happy rewards through good behavior.

These surprises were of various kinds. Perhaps something

good to eat which she herself had cooked in the huge kitchen of the hacienda. Perhaps a pair of toy animals fashioned from straw and tied with bright yarns dyed in berry juices. Perhaps—the best of all—if they had been really good, and had made her laugh instead of scold, and if at supper with their chins hardly up to the level of the table they looked as sweet as cakes and good enough to eat (as she said), she would be overwhelmed, at the age of six, with feelings of possessive devotion; and she would take the little boys to pray with her by her bed above which imprisoned in a little tin lantern was a tiny dazzling figure of Our Lady of Guadalupe; and when they were done making their acts of piety, with their delicately nostriled snub noses buried in their twitching paws held together into which they whispered their messages for God, she took them to bed with her and all three slept safe, warm, and sweet even though the night was huge and black, and filled with dangers no one could name.

So in her very young years she acquired experience that usually came later to women. She knew, and sought, responsibility. She came to know the male nature in such intimacy and innocence that it could hold no surprises for her. And as one in charge of other people, she learned the importance of facts, and how to assess them shrewdly. It was necessary to know everything, though all things were not equally important.

ii.

The house where she first saw the world was a world in itself. It had been much rebuilt since the Terror of 1680, and now stretched along through three patios in a row, all with inner doorways and covered passages connecting them. The river was over to the west a few hundred yards. From it came an irrigation canal to water the fields about the hacienda. A little spur of the ditch system brought sparkling, talking water in through the rear wall of the middle patio. The water was clear except in times of storm or flood on the river, and then it was as heavy as chocolate and nearly as dark. She once drank of it in that state expecting to taste sweet-bitter chocolate, and was so badly fooled that she burst into tears of anger. Everyone laughed at her so hard that she tried never to let anyone see her weep again, in all her life.

The depth of the hacienda walls made it resemble a fortress, and this in fact it was, for the horse Indians came sometimes, and had to be fought off. The big cottonwood gates were closed at sundown every day with effort great enough to make her think of ceremony. Then the house was secure, and all that went on within it assumed by its very independence and seclusion the air of being the *right way*. If anyone should ask her in after years why in her own family and household things were done in a certain way, she would always be able to reply that it was because the same things had always been done in that way, the right way, in the house of her father and mother. It was an answer, and a reason, that stood good in Santa Fe for many generations.

She was educated in every activity that went on in the house. She worked in the long, narrow kitchen with all its bright copper pots and its tiled ovens and its storage cabinets for the silver service and its clusters of geraniums in the sunward windows with their panes of mica. She worked in the bedrooms, each with its fireplace and its shrine. In the big hall where important festive gatherings were held, she helped to embroider coverings for the wallside benches of earth and tile. She tended flowers in the patio, she made butter and cheese in the cold storage room, she took her turn at dusting the family chapel, and in time she became expert enough at needlework to repair the vestments kept there for the visitations of the priest. She had a prayer for every one of these duties, and could rattle it off accurately, thoughtlessly, and without irreverence when preoccupied.

Where some people liked to have lists of things written down, in order to remind them of how to manage affairs, she could produce whole lists right out of her head, for she never forgot anything she had ever seen or handled, and the entire contents of the big household were expertly catalogued in her mind. So also whenever she heard her father talking business with his laborers, or with other farmers, she remembered every detail of the discussion, and astonished him later by her comment and her memory. One time he took her little head between his hands and looked into her eyes and said she should have been a boy, a son, to carry all the family burdens after he was dead and gone. She was shocked by the remark, for she knew her first duty was to be most truly a woman, and in her own time bear children, teach them, see that they received of the factual world all that was rightfully theirs, make sure that they would love God not once in a way but all day long, and, in the end, die in her own dust like an apple tree too old to blossom any more, but at peace in yet another doing of the right way.

It was true that the brothers whom she raised until they were adolescent showed little of her administrative promise. The older was the hot-tempered one who never seemed to know the difference between the truth and a lie, but who smiled so dearly when he spoke that few questioned his honesty till long after, and too late. The younger worked well in the fields, but loved best to hunt, and loved weapons so much that he was granted permission to take care of the family arsenal. Nothing else interested him.

Once, while going over possessions of the household, the father brought out his lockbox and opened it in the presence of these, his three youngest children. He took from the box a white elkskin bag tied with thongs. He hefted it in both hands and let the children feel its weight. They could hardly believe it was so heavy for its size. He nodded wisely and then opened the bag to show them what was inside. In sunlight that came through the kitchen window he displayed "fifty-four ingots and nuggets of gold, large and small, which weighed sixty-six pounds and twelve ounces," as the family records had it. Here was a great occasion of pride for the father. He knew of no other man in the kingdom, excepting perhaps the governor up at Santa Fe, who could display such a sum of wealth all in one place and in one precious substance.

The brothers wanted to touch the gold and, when they had done so, were satisfied. But she asked where it had come from, what it was worth, what would be done with it. Well, it had come from the mines of Peru, and it was worth a fortune, and nothing must ever be done with it, it must be kept as the private and solid core of the family's position, and in time more gold must be added to it, if possible, though gold almost never found its way to the kingdom of New Mexico.

There were papers in the strongbox also, and the father looked through them. Taking one up, he read it to his daughter as an example of how workmen were paid, and of what values she would do well to learn. To a master mason who had worked on the house a year or so ago, he had paid a combination of "goods and money" consisting of "18 pesos in two loads of logs, 03 pairs of shoes, 04 varas of unbleached muslin, plus 4 pesos which I gave him for making the chimney and the windows and putting in the floor." In another paper he found record of what he had paid Indians for two weeks' work: "4 hides and 8 thick elkskins," which were worth sixteen pesos. She should remember this scale of pay, and, if she ever had to buy adobes, let her remember that "for 900 adobes" he had paid "one load of wood and five bunches of tobacco," worth fourteen pesos. All such information she liked for its own sake. It attached her strongly to the world of how things really were done.

Her brothers hardly listened, but wanted to be at play. Their greatest excitement, the highest moment of their love for their father, came when he was summoned to Santa Fe in the early summer of 1720, with an order to appear under arms for duty in defense of the safety and integrity of the kingdom.

iii.

Early in life, then, the meaning of warfare came to her. Its terms were local but the feelings they brought were timeless and universal. She was a country child, and Santa Fe was the name for a great place in the big world, where almost all news came from, and the conditions of life for her and all her family. Preparing his accouterment, her father told the family what he had heard.

Soldiers of France were gathering far out on the great plains east of the kingdom. There they were training the Pawnee Indians in civilized warfare. Using the Pawnees as common troops, the French were moving toward Santa Fe. If they were allowed to come too near, it would then be too late to defeat them. Many councils had been held in the Governor's Palace, and it was plain that the only proper course would be to send the Santa Fe garrison, reinforced by volunteers and friendly Pueblo Indians, to intercept the French war parties, give battle, and save the kingdom.

As for where the French had come from, the rumor was that they had come from the Micipipi River, and to the Micipipi River they had come from the Ylinneses Indian country, and to that country they were supposed to have come from the Saint Lawrence River at the Atlantic Ocean. It could be imagined what the King in Madrid would think of any Spaniard who permitted the French to invade and seize Spanish lands. The father of this household was eager to do his military service. His little boy cleaned, oiled, and polished his pair of horseman's pistols and his firelock gun, and rubbed his sword blade with fine sand and vinegar till it shone. The father rode to the royal city leading two extra horses. At home, they knew they would not hear of him again before autumn.

But they were wrong. Long before the end of summer the news came to Santa Fe and from there filtered along the Great River road north and south, and spread to the homes which men had left for duty. Forty-two soldiers of the presidial company and more than again as many volunteers and Indians had marched to the eastern plains to find the French. The governor of New Mexico did not lead them himself. He was an invalid, suffering from an old wound, and, instead, appointed Captain Pedro de Villasur to command the expedition. The captain accepted the command in all obedient confidence, as was proper; but he had never before campaigned in command of movements against enemies in the field. Many a soldier, many an estate farmer from the country down the river, wondered at his appointment, but they followed him, and in due course he found the Pawnees encamped along the North Platte River.

There was no sign of the Frenchmen. But the captain knew that the French had been training the Pawnees, and he opened discussion with these Indians, using as an interpreter one of his men who spoke French. This man was himself a Frenchman, though now a Spanish subject, who had been an accomplice in the murder of Robert de la Salle, the French king's explorer who had come so near to Spanish lands by the great bay of Mexico. The Santa Fe Frenchman talked to the Pawnees in French. He received no replies. The Pawnees seemed not to understand him. The negotiations were useless. Some of the New Mexicans believed that the Pawnees understood, well enough, and were only pretending to be perplexed. But the captain believed they were really ignorant of the French, and camped his troops by the river for the night.

It was a strange night, full of restless early hours. To more than one soldier from Santa Fe, things seemed ominous and wrong. They heard swimmers in the river in the dark. Why were men swimming in the river at night? The captain did not send to find out. Later a dog in the Spanish camp barked in alarm. Why did he bark? Who disturbed him? The captain did not inquire. Spaniards awake in camp saw that no extra sentries had been posted in their lines. It was a night full of secret stirrings and sad thoughts, and in the dead of it, from the river, making their strange, flute-like whistle, the Pawnees attacked. The royal Spaniards took to their arms in the dark and defended themselves as well as they could, but—the swimmers, and the barking dog, and the perplexed Pawnees—the battle was won by the enemy before it ever started. All but thirteen of the men from the Spanish kingdom were killed. Among those dead was the Frenchman who had helped to murder La Salle. Those who escaped said that during the battle they came to recognize many of the Pawnees as Frenchmen in disguise. They said that these Frenchmen looked out especially for the murderer of their great explorer and killed him in revenge.

The thirteen survivors ran away and returned to Santa Fe to tell of the disaster. The word came down to the hacienda, and was told with all possible circumstance and detail, but nothing was so important and so full of change as the news that the father of the household was among those killed and left on the far eastern plains. It marked the end of childhood for the child-daughter of the house. She was ten years old.

iv.

About five years later she was the center of a series of events for which she had been prepared throughout her young life. Her mother had married again, for a woman alone could hardly manage a large and isolated river estate. Her stepfather and her mother one day received a visit at the hacienda from two friends from Santa Fe. One of these came to act on behalf of his godson, a young man in the service of the governor. Her hand was asked in marriage. After satisfactorily answering various questions about property, character, and goodness of intention, the godfather was able to return to Santa Fe with good news for the young man. A date was set, and, before a month was out, the wedding party converged on the hacienda.

The bride was surrounded with older sisters and female cousins and friends, all of whom managed to keep alive through several days an atmosphere of excitement and merriment. Her marriage portion was known to all. She would bring to her union "three hundred pesos in silver, four hundred ewes," and a "blacksmith shop" equipped with "anvil, screw hammer, and two pairs of tongs." The bridegroom was able to provide "five hundred ewes, twelve horses, one mule, a he-mule, twenty-four canvas paintings, one dozen silver spoons, one half-dozen china cups for chocolate, two Michoacan boxes and trimmings, two others of wood also with trimmings, and kitchen equipment of a pot, and an iron griddle and spoon." In addition, he gave her "one plain silk underpetticoat, another one of fancy spotted silk, some exceedingly fine cotton goods, and a fine scarf and head covering." For himself, he had ac-quired "a suit of Castilian cloth—cloak, jacket, and trousers; besides the one for everyday use." Waiting for them after the wedding was their new home—"a house in the city of Santa Fe, with a tract of land in front. . . ."

For they were going to live in the capital, where his work was, and where his whole family lived. The bride and bride-groom had never met until they were brought together for the solemn ceremony of betrothal, held in the presence of godparents, just before the wedding. They were married in late afternoon in the main patio, under an arbor of pine boughs, before an image of Our Lady of Remedies. The priest from the mission of the Pueblo of Santo Domingo performed the sacrament of holy matrimony. A feast fol-lowed, and dancing, with music from violin and two guitars in the hands of neighbors. Twice during the evening the bride came to show her dower costumes—the petticoats which she put on one after the other. She was calm, though high color showed in her cheeks. She and her husband had little to say to one another; but already she regarded him as hers to serve, to protect, and never to judge. She entered upon her compact with him in the name of the Father, and of the Son, and of the Holy Ghost, thinking less of herself and of her desires than of the family she waited to bring into the world. She knew much about the world. He would see.

v.

Her first impression of Santa Fe remained with her un-changed through the many years of her life there. It was this: things were better organized at the hacienda down the river than here in the capital. At the farm, they had always done everything for themselves, and never expected to do otherwise. Here in the royal city, where something over a thousand people lived, there were many persons who needed others to give them services in exchange for pay-ment. How unfortunate for those who were not self-suffi-cient, she would think, for, in the first place, there was no money in circulation, and it was more difficult in town to hand over a cow or a pig, or a portion of an animal, or a jar of beans, in trade. People maintained the fiction of money, though, and she often saw receipts that read in this fashion: "I received from ———— the sum of twelve dollars, paid with one young bull."

There were no apothecaries, and oils and ointments could not be bought, "or any other expensive things." When a paper had to be sworn, the petitioner had nowhere to turn to find a notary, for there wasn't any, except the governor, who swore his own papers. If a citizen fell ill, there was no doctor to cure him, but if he was lucky he knew a good and capable woman from a country estate now living in town who could administer homely remedies. She preferred her own prescriptions to the services of Xirón de Tejada, the "barber and phlebotomist" of Santa Fe, who described him-self also as "surgeon and dentist." He was no longer a young man, and his experience was valued by many, along with his impressive professional equipment, which he listed to include "three medical books; two cases for instruments, one with five razors, and whetstone, and the other one with six lancets trimmed with tortoise shell and silver; forceps for drawing molar teeth. Another small case with two lancets; one scarifier; one pair of scissors; three cupping glasses, one large and one small. . . ."

For many years José Garcia pursued his work as "tailor,

teacher, and citizen of this city," but when he died, they said there was no other tailor "who rightly understands" the trade. If Joseph Romero, "the master mason," was a resident of the city, and met many building needs of the slowly growing population, then for carpentry work people had to do their own, or wait until an itinerant carpenter came into town with his exact science locked up in his head and his tools bound to the back of his burro. His arrival, and all other important information, was called out for all to hear by Antonio, "an Indian versed in the Castilian language, acting as the common crier." From her patio a few houses east of the palace, the young wife could hear his preliminary calls, for his station was "near the guard of the royal garrison, as it is a public place." She would drop what she was doing and hurry out of the house and down the lane toward the plaza to listen.

It was impossible to think of not knowing the latest information, preferably before anybody else knew it. Her friends—and she soon had a great circle of them, and of visitors in search of charity, too, who came regularly for the best of reasons—everyone came to tell her all there was to know. By the same token, no matter how long afterward, they could come back and ask her anything, and, if she had ever heard it, she would be able to tell it. Everyone from the pastor of Santa Fe to "Francisco, the negro," and "Joseph the harpist" became her particular friend; for even as her family grew so fast, she seemed to have time for everyone and everything, until someone said that if anyone ever wanted anything done, the best person to go to was the busiest, and they laughed, and indicated her.

Through her husband, who knew all that happened at the palace, she was well informed and full of opinions about government affairs. In 1727 she knew it first when the Crown offices in Mexico opened an investigation of the disastrous and ill-conceived expedition against the French and Pawnees of seven years before. Justice might be slow, but perhaps it was wisely so, and in any case, though it would not bring back the soldiers and farmers lost on the plains, the penalty imposed on the governor of that time would earn them grace where they were now. For his bad judgment and negligence in ordering the expedition, the governor was reprimanded and fined "fifty pesos for masses for the dead of the expedition; one hundred fifty pesos for chalices and ornaments for the missions of the Junta de los Rios"—new missions far to the south on the Great River, in country which she could not picture.

What great differences showed in the relative abilities of men in official life! She knew by her own brothers, and by watching her own sons as they grew, that no two men were ever really alike. But it did seem that in any position of power over others, men should be always of the best qualities. Her husband quoted to her a statement from a paper he had found in a file at the government house. "If those who have been and are now chief magistrates of this city had been skilled in law, or had at least studied at the Institute, there would not appear in the documents the nullities therein contained."

One day her husband had to go to the jail cells at the west end of the palace and there read out to the prisoner Juan Romero who had "persisted in his bad life"—she knew all about him—"in spite of numberless demands and admonitions," a degree stating that "he should not create scandal and create a bad example in the kingdom and he not having wished to refrain from his public vices," he was forthwith "banished from this city to that of La Cañada for a period of two years." And what did Romero do when he heard it? she asked, and her husband replied that Juan Romero, "who, having heard and understood, said he would obey, and would depart immediately to fulfill his banishment."

It was really amazing how much loose behavior there was in the kingdom. There was a man down the river near Albuquerque who was a violent troublemaker. The governor was forced to have him notified that "under penalty of fifty pesos' fine and fifteen days in the stocks for the first offense, he shall not execute any writings or co-operate in same, because he is by nature peevish and turbulent; and that for the second offense he shall be banished from this kingdom. . . ." She sometimes felt that when the governor issued a proclamation prohibiting certain acts, it was as if he were administering a public scolding to his people, and she wondered how under proper shame they could continue—as she knew they did—their offenses.

For there was a proclamation to prohibit "concubinage, disputes, and other public sins." There was also a lawsuit —one of many like it—brought by a citizen against another man for indulging in "concubinage with . . . a mulatto spinster." And there were other suits for vagrancy, and "offending with indecent language," and "bad treatment by word of mouth," and murder, and assault, and theft, and the kidnaping of a married woman, and cowardice in battle against Indians, and open quarrels between husband and wife. What energy lay in human nature—so much of it wicked, when so much needed to be done for the suffering of souls, both here and in purgatory! The human appetites in all their greed kept the government offices busy enough, she knew. Laws had to be laid down against "exportation of grain, livestock such as cattle, sheep and wool." From Madrid came a royal cedula prohibiting in general "games of chance and staking a sum at cards." To this the local royal government, taking notice of habits in Santa Fe, added its own provision: "Nor shall the officers gamble with the soldiers in either public or private places. . . ."

Along with all others, she had an occasional relief from the scandals and troubles of home when knowledge of great affairs came from the royal court in Spain. In 1746 word came of death in Madrid, and Santa Fe heard an order calling for the "celebration in this kingdom of a requiem mass for Our King and Lord, Philip V (may he be in Glory)." This event was followed at once by "celebration in this kingdom of the oath of our King and Lord, Ferdinand VI," who succeeded to the throne. The mother prayed in her duty. She could have no notion what the actual men were like who wore the crown and died under it; but the crown survived, and she was an expert in matters of death and mourning, for in any family so large as hers and that of her parents before her, death must come many times in one generation. For dead kings or dead sons or brothers she held common vigil; and when any such death made her heart ache, she would burn away her tears in private with fierce thoughts of those things which lived on to demand all her uses—the Glory of God, which she could not see, and the authority of the Crown, which she could, for this was imitated in hundreds of ways all down the path from government to community life to family life.

Her greatest power lay in obedience. It was remarkable how fully she could express her own will through obedience. In the end, she almost always had her way in any circumstance; first, because she accepted the circumstance, and second, because once it was hers to use, she could turn it in time to her own sincere ends. Her husband, her brothers, her sons were otherwise. They seemed always to try to break the bounds of the authority they were sworn to defend. She now and then made a downward smile of ironic amusement at how willing were the men of Spain to impose on others the kind of restraint they refused for themselves.

When that reflection came to her, she was usually thinking of impositions upon Indians. She would sigh. They were human creatures, were born free, not in slavery, and had souls, and must find heaven. But angry as it made her to hear of unfair use of Indians by Spanish people, she must admit that the constant pressure of Indian menace, the promise of terror to those whom she loved and worked for, really required hard measures of restraint upon the natives. Threats could come from within the kingdom or without, and seemed constant from one source or the other. In 1748 a Spanish lieutenant rode down from Taos to Santa Fe with news of a Comanche attack on the Taos farms. He said that for days on the banks of the Jicarilla River there were "one hundred tepees of the enemy Comanches, and that there arrived thirty-three Frenchmen who sold them firearms." The result was a battle with many lives lost and captives taken, mostly Spanish women and girls. Evidently such a murderous trade in weapons with the savage people was not entirely an outside affair, for a local proclamation decreed in the same year that "no person, no matter what rank and condition he may be, shall lend or sell offensive firearms to the pagan Indians." She was shocked at the guilty implications of such an order.

In 1750 yet one more fatherly effort came from the government to take the roving Indians into the fold of community ways. At the Santa Fe palace arrived a policy paper from the viceroy, the Marquis of Altamira, which declared that it was the policy of New Spain to invite all roving Indians to take up settlements in Texas and New Mexico, where "they will be treated and regarded with all love and affection, without doing them the least harm." They would not be "compelled, obliged, or teased to be Christians"—she was not sure she agreed with this point—"if they voluntarily would not desire to be." The viceroy went on to note that in the kingdom of New Mexico, it was principally the Utes, the Chihuahuas, and the Moquis who were to be induced "by flattery, caresses, and all of the most reasonable terms and methods . . . to be converted and to assemble" near missions. There they would "be clothed and maintained . . . tools and the rest of the farm implements shall be given them for the cultivation of the land, until they shall be able to support themselves by the fruit of their labor." It was a wonderful picture; but did she not recall from stories of long ago that it had all been tried before? She knew as a mother of willful children how almost impossible it was for anyone to change completely the nature given into him by God. It was the nature of those open-land Indians to move over their plains like wild herds. How little did the City of Mexico and its royal offices know of the facts so far away in the northern kingdom! At least the viceroy was wise enough to allow of other possibilities than those he so fondly proposed to begin with.

For if the pacification were not successful, then those Indians "shall be destroyed," he commanded, "and exterminated by campaigns which shall be carried on for this purpose and in their own country." This decision was endorsed by the governor of New Mexico, who called "for its most punctual compliance and due obedience, *in so far as possible.*" His last phrase was sensible and honest. What looked so easy to the viceroy—a mass pacification or a mass extermination—was not really possible to carry out with so few soldiers, so little to spare in supplies, such great distances to rove with the cloud shadows, and such hard mystery at the center of the Indian soul. No, a little comfort might be had from the little things that could be done to keep peace, and the mother was glad to know that, if any Spaniard maltreated or killed "noncombatant Indians," he would be heavily fined—500 pesos for each offense—and one third of such fines collected would "be devoted to rebuild the palace," which, in the 1740's, was, once again crumbling.

The viceroy commanded one more measure of defense against the Indian raiders who had driven Spanish settlers from their towns of Santa Cruz, Chama, Los Dolores, Abiquiu, Ojo Caliente, Embudo, and Chimayo. Let these towns be retaken and resettled. But the men and women to whom the order applied knew that life in those places would be a combination of farming and fighting for some time to come; and the movement back to the abandoned villages was slow. Yet where a little town in the northern reaches of the kingdom had not been abandoned, it seemed to hold to its handful of earth and its mountain creek with an almost thoughtless strength. One such town was that of Saint Thomas the Apostle on the river of Las Trampas. It was firm enough not only to keep its place and live, but to put forth a division, like a family, as the mother thought, when she heard of what happened.

For in 1754 a new town was made of settlers at Trampas who moved to a new grant on the Rio de las Truchas, and there built in the shape specified by the government. They were given "one league of public land for grazing and raising of livestock purposes, with the understanding that the same shall be public to the new settlers; also the forests and watering places; as, also, with the right that they shall have the right to sufficient land to build houses; and which shall be united and adjoining, forming a square town site, closed and with only one entrance, only large enough for the passage of one cart, in a manner that the inhabitants and families may be able to defend themselves from invasions and assaults of the barbarous enemies that may try to destroy it; which defense they could not use but only through such arrangements; and being all united, they can be at any time ready to defend themselves; as, also, to the digging of ditches to irrigate their lands . . ." She could see it as very much like the hacienda of her childhood. But as the inhabitants at Truchas were not all of one family, she knew well enough what would soon happen. They would begin to straggle off from the fortified compound, until their later houses would sit alone up and down the little river—the Spaniard always trying to be alone in his community. Well, they each had an old firearm, for in the muster rolls of any new movement in war or colonization, every man was named and his weapons specified. Nothing was so important as for him to be armed; for nothing had such power over his daily life as the action of Indians trying to preserve their own.

For herself, in her own station of life, she did what she could about the Indian difficulties. She simplified them in her heart; thought of God's love for his creatures; and, over a course of many years, took in and raised with her own children several Indian orphans.

She did this without second thoughts. It was a simple expression of her nature. Life, young life especially, must be fostered, for its own sake, no other. How different the motive must have been, she said, when she heard that among certain chattels under legal attachment to the government pending settlement of suits at law there were seven little Indian boys and girls who had been stolen and taken away, undoubtedly for private use as slave servants, by the very officials charged with their care. It was not the only case of graft of which she heard. She knew Spaniards seemed to take on the air of owners when they went into public business—owners rather than servants of a trust. Among other things made off with by officials who felt themselves not only lucky but privileged were chamois skins, blankets, buffalo hides, elkskins, turquoises, corn, tallow, beans, three male mules, a branding iron, cows, horses, bulls, oxen, and one "half-fattened hog." The stolen—or appropriated—articles were duly listed in a document, perhaps by the very officers under whose care they vanished.

She could think of more worthy purposes to which goods should be put. For reasons that remained obscure, the Pope suspended "the ecclesiastical monthly allowances" for the kingdom of New Mexico during the 1740's. The vicar of Santa Fe was left to his own ingenuities to pay for what needed to be done in his work. She was his good friend, and she had a thump of pride in her bony little breast at the courage and resolution he showed. How could he raise income for his church? He looked about and saw that everyone was grinding wheat and corn in the manner of the Indians—that is, with two stone tools, one shaped like a flat bowl, the other like a roller to grind within it. What if there were a mill—a real one, where people could bring their grains to be ground? In 1756 he ordered "to be built a water mill, in order to grind wheat in this villa," and he named it "The Mill of Saint Francis," and to operate it, he named his "godson," who, he said, "is also my nephew, Phelipe de Sandobal Fernandez de la Pedrera, therefore . . ." he gave him the mill. People came to use it, and paid a small fee to have their grain made into flour. It was a sensible piece of business, like something in the life of a country estate, where all needs had to be met at home.

Who would not give what he could to maintain the church, which was a refuge for not only the soul, but, when need be, the body? It was the only sanctuary for anyone who ran away from the danger of the world. Once within the walls of the church, a man was supposed to be safe even from the police authority of the state. It was a terrible sin to violate the sanctuary of the church, though she knew of cases in which it had been done by self-important officials. The proper way to deliver someone who had fled to the church was that used by a friend of hers in Santa Cruz, who brought a petition to the governor at Santa Fe, "asking that his son, who is a refugee in the church of the pueblo of Nambé, be allowed to leave same. . . ." She thanked God for a harbor of mercy in the hard world.

vi.

She hoped her house was in some measure such a haven. When she first came to live in it as a bride it was listed as "a house of five rooms and an arched porch." One of the rooms was a great hall twenty varas in length. As the family grew, new rooms were added, and additional land was obtained by grant from the governor. It adjoined the original property.

She always liked the ceremony of possession. The vicar was present, and commented in a learned manner upon it, saying that according to Herodotus the ancient Macedonians had a symbolic ceremony of taking title to property, drawing a line with a sword around a patch of sunlight, and then gathering up the patch of sunlight in their cloaks three times. The early Germans had a similar custom, added the vicar. She was fully satisfied of ownership on her husband's part as she watched the plucking up of grass and weeds, the throwing of stones and clods of earth, and heard the royal official who established the grant "give shouts saying Hurrah for the King whom God our Lord will preserve."

When the family added to the house, there were eleven rooms, and she knew by heart the materials that went into the new part: "106 carved vigas, 564 boards, 214 corbels, 59 round vigas," with roofing of hewn logs. When it came to paying for adobes for the walls, she remembered her father's advice, and paid according to the same rate. Many new houses were going up on the heights of Analco, across the Santa Fe creek, above and beyond Saint Michael's church. But she preferred to be where she was, in the oldest part of the city, east of the palace, and in a line with it, and only a few houses away from it. It was best to be in the center of things. There was plenty of added land now if even further rooms might be needed.

And they were. The house having begun in the shape of an L, then became a square U, and in the end was closed on all sides, framing a large patio where she had two trees that were almost like children to her—one a mountain willow, the other a white lilac which bloomed the third year after she planted it from a cutting brought in from the country.

In as many years, she bore fourteen children, of whom eleven lived to maturity. Looking about her, she saw that, even as things were, this was an unusually large family. The knowledge gave her satisfaction. If so many children brought so many more chances for trouble and sorrow, as some women would remark, they also brought so many more chances for joy and pride. It was amazing that one who looked so frail as she should be able to give such abundant life to the world. She never grew heavy, as did so many women of her race. She kept the figure of a girl until she was a very old woman, and then she seemed to be made of the tiny bones, the little vaulted breast, the dried, cool flesh of a bird, that enclosed as it were impersonally a beating heart and a quick brain.

She was so busy all day long that her children of all ages would laugh and ask if Mamá was never tired, to which she would reply that she was dead with exhaustion, keeping right on with her task of the moment. It might do, she would say, to feel tired; but it would never do to act tired. They all marveled at how much she did, and how much she knew. She loved her duties, and took pride in knowing every detail of the family's existence. Of these, the catalogue of their possessions, which would have to be well kept in order to appear with strict accuracy in the drawing of wills, was one of her chief pleasures, for she kept it mostly in her mind, and could name any object, give its value, and if necessary produce it at once. By her vigilance, everything was always in its proper place. She made constant inspections of the whole premises to be sure of this.

Of her own possessions, she liked best her jewels. Though she almost never wore them, she often looked at them. She viewed them rather critically, as if to ask why so much value were imprisoned in such small forms. She concluded that it was just because they were such a pleasure to see, thinking of beauty without naming it. She had a small reliquary shaped like a purse. Its flat pouch was made of paper-thin gold. The gold looked as soft as kid leather. It seemed to give forth light of itself. She was supposed to wear it pinned over her heart, but never did. It was too valuable. She had also, "seven strings of black pearls, a necklace of large and small pearls, and one roll containing twenty-seven pearls," and a pair of earrings containing "pearls of the best kind." She could choose between two pairs of bracelets, one of jet, the other of coral, but never wore either. In a little locket "with silver frames" there were places for two small pictures. She wished someone could make a likeness of her husband to put in one frame, and of one of her brothers—she would never tell which— to put in the other. But there were no artists in Santa Fe, and what she did was trim out of an old prayer book two bits of wood-engraved images showing the Ecce Homo and Our Lady of Sorrows. These she put into the locket, and she wore the locket on great occasions.

They said at home that she had no vanity. The meagerness of her wardrobe reflected this. Her grandest piece of dress was a "purple blue satin cloak lined with bright pink satin." She could put "sleeves of English linen" into one of her blouses, and sometimes she wore a "lady's short cloak of yellow satin lined with blue silk." She had "a British skirt." For the rest, her few clothes were made of the cloth of the kingdom, good, sturdy, dark serge which she cut and sewed herself, according to patterns kept in her family for many years. The skirt was wide and full, like a bell, and the upper part was tight, with long sleeves. She had a choice of shawls—white lace, black lace, embroidered China silk, or plain black French silk with heavy fringes of black. She liked to wear the last. She drew it up over her head to go to mass. Her hair was fine and full, parted in the center, and drawn together at the back of her neck to be fixed with silver pins. Early in life it went gray, and then white. It made her eyes, which were gray, look both more brilliant and more dark. Sometimes when she glanced with an idea at somebody, they said they could almost feel her look strike them. Her children, whether young or old, knew what they meant when they said to each other, "Mamá looked at me." They meant there was no use trying to deceive her.

She often sorted through her husband's clothes. His wardrobe was far more abundant than hers. The vanity of the family was his, which seemed proper. Holding up his garments, she saw them as animated by him—his flesh, his movement, his character. For official use he had a "blue cloth uniform" and a pair of "blue velvet trousers" to be worn with chamois skin boots. She kept on hand "two yards of gold lace for military ornament and three skeins of gold thread" for the renewal of his uniform. He wore a pair of "crimson stockings from Geneva," and a hat, "half cardboard, three corners, with cord." About his waist went a "Tripoli belt with buckle." His dress sword had a silver hilt. His military cloak was of black "everlasting cloth lined with fur." He always took with him his silver snuffbox and his small leather "pocket folder."

Otherwise, he could wear civilian dress of some variety. He had another cloak, "white . . . lined in scarlet cloth," and another of "dieziocheño cloth," whose name meant that it had eighteen hundred threads to the warp, and also "a great coat of said cloth lined with blue flannel of this country," and trimmed with galloons. His other jackets included one of flesh-colored cloth, another embroidered, another of Castilian cloth, and another trimmed with *pianas*. For dress, he had "one ribbed silk shirt trimmed with gold fringe." His best waistcoat was of red satin, with which he wore one of his "eight sets of buttons— imitation silver." He had two pairs of "Chinese embroidered stockings," and others of plain yellow or black silk. About his neck he wore a scarf "trimmed with gold shrimps." His shoes were either heavy-soled or of fine, soft kid leather. He had two pairs of each.

In all these garments she saw his formal pride. If she half closed her eyes and tilted her head, she could see him as if standing off somewhere, the big three-cornered hat slanting forward, his coat collar reaching high, the tight back of his coat and its long square tails, his hand on his sword hilt and, drawn through his resting arm, the full long folds of his cloak, and all held up on the thin but strong lines of his legs encased in their elegant rumpled soft chamois boots. Adding the final sting of style, the line of his thin sword pointed straight out behind him.

She knew in detail the count of his arms and armament. In a separate room across the patio he kept "all the weapons of a soldier—musket, pistols, sword, lances, deerskin jacket of six thicknesses, leather shoulder belt with fringes, leather shield, ammunition, cartridge belts, saddle bags, saddles, bridles, and spurs." The spur buckles were "silver lions." There was an *esmeril*, that was, a small bronze cannon. One of the swords was large, "for horseback." Another had a hilt and guard of silver filigree. He stored the firearms in a wooden rack, except for a harquebus of the seventeenth century which had its own leather sheath and was hung on the wall. A bullet mold and a compass completed the contents of the armory.

In her own cupboards she kept supplies of cloth and leather which could be used to mend articles in the wardrobes or in the weapons room. She had bolts of English linen, and lengths of "flowered Rouen linen" from France, and "ten varas of narrow black ribbon with silver flowers." If this last item might have seemed like an extravagance when she bought it from a trader who had bought it from the City of Mexico, still, it was gratifying to discover how many uses the ribbon could be put to. No such qualms ever troubled her about the piles of chamois skins, elk hides, and buffalo hides in the storeroom. Leather, next to wood, was the most useful of all materials.

She was at her most sharp-eyed when she went to inspect her stores of food. Though she was the principal cook, she always took along one of the Indian women who served in the kitchen, and to her she would point out what was good and what bad in the rows of hanging meat cuts, or in the pottery vats of flour, or the wooden bins full of grains, or the strings of dried fruits hanging overhead. The fruits were kept against the wintertime, when fresh vegetables could not be had. In summer, the fields beyond the patio yielded fresh corn, beans, onions, lettuces; and the family's "sixty-three fruit trees" brought peaches, plums, pears, and apples. How, she sometimes wondered in a side notion, how could children grow up without an orchard? Fruit trees were so safe—their branches sprouted within reach of enterprising small limbs, and they spread wide and upward so gently that once in a tree a child could climb almost as if by ladder. Nobody knew how it delighted her to see both children and apples in a bounteous tree in full summertime.

As for the rest of her food stores, she kept a narrow tally of those precious articles that were imported from Mexico at great trouble and expense. These included "sixty-eight pounds of base chocolate," and "eighty pieces of maple sugar." In a corner of the storeroom was a barrel containing whisky distilled by the friars at El Paso. She used it chiefly for medicinal purposes. In a corner from the heavy unpainted log beams were hung one hundred bundles of tobacco. These, too, were imported and left in the raw state until, in private use, the owner was ready to crumble the leaves and smoke them. Under the law, no province of the Spanish empire was permitted to use its own crops of tobacco for local manufacture of cigars. The home country maintained its monopoly of the tobacco trade. It was something much talked about in Santa Fe, and, she supposed, elsewhere, for people anywhere would surely object to such a law.

When she considered the contents of her house, she turned first to the kitchen. She loved her most useful objects the best, for these she handled more than any others. They included all sorts of clay pots made by Indians in the pueblos, and a whole set of wooden bowls shaped like flat, narrow boats, in all sizes, that came from the old province of the City of Mexico. She had copper kettles, an iron griddle, a brass mortar and pestle, and large flat trays cut from cottonwood which through long use and many washings grew soft as velvet to the touch. In her "two chocolate boiler drums" she melted down and refined the raw chocolate stored in the larder. Her glassware came from Puebla and from Toledo, and her table porcelain from China through the Pacific trade at Acapulco and Mazatlán, by way of Manila in the Philippines.

In cabinets with carved openwork doors she kept her table silver. Its various pieces did not match, but all were heavy and rich to hold. She had silver forks and spoons, a salt cellar, a "waiter with cover," and a silver cup "which could hold a quart." Set side by side on a wooden shelf she kept several pewter plates. All these looked well if she brought them out together for a grand party, when the long dining table at one end of the kitchen was laid with one of her best "Germanic tablecloths." The cloth was perfectly smooth, for she had a flat iron, which was a rarity in Santa Fe.

Throughout the living and sleeping rooms, most of the furniture was homemade in the carpenter shop at a corner of the patio, where the tools were kept—axes, an adze, a drill, knives, nails, and various chisels. The beds, tables, and chairs were sturdy and plain, with squared lines. Skins were thrown over the seats, and blankets woven by Indians. Of these, the blue ones shot with red patterns were the softest and best. They were also something of a grim reminder, for the yarns of which they were woven came from Spanish uniforms taken by Indians from soldiers dead in battles and skirmishes.

But beyond such plain pieces of furniture, she had a few treasures which gave to a wall or a corner something handsome to see and to use. She had two painted chests, made in Michoacan—part of her marriage portion—and two mirrors with gilt frames that she hung above them. In the formal room, there was a round table which by its shape was a local curiosity. Her best piece was an "old desk with drawers painted." She did not know where it came from, except that it had always belonged to her husband's family. But of course many of her household possessions had come to her in his dowry. The two dozen paintings on canvas which he had brought to her at her wedding were displayed in two rows, one on each side of the big room.

They were religious pictures, and much prized for being on canvas. Most of her other sacred images were painted in pale brown and blue berry colors on elk hide, and were hung unframed, like pieces of tapestry, high on the walls. One showed "the crucified Lord," and another, Saint James, and another, the Infant Jesus. These holy presences lived as part of the family, and presided over all the lives of the house—even to the animals out in the farm corral between the house and the fields. There were horses, pack mules, chickens, hogs, turkeys, cows, and the "five oxen trained to *whoa!* and *stop!*" marked with the branding iron which was kept in the blacksmith shop along with the tools she had provided at her marriage.

With all of these possessions, inanimate or living, she felt a thoughtless intimacy, for in any of the activities or uses which they represented she could find herself.

There was only one kind of thing or use in her house from

which she felt excluded. This did not trouble her, for she refused to be troubled by mysteries beyond her grasp. To her it was a mystery that her husband should possess books, and sometimes read them. She had picked up a little skill at reading simple and familiar lists of supplies or tasks, but to imagine herself sitting down with a book and calmly working her way through it page after page with her eyes—this was beyond her. But she had great respect for those who could read, and when on occasion—perhaps once every two months or so—her husband stated that he would read for a while, she ordered absolute quiet in the house, and watched with remote approval the ceremony with which he approached his exercise.

She knew his books by sight. He had "three volumes of ordinances; one volume: *The History of Gibraltar;* one volume: *Concourse of All the Sciences;* two volumes: *Historic Abridgement of Religion;* one small book: *Castilian Orthography;* one small book: *The Philosopher Sueco;* one *Christian Catechism;* one *Guide of Foreigners With the Regulation of Garrisons.*" It was an impressive list, and she knew of only four other people in Santa Fe who read for the enjoyment of it, aside from reading the things that were necessary in business or government.

Her husband would go to his bookshelf and run his finger along the backs until he came to the volume that met his interest, and then he took it out, went to his desk with the painted drawers, seated himself, placed his book, took from one of the painted drawers his "pair of spectacles with silver rims," set these well down upon his nose—no wonder they were called "in-front-of-eyes"—opened his book, pulled his candles closer, and with one forefinger on his lower lip and the other slowly traveling just below the line he was reading, he applied himself to the absorbing work which seemed to bring to him a wholly incommunicable pleasure. There was nothing she did not know about him except this one thing—whither his mind went when he was reading.

vii.

Important family papers were rolled up and kept in a sheath of soft elk hide, and tied with thongs around a button in the form of a small stuffed ball of the same leather. There she could find property deeds, and records of birth, baptism, and death.

She had many receipts for the charity given with full heart to the dead. These read variously, "I paid for twenty-five masses with a yoke of oxen," or "three masses paid for with the silver buckles," or "six masses paid for with one bull," or for the digging of a grave in the floor of the Chapel of the Virgin, "one and one-half fanegas of piñon." In 1758 the elkskin wallet was again put to use, for in that year her husband fell ill, and soon it was clear to him that he must make his last will and testament, which would be placed with the other family records.

It was an awesome occasion, and yet, too, it required the help of so many persons that it seemed at times merely formal. A penman from the government houses was summoned to take dictation from the dying man. Several witnesses came to hear the document take form, and to identify the chattels and other possessions specified in the bequests.

Many people outside the family learned much of the family's business in the process. The mother could not help regretting this, yet accepted it as necessary for others to know the number of spoons, cups, animals, and the rest that belonged to the household.

In the usual style, the will was drawn "In the name of God Almighty." It offered the soul for "a most clear career of salvation" and the body "to the earth from which it was made." The corpse was to be "shrouded with a habit of the Third Order of Saint Francis." Most of the property was left to the mother, with a few provisions for each of the eleven living children. To a son went a certain room of the house; to another, a garden plot; to various daughters, sacred images or pieces of silverware. If the mother should die soon, any unmarried children were assigned to brothers or sisters "that they may rear and shelter them as their adopted children; instructing them in the holy fear of God; protecting them; as I transfer for all the paternal right which pertains to me."

The will contained a full listing of all properties, including various plantings of grain in different places—"a bushel of wheat and a half of corn at the ranch of Juana de la Ora, a bushel of wheat at Santa Clara Pueblo, another at Chama, another at Tesuque Pueblo, and more plantings at Pojoaque." The land at Pojoaque, after the harvest, was willed to the Indians of the pueblos of Santa Clara, Pojoaque, Tesuque, San Ildefonso, and San Juan "in equal parts," for their own future farming.

In such an exercise of final responsibility, even the most secret truth must be told if duty depended upon it. Years ago one of the orphan Indian servants of the household bore a child whose father was never named. The mother of the household took it in and raised it as one of her own. Without being told, she knew who the father was, but no one else ever knew what this knowledge cost her. Now, as her husband on his deathbed made his will, she knew what must come; and she heard him bequeath "to the orphan serving maid, by reason of the deceased being the debtor of her virginity, two hundred pesos in order that she may have wherewith to be able to be married, and if she should not desire to, in order that she may be able to alleviate her needs and"—it was this that made his wife finally bow her head before wide nature—"and unburden the soul of the deceased." The witnesses now knew for fact that which had been the subject of gossip long ago. Judgment would soon pass from them to Almighty God. Who among them had not sinned? Who would not suffer in his turn? They signed the will, if they could; and if someone couldn't another wrote by his mark, "I signed for him as he did not know how."

It was important that all be recorded and understood in utmost clarity, for if the will should later be the subject of civil inquiry by the government, settlement of the estate might take years, and the costs would be considerable, and tiresome in their detail:

	Pesos
To four instruments presented, one with exhibits	5
To eight writs at one peso each	8
To two correlative answers	2
To service of four writers at 1.25 pesos	5
To depositions of nine witnesses examined, less the fifty cents for each question at pesos each	18
To the notification of decision at fifty cents	.50
Total: thirty-eight pesos and four reales	38.50

Such a bill seemed to say that if grief in time went away, practical affairs were everlasting. Perhaps, in a habit of mercy, one helped to dissipate the other. She had lived with him for thirty-three years, and was destined to survive him for a longer span.

Now supreme authority in the family passed to her when he died. She was forty-eight years old. Two of her eleven children were grandparents, the rest were all fathers and mothers but two younger sons and one grown daughter who was unmarried. The daughter went to live with one of her married sisters in whose house she would remain as maiden aunt, governess of the children, and godmother, an aging family fixture who would be loved for her eccentricities and feared for her chaste wisdom.

The matriarch could see in her ever-growing tree of descendants and dependents—including the Indians whom she had adopted—examples of most variations in human nature. Some of them gave her concern, but, as the years passed, she found herself less able to feel tormented by suffering when one of her own people broke the laws of God and King. After having given them the supreme gift of life, she had done what she could for them, and the rest belonged to prayer. She went daily to mass and prayed for those whom she loved and was responsible for, and, if they fell into evil, she prayed that God's mercy would comprehend them even as they were.

One of her sons was a famous gambler. At first he had been lucky, winning "many horses at the game of cards, as well as Indian servants, hides, and other things." His success seemed to him—and she must admit to others, including some of his brothers—like a justification of his ways. But it did not last, and she was drily ashamed that a legal record existed stating that he "would gamble and lose whatever came into his possession, in the towns of this kingdom. And . . . he would at times run away from his father on account of his many crimes." She heard that people went about saying that he had gambled away twenty thousand pesos. The rumor was so absurd that she disdained to answer it in any way. After his father's death she refused this son any more money. He was amazed to find her stronger than his father. After his first anger, somehow he knew that her strength represented a truer love than his father's exasperated indulgence had done. He viewed her with new eyes.

She had become a power; or perhaps all that in her which for so long had been humbled before her husband now simply came into view. It was not that she was the official head of the family—the eldest son held that position. But in her widowhood, age, and experience, all her children turned to her for guidance and approval.

So, in time, did many of the leading families of Santa Fe. Making no effort to do so, she gradually became the source of important opinion, just as for so long she had been the expert on matters of general information. Her interest was as lively as ever, but her manner came to show a new dignity, as suited her position and increase of years.

As one who knew how things had always been, she came to be regarded as one who knew how they should always be.

So small in person, she contained a power like that of the Spanish Crown—a power whose first purpose was conservative. Let that which has made us, and which is good —so this power seemed to say—remain unchanged, no matter which way the world may move. For nearly fifty years more, following the death of her husband, all unknowingly she represented for Santa Fe the empire of Spain in the eighteenth century.

viii.

Of the great affairs that came naturally to her notice and demanded her touch the most enlivening took place in 1760. This was the official visit of the Bishop of Durango —the first such visit in thirty years.

For many days while preparations were going forward at Santa Fe, it was known that the bishop was toiling his way northward along the valley of the Great River toward the royal city. Late one May afternoon with his small train of accompanying chaplains, secretaries, and soldiers, he was received half a league from the city by the governor and "a numerous and brilliant retinue," as the bishop put it. There were mounted gentlemen, and ladies in carriages and wagons. One of these was the matriarch.

With the rest, she turned and followed when the bishop and the governor proceeded into the city in the governor's coach. The streets were full of welcoming people. Cloths and rugs and banners were hung on the houses. The procession passed under arches of greenery and flowers, to salutes from artillery and bells.

At the very edge of the plaza the procession halted, and there the bishop stepped down and was vested with miter and cope. The clergy took up positions, and, with intoned declaration and response, and use of holy water and crucifix and lighted candles, the bishop made his entrance to Santa Fe with the same observances that the Roman ceremonial prescribed for a bishop's entrance into a cathedral. The act was solemn, and, through the person of the prelate, shimmering in gold and silver bullion embroideries on cope and miter, it had splendor. The whole city seemed like a church. When the grand observance was completed, the bishop was taken to the palace where to make way for him and his suite the governor had vacated his own rooms and had moved to another house.

On May 25, which was the Feast of the Pentecost, the

bishop "with all possible solemnity" made his official visits to the churches of Santa Fe. He preached in the parish church of Saint Francis at the east end of the plaza, and inspected all its facilities, noting that it was "large, with a spacious nave and a transept adorned by altars and altar screens." He went to see Saint Michael's across the creek, where the roof was under repair, and described it as "fairly decent." In the plaza a new church was being built. It was the chapel of the royal garrison, dedicated to Our Lady of Light. He saw with particular interest that a richly designed altar screen in three tiers was being carved out of a "very white stone" which was quarried eight leagues from Santa Fe. The carving was nearly completed when he saw it. It was handsome. The sculptor had come from Mexico. He carved six main figure pieces, showing Our Lady of Valvanera, Saint Francis of Solano, Saint John Nepomuk, Saint Joseph, Saint Ignatius of Loyola, and, at the crest, the Eternal Father. These were framed in heavy borders and supporting urns on pilasters, all treated with carved leaves, garlands, flowers, and grapes. It was massive and from a little distance looked like the encrusted embroidery seen on the richest liturgical vestments. Evidently the figures were to be delicately tinted, in the polychrome technique of the Renaissance. The chapel and its treasure stood across the plaza from the palace.

The bishop was much occupied with business of the church—cases to be heard under canon law, discussions of administration with the local priests, inspection of church accounts, confirmations, and the rest. But he had time to make a general observation of the city. He was told that there were 379 families, totaling 1,285 people. But how could this be? he asked, when by actual count he had confirmed 1,582 in Santa Fe alone? Those charged with keeping the census must be in error. "I am convinced that the census they gave me was very much on the low side," he said.

He observed that the whole city—churches and houses— was built entirely of adobe. He was amazed to see that the houses were far apart, for, because of this, he remarked, the city did "not have the least defence." It was extraordinary that there was no actual fortress at the capital, and not even a formal headquarters and barracks building for the garrison.

"If there had been a fort," he said, "at the time of the uprising in the year 1680, the Indians would not have dared to do what they did."

He saw that water was scarce, and it was agreeable as an adjunct to his visit that during the day on Pentecost Sunday heavy rain fell, followed by hail, and the mountains above town were covered by snow, which soon melted. The weather made everyone rejoice, for "such early precipitation augured a good winter."

After a few days in the capital the Lord Bishop of Durango left for Pecos and Galisteo, where he visited the missions and confirmed many men, women, and children. He returned to Santa Fe in time for the Feast of Corpus Christi, the second Sunday after Pentecost. The city was decorated with "branches and splendid altars," he noted, and after celebrating pontifical high mass he appeared in procession "with His Divine Majesty." The streets were thronged and the bishop was gratified by "salvos from the military squadrons." After another few days he arranged to continue his tour of inspection, with plans to proceed through the pueblos along the Great River to the north, until at Taos he should see the last of his far-flung parishes. Before he left, he accepted an invitation to dine with the matriarch upon his return from Taos.

He was back in town about the middle of June, and in due course came to dine. His hostess received him in the entryway, and conducted him to the big room, where places had been laid at two long tables set up for the occasion. Her Germany tablecloths were on, and all her silver, and the best Toledo glass, and ranks of candles. The walls were freshly washed with white lime, and the gold frames on the painted canvases had been polished. The bishop exclaimed at the beauty of the room and its air of state. He sat down in a great chair with arms and a high back over which she had cleverly fixed a piece of purple Flemish velvet. The maids had been well rehearsed. The sons and daughters of the house were sober guests.

The bishop, once the introductions and presentations had been made, found himself next to his hostess at table. He found her easy to talk to. He did not have to explain anything too much. She understood his point readily each time. You might have thought she had grown up at Court, for the grace of her manner and the ease of her exchange with lord bishops. He was amazed to hear that Santa Fe was the only city she had ever seen and this kingdom the only land. By the same token, she would understand all the better his concern for a condition here which he had repeatedly encountered.

The Christian Indians did not make full use of the sacraments. The worst case was that of confession. The Indians said they did not know Spanish, and the friars said they could not themselves speak or learn the Indian tongues. There were one or two native interpreters in each pueblo, but the people were reluctant to go to confession through a third person. It was an appalling condition to find, and the bishop told her that it "saddened and upset" him more than any other "in that kingdom." He was vigorous in chiding his clergy for their neglect in the matter, urging its extreme importance "for the good of those souls." He said if they would formulate catechisms and "guides to confession" in the Indian sounds, he would pay to have them printed.

The whole problem was complicated and troubling, and he could remember himself just how baffled the fathers could be, for when he was a young priest on parish duty at Caracas, in Venezuela, he had had the same difficulty with negroes brought from Africa by English traders. Still, he did notice here in New Mexico that, when it came to certain affairs, the Indians could make themselves understood well enough, and grasp the meaning of what was said to them in turn.

She nodded. She knew what he meant.

"In trade and temporal business," declared the bishop drily, "where profit is involved, the Indians and Spaniards of New Mexico understand one another completely." In such matters, he added, the Indians were "knowing and avaricious enough." This habit of understanding did not extend into the spiritual realm, with regard to which they displayed "great tepidity and indifference." The result was "wickedness." He sighed. Mysterious creatures, Indians. On his recent travels to the pueblos, he had twice been promised encounters with hostile Comanches. One of his warnings came from "friendly Apaches."

However, no battles had developed, and he had proceeded on his way. The water at Nambé was heavenly to drink, though in the same pueblo he met with bedbugs. "A plague," he said, "a swarm . . . a multitude." At Taos he heard about the annual Comanche fair, but was unable to wait for it. But he understood the plains people brought "captives to sell, pieces of chamois, many buffalo skins, and out of the plunder they obtained elsewhere, horses, muskets, scatter guns, munitions, knives, meat," and so on.

True, she murmured, many of such things found their way to Santa Fe through commerce. It was curious that from such savages so many useful objects were obtained.

Yes, he added, he understood the Comanches came in great numbers, quite seventy of their buffalo hide tents would be set up on the outskirts of Taos. They did not sell their wares for money—there was of course no money —but traded for other goods. And amazing: while some Comanches were trading in peace at Taos, others of their nation would make war on pueblos elsewhere in the kingdom.

He would say that they were oddly aware of themselves, for the governor had told him how the trading Comanches had said on occasion, "Don't be too trusting. Remember, there are wretches among us, just as there are among you. Hang any of them you catch." It was a strange land, and he had much respect for those pious and hardy Spaniards who made their life here through many generations.

She exchanged a look with him, and accepted his compliment.

The dinner party was a success. It lasted three hours, and when it was over, at seven in the evening, he toured the house, blessed the rooms, and gave his hand so that all of the company might kiss his ring. Despite his marks of rank—the violet silks, the heavy lace, his great gold chain with its jeweled breast cross—he seemed close to them all. The family, like the whole city and, in fact, the kingdom, felt restored by his presence. His see of Durango was fifteen hundred miles distant. He had come to them through hardship and danger—they knew how much and what kinds —and must return the same way. They were moved by his care for them.

He left the royal city "for the outside world," as he said, in early July.

There was an odd, a scandalous, echo of his visit to Pecos. The story reached Santa Fe in September, and the matriarch was much shocked by it.

An Indian of Pecos, having attended the bishop's ceremonies in May, turned himself into a bishop in September and paid a burlesque visit to the Pecos Pueblo. He made a miter of dried sheep hide and stained it with white earth. Out of an ordinary cloak he fashioned a cope, and a rochet out of another. His crosier was a long dried reed. Another Indian played the part of the father president of the kingdom. He wore an imitation of the Franciscan habit. Another painted himself black and impersonated the bishop's negro body servant. Riding on mules, the three wretches made a ceremonial entry into Pecos. Drums rattled. The people knelt down. The Indian bishop gave his blessings right and left and walked to an arbor where there were two thrones. The people were then ordered to come forward for confirmation. With water, he put a cross on the forehead of each, and "gave him a buffet," and dismissed him. When all had been treated, a feast was served, and

then all took part in a dance. The shocking imposture
continued all the next day, with the false bishop pretending
to say mass in the arbor, during which he distributed a
mockery of Holy Communion, using broken tortillas for
the sacred wafers.

After a third day of such blasphemous nonsense the joke
ran dry, and the Indian bishop went off to tend his cornfields near the Pecos River. He sat down under a cedar
tree and gazed at his cornfield. There his punishment overtook him. Walking straight out of the mountain to the
cedar tree, a bear came to him and without warning attacked him from behind. The bear tore away the skin of
the man's skull from just above the place "over which the
miter must have rested." The man's right hand and heart
had sinned in blaspheming the sacraments, and the bear
bit him on the hand, and then on the breast. And then,
not even glancing at the ripe corn which ordinarily he
would have raided, the bear turned around and went
straight back to the mountain. It was clearly an inspired
retribution, as these details indicated. The matriarch knew,
further, that bears did not ordinarily attack men unless
men chased them.

The foolish Indian bishop was taken home. There he
said to his son, "I have committed a great sin, and God
is punishing me for it. And so I order you that you and
your brothers are not to do likewise. Counsel them every
day and every hour." He then died. It was an edifying
tale, worth many hours of conversation. Indians. There
seemed no limit to the mysteries and powers that resided
within those people.

ix.

Her interest in knowing the life about her in all its
aspects was like another affirmation of her vocation, which
was to foster life. She had no book learning. She learned
all she knew from facts to be seen, and from hearing the
Gospels. So as the great age that was granted to her took its
course with the eighteenth century, she continued her stor-

age of information about the city, the military, the law, the government, the faint touches that reached her city from "the outside world," as the Lord Bishop of Durango had called it.

The Comanches gave battle at Taos in the summer of 1760, and again, and far more fearsomely, in 1761. Their terrors came intermittently through the years, and once again the outlying towns were abandoned, until in 1779 the population of the capital had been much increased by refugees. The royal cavalry troop consisted of twenty-four soldiers. During the summer months half of these were stationed at advanced posts near Galisteo to guard against Comanche sweeps from the eastern flatlands. The armament of the kingdom "contained of weapons, eight guns, one without carriage, and eighty-four serviceable muskets."

In 1781 the reigning governor Juan Bautista De Anza made the startling proposal that the capital be moved from Santa Fe plaza to one of two places. Let it be re-established either on the heights of Analco beyond Saint Michael's church across the creek, or let it be uprooted and transplanted at a site "ten leagues distant from the city of Santa Fe" on the Great River. The governor had in mind "a clear and spacious locality, not so cold in temperature and much more pleasant than that of Santa Fe. The proposed place was about "four and a half miles in length, and two or more miles in width, with farming lands sufficient for raising plentiful harvests of wheat and other grains, and to make gardens." It stood halfway between the pueblos of Cochiti and Santo Domingo. There was "an abundance of water because of its proximity to the Rio del Norte, whence it can easily be taken with no expense and very little work." Also it abounded in "good grazing lands, and two mountains at a distance of less than five miles, one to the south and the other to the west" would "furnish all the necessary wood and lumber; and stone, lime and other materials for building" were not lacking.

To put his plan into effect, the governor thought of a way of bringing the citizens around to his will. "The easiest thing would be the speedy transfer of the garrison," he believed, "as by this example, the greater part of the settlers would voluntarily do the same on account of the intimate relationship they have with members of the troop." At the same time, he would leave a hundred "wealthy settlers" at Santa Fe so as not to abandon entirely that northern outpost of defense. The officers and men of the presidial company agreed to put up 2,165 pesos toward the resettlement, and the governor asked the viceroy in the City of Mexico to provide out of government funds another 2,000.

But the population in general did not accept the idea of the move, and the matriarch agreed with them. The royal city, with all its problems and difficulties, its establishments and memories, remained on its high plateau, where the air was so clear, the light so bright. She once asked an Indian in her household what the Indians had called the place long ago before the first Christians came. She never forgot the reply.

The Indian said his ancestors called it the dancing ground of the sun.

The expression moved her, not because it seemed to her picturesque, or beautiful, for she never thought of these qualities, but because it seemed to say so plainly that the Indians loved their land, for they worshiped the sun, and they did so through dances. They belonged there, those people, as no other people could belong. She was always one to be troubled and indignant when Indians suffered injustices. This was her own everyday Christian charity at work.

In 1783 she was furious in a particular way when she heard how Indians were being forced to abandon their own dwellings in their own towns because renegades of the Spanish society were persecuting them. There was, it seemed, a floating population of "Spaniards, negroes, mulattoes and half-breeds—men of turbulent and bad conduct, thieves, gamblers, vicious and vagrant persons." These undesirable persons would enter a pueblo of the Indians and "besides treating them badly, make them serve them, and teach them their bad habits and idleness," and "also some errors and vices which tend to corrupt them and thwart the just benefits desired for their salvation, increase, and tranquillity." All the Indians could do "to escape injury from them" was "to leave their pueblos and premises." It was disheartening to see people driven from their homes by the worst expression of the Spanish character. It was good to know it when the governor, taking cognizance of the miserable situation, issued orders that bad citizens who went about the kingdom from pueblo to pueblo doing harm must settle down in Spanish towns, and practice a trade, and, if they had no trade, they must learn one.

There was useful work to be done in the city, for new buildings were wanted. Skilled craftsmen were still lacking in the 1780's. It was at last decided to build a military headquarters for the presidial troop, and also to put up quarters for the troopers. In 1788 the military chief of Santa Fe reported to his superior at Chihuahua that he had "already cut and piled all the timbers which must be used in said building." He had "also gathered straw and other necessary materials for making the adobes during next spring." The buildings were laid out on a most suitable site, west of the palace, and in a line with it. The matriarch walked past now and then to see how matters progressed.

It was the first ambitious, official building venture undertaken by the government in well over half a century. Heretofore, the governors had done little except to repair the palace when time after time it seemed ready to collapse. She remembered that one governor, in fact, had been ready to tear it down until stayed by the viceroy. The new buildings would include some stonework. Where would they ever find a master mason? she wondered. Now and then the home government in Mexico would pick out some workman who had been convicted of some criminal act, and would send him, instead of to jail, to serve his sentence as an exile in some far province. Many of the troopers came to Santa Fe under similar dispensations. She was not surprised when the governor told her that he had asked Chihuahua "to be pleased to forward . . . an expert mason who may have been sentenced to some house of correction." She nodded.

"Those who are here," he added, "know very little, and it is necessary to watch them constantly in order that they may make fewer mistakes."

The work went slowly, but by fall of 1791 the military headquarters building was completed and in use. It was a hot and dry year, quite typical of the several years past. If all went well, and the dry spell lasted, the troops would be able to move into their barracks in August. But the weather broke, and the first thing the matriarch thought of was the great pile of adobes ranked and ready for use in the soldiers' quarters. It rained every day, and heavily, from the middle of July until early September. Work was halted, while "about 100,000 adobes" melted away in the torrents of rain. It was late in the autumn when the barracks were completed and the workmen paid off.

This matter of payment was exasperating in its form, she knew. On a great scale, it was just what happened in a household, and she knew what the military commander was going through to complete the financial transactions of his new buildings.

To accomplish the payment of wages, "it was necessary," he wrote to the commanding general at Chihuahua, "to place together all assets, merchandise, and wares furnished to the workers," and to call all such commodities by the name "pesos of the country." All of these were "apportioned accordingly; each one of these corresponding to three royals and five grains in silver." As the general would understand, this system of using an "imaginary currency" was "subject to great confusion . . . because it has no fixed value, and varies greatly."

The commandant illustrated what he meant. "For in our part of the country, one vara of Brittany linen is worth 2 pesos, currency of the country." And yet in Chihuahua, "the same is valued at 10 royals of silver. Likewise one vara

of unbleached muslin is worth 2 pesos here, and in Chihuahua, 2½ pesos." It was a bore, and clumsy and time-con-
suming, but the only way any proper accounting could be
arrived at with "these unequal estimates of value for the
same articles" was to send lists of the articles to Chihuahua
where the "proper accounting" would be calculated, which
would make "payment of wages possible." It was a journey
of several weeks to Chihuahua. The workmen must wait.

And still there was building to be done, for the junior
officers of the garrison had no quarters of their own, but
took rooms in private homes near the headquarters. One
day officers' quarters would have to be built. The commandant admitted to her that he was not eager to undertake
that effort also. The only thing he could say was that, so
far as he could remember, it was easier now to obtain money
from the government for frontier military purposes than
during any other period of his service.

Yes, she nodded, and for a good reason, since the French
were permanently settled at the city called Saint Louis on
the vast river they had heard about in Santa Fe; and those
other people, of that other country, the British Americas,
were fighting for their independence from the British crown.
All revolutions were not only foolish and sinful, she said,
they were also dangerous, for they destroyed so much by
which the young people grew up; and when that was gone,
what was left? The world would change, and that would be
wrong. It was, therefore—to return to the military budget
—high time the government was willing to spend more for
protection of frontiers, so that foreign ways might be held
at a distance.

x.

In May, 1792, it seemed a valid idea to discover as much
as possible about the French in their town of San Luis de
Ylinneses. The governor picked a man to send on a tour
of investigation. He was a Frenchman long resident and
trusted in Santa Fe, Pedro Vial. He left for Saint Louis
of the Illinois in May and was home again in October with

his report, which was sent to the viceroy. It did not really reveal much, and Santa Fe told Mexico that "of the country he crossed he gives no descriptions," which was to be regretted, for one of the purposes of his journey was thus unfulfilled. Someone else must undertake the same mission later. "It is desirable that similar explorations be made by persons of greater intelligence and broader interests," concluded Santa Fe.

However, Vial had adventures of his own to talk about, and he and his two companions were much in demand, for a while, with their narratives. They told mostly of encounters with Indians. The Kansa Indians captured them and held them for two weeks, during which they had been forced to live naked. They were then released—why, they could not say. They would never pretend to understand Indians.

The matriarch knew what they meant.

For example, to continue: One night—it was the seventieth night of their return journey from Saint Louis—one of the Santa Feans woke up to see a horse standing saddled instead of unsaddled for the halt. He called Vial and said, "Look here, there is a horse saddled. Perhaps it is some Comanche who is coming to attack."

Vial took up his weapons and went forward to see. But it was not an enemy horse, it was his own, which should have been unsaddled by the Santa Fe soldier whose duty it was. Vial scolded the soldier.

But the soldier pointed to an Indian guide sleeping in the camp, and said "he thought the Indian might have saddled him to steal him."

Vial went to the Indian and woke him up.

"What has happened!" exclaimed the Indian, awakening with too much expression, so that Vial knew he was "simulating fright."

Vial said, "You saddled my horse."

The Indian felt abused. No, he said, on the contrary, they were encamped on a Comanche burying ground, for he had heard Comanche whistling in his dreams, and the fact was, the horse had been saddled by "some of the dead."

It was an elaborate story, and like such, it had to be made even more so to justify itself. The Indian asked Vial for some tobacco which he would bury right there in order "to quiet the dead." The Indian raised his arm in a solemn and ghostly gesture, which did not persuade anyone. Vial and his fellows stayed awake the rest of the night, watching over their horses. In the morning he sent the Indian guide away, after "presenting him with some little things."

But Pedro Vial and his two men had gone and had returned, across the grand plains all the way to Saint Louis and the Mississippi River, and if they had done it, thought the matriarch, so could other men, for that was how a trail was found, and how it grew. The thing to remember, she said, was that no trail led only one way. If men could go out from Santa Fe, others could come toward Santa Fe. It was not entirely desirable that this should happen, in her view.

xi.

In 1804 she was ninety-four years old, and her thoughts came more slowly, but they were clear, and they all had sensible reference to the events of her long life.

She never left her house now except to be assisted to mass, but friends came to see her, and so did her children, grandchildren, great-grandchildren, and great-great-grand-children, to pay little calls upon her, and give respects to this source of their own being.

She had borne her first life in her girlhood, unimaginably long ago. Small and frail, she seemed to be made of dried twigs and fine parchment. But in her eyes there was still much light, and in her presence there was much manner. When they spoke to her, she heard, and though it might take a little while for her to answer, when she replied in a clear whisper that sounded deep in the little cave of her mouth, they all knew again how much life interested her.

They told her of echoes from the outside world which were years old by the time they reached Santa Fe—reports of disruptions and furies which were changing whole nations. France was still trembling after a revolution. England had lost the eastern shores of America. Not only lands and kingdoms, but even the minds of men were visited by strange and fateful turnabouts. Ideas were abroad that seemed to start fires in men's thoughts, until whole societies began to burn.

Only Spain, the father kingdom, seemed safe in the midst of so much fury and menace. Spain in its wisdom shut its doors to science and the new philosophies and the smoking torches of revolution. Spain and its empire, the kingdom of New Mexico, and the royal city of Santa Fe, though they lived through the time span of the eighteenth century, seemed to remain in the seventeenth until the nineteenth was ready to break upon them in all its rude power. Nobody could see what was coming, of course, for few men were gifted with prophecy.

But the government was true to itself, and did its best to meet the mutterings of a new world wherever these might be heard.

In the early winter of 1803, a secret paper reached the governor at Santa Fe from the commanding general at Chihuahua. It described the infiltration of most alarming threats into the kingdom, which must be met with speed and determination. One of the matriarch's grandsons was a trusted member of the governor's office, and so was in a position to have access to the secret document and to talk about it. His grandmother was much interested in it. It said:

> To the Lord Governor of New Mexico:
> I have reliable information that the enemies of good order, in continuation of the depraved system of propagating the maxims of liberty and discord with which they are trying to destroy the Throne and the Altar, have introduced into this kingdom different copies of the perfidious writings entitled "Contrato Social" of Juan Santiago Rousiau and "La Monarquía, or, the Victim of the Inquisition."
> In order that they may not go unpunished, I have deter-

mined to advise Your Excellency that, with the prudence and
tact which your devotion may dictate, you shall endeavor to
collect any copies of the aforementioned writings that you
may learn exist in the district of the government under your
charge; and those you shall obtain thus Your Excellency
shall remit to me with suitable security for the purpose of
avoiding their being read on the road.

God guard Your Excellency many years.

Chihuahua, 1 November 1803

Nemesio Salcedo/rubric/

She had no idea who these authors were or what their
books were like, but they must indeed be perilous for the
good estate of Spanish life if the government moved so
sternly against them. She approved but, though she did not
say so to her grandson, she did not think the measures
adopted would do much good. It was her observation that
men—even Indians, even sons—made of their own thoughts
what they would.

As to protecting the frontiers of the kingdom in another
quality, it seemed to her hardly adequate that in 1804 the
"useful appurtenances" of the presidial troop of Santa Fe
consisted of "two 4-caliber cannons with gun carriages, one
measuring spoon, one ramrod, one wad hook, one punch,
one sponge, three boxes for carrying ammunition and
powder when campaigning, with their locks, one small
trunk for the same purpose, four mattocks, two more of the
same, one coal hatchet, and one bullet mold with its spoons
and tongs."

But again she reserved her opinion, even when she heard
young soldiers in her family discussing news that the whole
city was gossiping about. Word had come from Luciana,
or "Louisiana," that a certain captain of the United States
of North America proposed to explore the Missouri River,
in order to extend the boundaries of his country. The
government in Santa Fe made plans to advise the Indian
nations to the east "to preserve and defend their lands and
dwellings." Santa Fe's first defenses lay out on the plains.
But the great continent was in the same year opened to

another reach toward its western approaches. In 1804 the Santa Fe government received and acknowledged orders sent out by the King of Spain to give aid to members of "the Russian American expedition under Captain Krucenstern" in case they made forced landings at Spanish ports of the Pacific Coast of the Californios. With the dawn of the nineteenth century, the royal city, long lost in the northern kingdom, seemed about to yield up its secrecy.

xii.

After so many decades without one, the Santa Fe garrison at last had a surgeon, a certain Dr. Larrañaga. While his duties primarily were concerned with the military personnel, he did what he could for the civilian population, even to touring the outlying Spanish towns and Indian pueblos to administer vaccinations against smallpox.

On his return from one such trip he was asked to come in attendance upon the matriarch, who in 1805 in her ninety-fifth year lay dying.

But when they brought him to her, she dismissed him with a kindly whisper. She did not need him. Her life was ending under the touch of nature itself. She knew she was dying of life.

In the same year, a North American, James Pursley by name, arrived at Santa Fe. He was the first citizen of the United States to enter the royal city. He was not detained under arrest, but neither was he permitted to leave the city or the kingdom. When it was learned that he was a skilled carpenter, he was put to work and given plenty to do, for which he was paid. Because of where he came from, with him came all the implications of the nineteenth century.

But the matriarch had been spared wars of independence, and the fall of crowns, and the change of flags, and new ideas and ways of government. In all her long time she had seen little change in the life about her. She died at peace with the world she knew.

BOOK TWO:

UNDER MEXICO

VI

The Missouri Trader: 1821

i.

HE SAW THEM first early one afternoon in November, 1821. For a long time he tried to make Indians out of them, but they would not conform to the outlines of Indians, and when at last they were near enough to be clear in his glass —he was the only member of his party to carry a telescope —he saw that they must be a little squad of New Mexicans. He studied their outlines, and reported aloud the great disks of their hat brims, and a long capelike affair tossed over one shoulder, and short jackets, and tight breeches flared over the boot, and the enormous, even fanciful, spray of metal spikes serving as rowels to their spurs. Their horses were small and nimble. They were coming toward the party of Missourians of which he was the newest and youngest member.

He had been on the plains with his companions for sixty-two days. Their purpose was to trade with roving Indians for horses. More precisely noted, his purpose was to go along as a supernumerary member, to do what chores he could toward the general welfare of the company, and particularly to test the theory of his family physician at home in Missouri. The theory concerned his health. A few months on the open plains, in the opinion of the doctor, would either kill him or cure him.

He had left home so weak that he had had to be assisted into the saddle. For the first few days the rough food of the camp had produced symptoms in him very like those of the cholorina. The vast empty distances of the prairies had at first filled him with fear, so impersonal they were, so small he, so oceanlike the immensities all about.

Nightly, as the last light lingered in the illimitable west, he wrote in a black wallet notebook his impressions of the day. When at the end of two weeks he reread what he had so far written, he was amazed to discover that after the entries of the first few days, all of which described his miseries and their symptoms, his diary referred less and less to himself and more and more to the new wonders all about him. He forgot himself in the variety and robustness of the new experience he was helping to bring to life.

It was an experience which, as he noted, "seemed to call out into play all the powers of the young United States of America—imagination and enterprise, spirit and body, as the Far West waited to be examined." The young trader was conscious of his country's strong romance for the west, and he felt representative of it. He felt, also, a conviction of superiority to those other human beings whom he encountered on his travels, the various parties of Plains Indians, and—now as they came into hailing distance—the men from New Mexico. He believed that an enlightened superiority was the best point of view from which to examine new or unfamiliar exercises of the Divine Will, and he derived his own from two sources. One was his citizenship of the United States. The other was the tone of his mind, for which he could be persuaded to take the credit, as it was the product of his unceasing diligence in self-improvement.

The approaching New Mexicans were few in number, fewer, in fact, than the Missourians. They were polite, sweeping their great saucerlike hats in wide gestures and bowing in their saddles so heavily studded with carved silver. The young trader had included Spanish among his studies at home, and he now represented his party in conversation. The New Mexicans smiled at his pronunciation, and helped him all they could. With good will on both sides, understanding was possible. As the conversation unfolded, he could not suppress an excitement which the other Missourians noticed. What was it, they asked, crowding up to him, wrinkled in perplexity and suspicious in their exclusion from the dialogue. He waved them calmly to wait until he could hear more. The New Mexicans were all smiles and ease. They chattered like brown monkeys riding on little doglike ponies. The young trader thought finally that he had enough of their gist to give it to his companions, and he turned to amaze them with his news.

The New Mexicans were from Santa Fe. During the second week of September, New Mexico had signed an oath of loyalty to the new nation of Mexico. Led by a Colonel Agustín de Iturbide, Mexico had broken away from Spain. Spain had always worked to keep foreigners out of her provinces—especially North Americans out of New Mexico. But now it was of interest to many New Mexicans to invite trade with the United States, and these present travelers from Santa Fe asked if, with their pack animals loaded with goods to be traded, the Missourians would not accompany them back to Santa Fe where without any doubt they would sell all their goods in a few days at excellent prices.

The Missourians were inclined to be shrewd. They asked further questions, and they squinted above their beards in order to detect any traps that might be hidden in the offer, and then they withdrew a little distance to consult. Presently they returned and declared that they would give their answer in the morning, if the New Mexicans would camp nearby for the night. By firelight, later, the Missourians made lists of their goods and set down a price opposite each item. When they added it up, the total was astonishingly large. It was a mild autumn, and there was yet no sign of winter. The plains were dangerous when snow came, but the stakes were great, and so far as they knew the Missourians would be the first Americans to enter Santa Fe as businessmen in trade. Far West was in their blood. The next morning they gave their answer, and went on toward Santa Fe with their new guides.

The young trader worked to improve his Spanish in conversation with the New Mexicans. His grammar was better than his accent, for he understood system better than character. They had several weeks of travel still ahead of them. Each night he had much to enter in his black wallet notebook. It was fortunate that he had brought three of these with him. Naturally frugal, even he was amused to observe how precious could be so common an article as paper when there was so much to write and so little space in which to write it. He fell asleep on the plains each night, as healthy as anyone of his party, and, more than any, filled with the particular sense of gratification that visited an educated man, however young, who felt his powers of analysis responding to the challenge of new objects of study. It was an emotion which he prudently concealed from his associates, some of whom already thought of him as "pee-culiar."

He had often been made to feel like a changeling in his society. A child of the hardest frontier, he had come to show early in life a devouring interest not in hunting, killing, building, but in reading, thinking, knowing. His mother saw him as a sad child likely to be a disappointed man, but her duty lay to his nature as it was, not as others would have it be, and she persuaded her husband to use their small funds whenever possible to acquire for their son the books he craved. With loans of printed works from an occasional neighbor—a medical doctor, a clergyman, an itinerant philosopher such as now and then turned up at the last edge of the nation as it spread westward—the education of the young trader was rapidly advanced.

Most of what he studied came from the literatures of Europe, for American works were not so widely available. Among his favorites were *The History of the Decline and Fall of the Roman Empire,* by Edward Gibbon; *The History of Charles XII,* by Voltaire; the philosophical writings of John Locke; and *The Life of Samuel Johnson, LL.D.,* by James Boswell. In this last work he drew his pleasure not so much from Boswell's simple, daylight ramblings about his subject, but from the quotations of remarks by Doctor Johnson, in all their terrific honesty, bad manners, and crushing weight. If he himself desired power, it was power in terms of such majestic unpleasantness as Doctor Johnson's. But such a hope was only a daydream, and he allowed himself little time with it. He devised a maxim to frame his ideal of living and writing: *To combine precision with elegance and to fortify sharpness of taste with inflexibility of standards.*

In no field was his opinion already so fixed as that of religion. Religion to him was merely an organized expression of the rational mind, and its impulse at its purest was simply derived from man's ethical sense. He believed that emotion in matters of faith was unsuitable. The revival meetings of the woods clearings on the frontier turned him sick physically.

His surest recovery from the debilitating rages which the coarseness or stupidity of his fellow creatures often put him into was to turn to some branch of natural science. He studied physiology, biology, botany, and geology. He read what he could find of the works of Baron Alexander von Humboldt, studying German for the purpose. He saw no reason why he might not become the Humboldt of the newly opening Far West. He believed that in time every man must through education and elevated sensibility become a "universal man," and there had to be one here, a few there, to set the example. In his small, rude, and intimate frontier community none of his fellow citizens knew what to make of him. The discovery of this made him odder than ever, until he was ill. His recovery on the prairies, in the face of primitive challenges, gave him the first happiness he had ever had in common with other men. He loved the prairies, in consequence, and so traveled toward Santa Fe, as he wrote, "with indulgent high spirits."

One day on the plains another party of horsemen appeared in the distance. The Missourians and their New Mexican guides approached with care, and all redoubled this when a New Mexican hissed, "Comanches!" The Missourians closed the formation of their pack animals, which carried their stock in trade. It seemed a long time before the vaporous distance yielded up the separation between the two parties, but at last they met. A remarkable personage sat at ease on a magnificent horse before the Indian line. He was their chief, and said so, lifting his hand, and repeating his name, Cordero, several times. One of the New Mexicans had a few Indian words, and between him and the young trader with his priggish Spanish the two parties communicated.

Cordero was tall and erect. He was about seventy years old. His eyes were black, bright, and piercing, and his nose was like the bill of a hawk. He held himself with a military air, which was enhanced if not inspired, as the young Missourian noted, by his costume. The Indian wore the "complete regimentals of an American colonel—blue coat, red sash, white pantaloons, epaulets, and sword." His painted followers wore blankets, quill ornaments, feathers, and leggings. All were mounted and with them they had a large band of extra horses.

The senior Missourian gave word to ask whether the chief would trade his horses for goods. The chief asked for a look at specimens of the goods, and indicated that he would trade. The Missourians then said they were going to Santa Fe, and would like to meet the chief on their return. At this, he gave a great scowl and stared at the New Mexicans. It was plain that he regarded them as enemies. What were the Missourians doing in such company? he demanded. The answer—doing business—did not convince him, but he gave thought for a moment, and then said that he would watch for the party on its return, and, if they were destined to meet, he would trade some of his fine ponies for what they had in their baskets and sacks. He then raised his right hand to make significant motions in the air, and in sequence managed to convey a stern warning, a mocking opinion, and a perfunctory blessing. The parties drew apart from each other, and the traders rode in silence, pondering the doubts raised in them about the New Mexicans by the Comanche colonel.

Several hours and some miles later, the New Mexican spokesman as if answering their thoughts pointed out that for generations his people had been terrorized by Comanches, with only a few interludes of peace. If distrust was to pass between any two companies, it would do better between Christians and Indians than between two civilized peoples. The traders thinking this over could not but agree. A sense of good feeling returned to the whole party.

ii.

Toward evening of a December day they came in sight of the capital. Part of the sky was overcast, but above the mountains there was a rift in the clouds that let a golden pour of light fall over the snowy peaks. The light was caught in ascending columns of smoke which rose out of low, rectangular bars of some substance resembling earth, by which long shadows were cast. The sight possessed such clarity, its colors were all so strong, the cold air was so sweetly laced with scents from burning pine that the young trader halted to bring order out of the confusion wrought in his senses by all these. It was Santa Fe, and those were houses that looked to him like "piles of unbaked brick in a kiln yard." The high plateau embraced so generously by mountains within whose protection the city lay so intimately was like nothing he had ever seen before. His heart made a heavy beat, and he told himself that he must be calm, for feeling was not to be permitted to take effect ungoverned.

When he rode forward again, he observed that from the mountains came a clear small river flowing through the city. He noted that the city was "three streets wide and a mile long," all parallel to the Santa Fe River. As he came among them, he saw that many of the houses were white-washed on the outside. All were one story high and flat-roofed.

Bearing themselves like personages conducting a triumph in public, the New Mexican guides led the Missourians to the plaza and to the palace. There they dismounted, their animals were taken in charge by native sentries, and they entered the palace through a gateway crumbling at the edges. In a few moments they were in the presence of the governor of New Mexico. Once again it fell to the young trader to serve his companions as interpreter.

The governor was short and fat, and, if these were deficiencies in a public personage, he made up for them in amplitude of manner. He shook hands with the visitors, indicated his walls, rafters, ceiling, and told them they were all theirs, promised them supper, welcomed their purpose as traders, and assured them that in the grand day of the new nation of Mexico, free and independent, a great future lay waiting in the friendship between his country and theirs. As an example of this, he declared that Spanish passports held no validity any longer, and that the old Spanish system of heavy charges upon imports would no longer be applied, and that the Missourians were at liberty to sell their goods when and where they chose to do so. The governor seemed to be "well-informed and gentlemanly in manner; his demeanor was courteous and friendly." The young trader satisfied his companions on all counts as to their freedom of action. The older men of his party, who had the best eye for business, took charge of the commercial arrangements, and were assured by the governor that they would be permitted to rent a house near the plaza where all their goods could be displayed for sale.

As they moved to go to set up their arrangements, the governor detained the young trader for a moment. He shook his hand again, holding it in both of his, and asked him to return when he could, the sooner the better, as there was much he wanted to discuss with so intelligent and so responsive a man from the North American republic. The governor had once made great friends with a distinguished officer of North America, Lieutenant Montgomery Pike, who entered the kingdom "by error" in 1806. Though a hero of fidelity and loyalty to the Spanish Crown so long as it ruled over him, the governor was now no less passionate in his dedication to Mexico's freedom, and—so he assured the trader—he felt convinced that great and ideal relations with the United States of the North must be a cornerstone of Mexican policy. Would he not return soon to discuss this and other absorbing topics? Santa Fe was far from any of the great centers of learning and information. It would be a pleasure to converse with a man of cultivation. The young trader gravely agreed to return for the purpose submitted.

In his later conversations, then, he seemed to inspire the governor to talk freely about the events of his recent lifetime which had seen so many changes of significance come so swiftly over the kingdom.

The governor said he knew what it meant when Lieutenant Pike and party appeared on the upper Rio Grande in 1806. Even though they were brought to Santa Fe for interrogation as prisoners of sorts, and later sent on to Chihuahua under custody, he knew. They were signs of the future, and he, for one, was glad to be on friendly terms with them. He admired Pike, who was charming, intelligent, honorable, and courageous. There were still some men in the kingdom who believed that the United States must be excluded from entering. The present governor was not one. North America was surely large enough to contain everyone, and to let them trade in peace. Yet throughout the last years, the home government of Spain had persisted in its exclusive laws, though two things prevented their consistent or proper execution. One was the fact that New Mexico had no money and few troops to erect a firm defense. The other was that the home government was in difficulties, mostly owing to the dreadful operations of Napoleon Bonaparte. In 1808 Ferdinand VII, the rightful king of Spain, was deposed by Napoleon, and Joseph Bonaparte was set upon the throne instead. The Spanish government retreated to Cádiz at the sea where the parliament continued to sit. Now Spain needed all her sons. In 1809 the Cádiz assembly decreed that for the first time delegates from the new world provinces must come as full members to take seats in the Spanish home government. Santa Fe sent a prominent citizen, Pedro Bautista Pino.

All the way to Cádiz? asked the young trader.

All the way, declared the governor, and while there he presented the needs of New Mexico with eloquence and loyalty. He asked for the establishment of a bishopric at Santa Fe; the founding of a "seminary college of higher learning, and of public schools for the instruction of the youth"; a system of "uniformity in military service, the addition of . . . five forts . . . and payment of salaries to all settlers who may be enlisted."

Did that indicate, asked the trader, that the militia served without pay?

So it did, answered the governor, and, what was more, the militiamen had to furnish their own horses, and if these were injured or killed, the owner had to bear the loss, as the kingdom could not pay the damages. Pino's request of the Assembly was only just and fair, and, after all, the militia of other states received pay—Durango, Sonora, Texas, and so on. To conclude, Pino asked also for the establishment of a civil and criminal court at Chihuahua, which was only six hundred miles away. The one at Mexico City was over three times as far. It could be imagined how few citizens of Santa Fe could travel to Mexico City to obtain justice in a law court.

These seemed not only like enlightened measures, thought the trader, but real necessities that deserved fulfillment. Did this come promptly?

Ah, no. Even as the parliament opened its sessions, the spirit of revolt broke out in Mexico. In 1810, on September 16, Father Miguel Hidalgo gave his *"grito"*—his cry of liberation, and Mexico rose up in arms to join him in battle against Spain. The parliament could hardly grant benefices to a kingdom in revolt. When Delegate Pino returned from Spain, having been able to bring them nothing that they needed, his fellow citizens of Santa Fe sang a little song—

> Don Pedro Pino went;
> Don Pedro came back.

It told the whole story.

As for the revolt, it was put down by the royal forces in Mexico, and the Cádiz assembly, in the name of their exiled king, offered amnesty to the rebels of 1810. The governor had to confess that this parliamentary act had settled a number of "doubts, qualms, and points of discussion" in Santa Fe and elsewhere. The decree was notable for other effects—it affirmed equal rights before the law for people born, or descended from those born, in the colonies—including Indians, mind you—and the Spaniards of the homeland. These rights included that of equal representation with European-born Spaniards.

Such measures were much wanted by the new world. Perhaps they were granted out of duress, as the home country felt the menace of Napoleon, and needed all the help it could get. When the documents asking the colonies for such aid arrived in Santa Fe in 1812, they were thoroughly discussed, but it was difficult to think of any ways in which the New Mexican province could help the home kingdom against the "modern Attila." It all seemed so far away— the battles on the Iberian Peninsula, and Lord Wellington, and the French emperor, who was said to have gone into Russia. And in any event, the war was suddenly over, Joseph Bonaparte ran away from Madrid to France, and King Ferdinand resumed his throne. In February, 1813, the Spanish assembly, acting still from Cádiz, issued an order in the name of Ferdinand VII which Santa Fe received and obeyed later in the same year. The governor had a copy of the order which he kept as a model in case of future proclamations of a similar nature. He handed it to the Missouri trader to read, and together they arrived at a translation.

Appearing by the noble triumph of our illustrious Ally the Emperor of the Russias against the Armies of the Tyrant of Europe and their influence in the liberty of Spain and the tranquillity of the universe, and being but just that the Spanish Nation should make a public testimony of the live interest that it takes in the exaltation and glory of that Empire as well as in the humiliation and ruin of our common enemy:—The Royal and Extraordinary Courts decree: That in Celebration of so glorious a success a *Te Deum* shall be sung in this Capital and also in all other cities and villages of the Spains, and let there be illuminations, artillery salutes, and bell-ringing in general . . .

Cádiz 16 February 1813

The trader handed the paper back without comment. To himself he said that it smacked of Romish and royalist claptrap; but he could not explain the little tingle of nerves about his spine that the words of jubilee, so fully the expression of a national character in all its ardent faith, secretly gave to him.

In the years that followed, the governor observed, a number of intrusions took place upon the boundaries of the kingdom. These were effected by hunters and trappers looking for beaver in the northern mountain streams and lakes.

Where did they come from?

Many from Canada, Frenchmen. Others from the North American states. They did not often venture into Santa Fe of their own free will, preferring to lurk in the mountains and to enter Taos when in need of supplies or human company. But the government took a number of them from time to time.

What became of them?

Naturally, they were imprisoned. If they had accumulated stores of pelts, these were confiscated. One such haul brought the value of twenty thousand dollars. If the men gave trouble, they were sent south to Chihuahua under guard where no doubt they rested in jail even now. Actually, there had been a few such men in jail at Santa Fe, in the west end of the palace, until last year, 1820.

Americans? In jail? The young trader was incredulous. How had they been released?

The governor shrugged. For himself, he would gladly have let them go long before, but the central government had ordered all foreign hunters captured and imprisoned until further notice. However, events in Mexico, the glorious birth of a new nation, had brought about new policies. It was somewhat sad, in its way, how the old empire had felt the new world's intention and desire before these had actually burst into the light. For example, the governor could recall an order which he received from Madrid, and which he published in Santa Fe on the last day of 1820. It was a decree of the royal court commanding allegiance to the Spanish government and the constitution of the monarchy. What could this mean but that the home power felt its grasp weakening upon the other Spains, and was trying to hold fast? Anyone who gave allegiance elsewhere was to be "deprived of all honors, employments, emoluments, and prerogatives proceeding from this jurisdiction." Further, he was to be exiled "from the territory of the monarchy." And finally, if he was a priest, like Father Hidalgo who led the revolt of 1810 and died for it, he would "suffer deprivation of the temporalities."

Temporalities? The young trader wondered what these could be.

They were those exemptions, privileges, and grants of material support which the state made to the church.

The trader pressed his lips together in a thin smile of uninformed disapproval, but said nothing.

And then, and then, all these precautions meant nothing, for earlier this year, an army colonel of the royal forces in Mexico raised a cry of revolt. This was Agustín de Iturbide, and by August the amazing fact was achieved: complete independence of Mexico from Spain. Even the Spanish viceroy recognized the new movement. Colonel de Iturbide found an army springing to life all over the country. Wherever he went he conquered with the mere idea of independence. It was hard to believe, but it was true that the revolt was accomplished without any battles. The royal forces seeing how universal was the response to the rebellion gave way and finally retreated to the fortress outside the port of Veracruz—the castle of San Juan de Ulloa.

On the eleventh of September the oath of allegiance to

Agustín de Iturbide as new ruler of Mexico was taken at Santa Fe. The governor led the ceremonies. The official celebrations would take place in a few days. Preparations were even now under way. It was strange, to know that the long fatherhood of Spain was done with. The Crown may have been heavy, but it stood for the control of those things in life which no band of citizens by themselves could manage.

Ah? The trader was quick to cite the processes of government by free election, congressional representation, and judicial review which the United States had followed successfully for all of forty-five years now.

The governor sighed. Liberty was becoming fashionable, and he would do his best to learn what could be managed with it. Anyhow, Colonel de Iturbide was addressed as Serene Highness, and it was thought that he would end by assuming the style of emperor. Meanwhile, the preparations for Santa Fe's celebration of his triumph must continue, and the governor wondered if the Missouri trader as a member of a free nation might render assistance with advice. The trader regarded the request as perfectly appropriate, and agreed to serve as an authority on jubilations of independence.

A few days later he met with officials who drew up the program. They asked him what he would propose. He gestured in the direction of the plaza before the palace, and said that there, in the center, a "Liberty Pole" should be erected. When they asked what this might be, he explained. They then enthusiastically appointed him to carry out the project, promising him all the assistance he might need.

He gathered a party of men and went with them to the mountains after timber. He selected two trees whose length totaled seventy feet. These were cut down and brought to town. In the plaza they were made into a flagpole. The next problem was to decide upon a flag to fly from it. There was yet no flag of the new nation, and it would of course not do to fly the old yellow and scarlet royal banner. The trader waited tactfully, but, as no one made a move, he designed a new flag himself. It showed clasped hands, "in sign," as he said, "of brotherhood and amity with all nations." With "cordial female assistance" the design was carried out in fabrics and colors.

He noted that the people of Santa Fe became more animated as the day drew near for the celebration. Excitement was visible wherever preparations were under way. Christmas intervened with its religious exercises, which he observed with barely concealed impatience, and on the twenty-sixth of December a courier brought word from Mexico of the triumphal entry of the new "Serene Highness" into the capital city. Eleven days later the capital of New Mexico was at last ready with its own triumph.

At five in the morning of January 6, 1822, the young trader went to the governor to tell him that he must now come to raise the flag on the Liberty Pole as the first act of jubilation. The governor's answer astonished him.

"Oh, do it yourself," he said. "You understand these things."

"So," noted the trader in his wallet notebook, "I raised the first flag in the free and independent state of New Mexico."

He did it in style, for he had arranged for cannon salutes. The cannonading brought the city out. People came at a run, pulling on their clothes. The great day was launched. A parade followed, and later, at the palace, a grand entertainment, which was given against the background of new decorations painted for the occasion by the postmaster of Santa Fe. The head of the city council led a cotillion, which opened a ball, and, as a climax to the celebration, a tableau in three scenes was staged to illustrate the three principles of the Plan of Iguala upon which the Most Serene Highness Agustín Iturbide had based the appeal of his revolution. These were the continuation of the Catholic Church as the official church of Mexico; the establishment of an independent nation with a limited monarchy; and equal rights for Spaniards and colonials. Prominent citizens and members of the clergy enacted the allegories, after which the dancing was resumed.

If the trader thought that this would conclude the festivities, he was wrong. For five days they continued. He was offended by what he saw.

"All classes abandoned themselves to the most reckless dissipation and revelry" indulging in "thoughtlessness, vice, and licentiousness of every description," which persisted through "night and day" with "no time for sleep. Gambling tables surrounded the square—dice and faro banks." All were "infatuated with the passion for gaming. Women of rank were seen betting—money, even their jewelry." On the second day a large company of "handsome men and women in fine cotton cloth and coral and silver jewels came and danced in the plaza, to drum and chorus." They were Indians from San Felipe pueblo. The liberated Spaniards watched until another Indian throng suddenly appeared. These were Pecos Indians "dressed in skins of bulls and bears." They were fearsome. The Spaniards took fright and ran away from the plaza until the Indians departed. During the next days, while the citizens exhausted their joy and his fellow traders peddled their goods, the young Missourian enlarged his impressions of the city.

iii.

He thought there must be about six thousand people in the capital. He was told that the last census in 1808 had indicated a total population of 34,745 in the kingdom. The figures included Christian Indians. Such records were kept in the palace—though he could not imagine how they were kept dry and safe. The palace, and its supplementary buildings, were "disintegrating in decay," and he saw very few soldiers stationed about it, and no workmen trying to stay the crumbling that daily took toll of the walls and roof. He thought the whole establishment occupied about ten acres. An outer wall eight feet high enclosed all the buildings behind the palace. It was of course interesting to find a structure so ancient in civilized North America.

When he asked the governor why it had not been better kept by the government, he was told that its present repair was a great improvement over its state in earlier years. In 1810 it had been actually vacant in the prolonged absence of the then governor, and an old paper in the files described it: "The outside walls are sagging with the constant snows of winter and the summer rains, causing many of the rain spouts, which are made of inferior wood, to decay, and other deteriorations caused by time." When the governor left the province in 1810, the "main door . . . did not have a key in order to protect the entrance hall, courtyard, and even some of the kitchen rooms." If anybody left the great sagging gates open even a crack, "there would enter the house, asses, hogs, and other animals which would tend to dirty and damage it more." The acting governor asked the authorities in Mexico what to do about it, and was granted permission to make those repairs "which may be absolutely necessary to avoid the deterioration of the said house . . . with the understanding that it will not cost more than 25 or 30 pesos." It was plain to see that little could be accomplished with such a sum.

The young trader remained politely silent, until he could change the subject. What, he wondered, was the condition of a typical family of Santa Fe? The governor took thought for a moment in order to frame a reply, and then extending his forefinger and shaking his lace cuff he had the answer. From a large vellum envelope containing many papers he withdrew a paper which he handed to his visitor. It was the will of the first sergeant of the Santa Fe company. It had been filed recently. In its record of a dutiful man's possessions, the circumstances of a family could be seen.

The first sergeant was the father of eight children. He had been married for thirty-eight years at the time he dictated his will. His dwelling house had seven rooms, a thatched shed, and a stable with its piece of land out in back for an orchard, measuring 1,520 by 189 varas. The rest of his property consisted of "a cutoff regulation gun, 1 cartridge box, 1 leather shield, 1 saber, 1 scabbard, 1 pair of spurs, 1 saddle, 1 new uniform, a pair of trousers, 1 new red waistcoat, 1 pair of buckskin trousers hemmed, lined, and never used, 1 worn cloak, 1 worn hat, 1 colored blanket, 1 white blanket, 1 serape of blue color, 1 change of underclothing much used, 1 embroidered pouch, 1 ordinance manual, 2 pair of oxen, 1 horse, 1 mule, 2 spits, 1 big ax, 1 adze, 1 chisel, 1 branding iron, and 2 plow points." The young trader handed the paper back, saying that he supposed this was an example, then, of the wealthiest class of citizen?

The governor raised his eyebrows. Not at all; there were certain families who managed to gather great stores of the world's goods. He had seen wills filed only five or six years ago in which one family represented its fortune as totaling more than 32,000 pesos and 696 cattle, and another gave about 35,000 as its figure. One of these families had the prudent knack of gathering all the available currency into its hands, which as could be imagined caused inconvenience to the rest of the population. Laborers were hired for "about three dollars a month," but of course were paid in goods, not in money. The tasks for which they were employed were usually those of herdsmen.

From what he had seen, the trader concluded that the New Mexicans, "like the French," about whom he had read, lived in villages, "the rich keeping the poor in dependence and subjection." He was forced to find a contrast in his mind between such conditions and the five churches of Santa Fe, which in spite of their adobe construction he regarded as "very splendid . . . embellished with pictures, and ornaments of gold and silver in the most costly style. The chalices were of pure gold and the candlesticks of silver."

When he gave his attention to the farms surrounding the city, he saw that they were without fences or walls. During the growing and harvesting of crops, the animals of the farms had to be gathered and confined. The farmers raised peas, beans, corn, wheat, red peppers, and onions. The onions were planted a foot apart and, irrigated with water from little ditches along the rows, grew to sizes of from four to six inches in diameter. Potatoes and turnips were unknown. He saw peach trees but none of apples, pears, or cherries. Everyone, it seemed, had sheep, goats, asses, and cattle, but hogs and poultry were scarce, and only the rich people had horses and dogs. He was always amazed to see a few farm animals at large in the plaza. He made a note of what the stud horse of a stable was called: *"caballo maestro."* When he asked what land was worth, he was told that property near an irrigation source sold for one hundred dollars an acre!

He made judgments upon the people. In his view, they lived "in a state of extreme indolence and ignorance. Their mechanical improvements" were "very limited, and," it seemed, they knew "little of the benefit of industry, or the advantage of the arts." One time he was asked if Napoleon Bonaparte and George Washington were the same person, and again he was asked if the United States of America were as large a place as Santa Fe, and, again, whether Europe were a province of Spain. He decided that he "had seen enough of Mexican society to be thoroughly disgusted with it. I had not supposed it possible," he noted in his small careful, sloping, wiry handwriting, "for any society to be as profligate and vicious as I found all ranks of that in Santa Fe. The Indians are much superior to their Spanish masters in all qualities of a useful and meritorious population." In the manners of the New Mexicans, who meant to be amiable, courteous, and cheerful, he found only "a false glare of talent, eminently calculated to mislead and impose."

And the everlasting bell-ringing! Three times a day, when the bells of all five churches rang out in some established sequence of peals which he recognized but did not wish to memorize, everyone went down to kneel and pray.

Well. But was there any enlightenment for the mind? Books? Did anyone read? What did men of parts do with their thoughts when the world's affairs briefly granted them leisure?

Certainly. The governor knew of a book collection, fine if small, that belonged to his old friend a retired captain of the garrison. He conducted the trader to his friend's house and there exhibited thirty-eight volumes of miscellaneous works all in Spanish. The owner unfortunately had died a few years ago, but his family kept the collection intact. The trader received permission to examine the titles. He found the *Works of Charles V* bound in parchment, and three volumes of the *Lives of the Saints, The Light of Faith* (1 volume), a life of Saint Agnes, a manual for Holy Week, another prayer book called *Daily Exercise,* and two curious works about the Jews—the *Hebrew Monarchy,* in four volumes, and *The Persecuted David,* in three. There was a treatise on agriculture, and another on *Criminal Practice,* and a two-volume grammar called *Writer's Style.* As the owner was a soldier, he had owned three volumes of *Military Ordinances.* Miscellaneous biographies included one about Salomon Coronado, and another about Estevanillo, and—the young trader made an inward hiss of pleasure when he saw it—Voltaire's *History of Charles XII.* It was one of his favorite books.

As he read the remainder of the labels, he began to frame an intention. A work on *The Conquest of Mexico,* a volume of *Mexican Theater,* and eight volumes of selected novels completed the library. He must admit that the owner had been a cultivated man with varied interests. Who read these now? he asked, and the answer had to come: nobody, as the captain's survivors had never developed the habit—the ability—for reading. The trader was pleased to hear this, for he was now ready to reveal his hope that the family would consent to his purchase of the volume by Voltaire. He would like to have a copy in Spanish to sit beside his own in English. There was a whispered conference by the women of the household, and presently he was granted his wish, a price was named, and he left with the little leather-bound volume pressed in his hand, happy as only a booklover could be with a new, odd, and unexpected acquisition.

Regarding him, the governor was cast into a brief silence. For all his good feelings for the North Americans, they were a strange people. Here was one, a young man, who was not only a man of action, but a scholar, whose energies expressed themselves in many directions. What was to be done with such men? What in the end must be the will of their nation looking to the west? The governor's heart filled with secret valor. His nation, too, had its own will, the freedom of Mexico, and the preservation of her old imperial boundaries. Had he been too liberal in his reception of the Missouri traders? It was useless to think of it. Only time would tell.

A day or so later the governor was again filled with sorrowful doubts about the good intentions of the Missourians when a band of Comanche plainsmen appeared in the plaza and asked about them. It was Cordero, the uniformed chief, with thirty of his riders. The chief entered the palace and asked for a council to be attended by "Spanish officers, magistrates, and principal citizens of Santa Fe." It was an extraordinary demand, coming from a wild Indian; but Cordero was so full of dignity and a grand sense of power that his request was granted.

The traders heard of it, and came to sit with the others. Cordero said he had come—so the young trader put it— "to ascertain if we were at liberty." He was gratified to see that they were. Dominating the conference, he was then pleased to turn it into an exercise in diplomacy with the United States. He seemed to have contempt for the New Mexicans, said the young trader, and "spoke to them always as an equal or superior." Still, he was glad that instead of finding that the United States visitors had been thrown into prison by the New Mexicans, he found all on friendly terms. He then urged that the United States establish trade relations with the Comanches, and he regretted severely that the United States traded with Osage Indians—his enemies—and even sold them arms. He was persuasive, and the young trader found that "the old warrior spoke like an orator and looked like a statesman." When his speech was done, he gathered himself to depart, reminding the traders of their rendezvous with him on their homeward journey. In his blue, red, white, and gold, he was the most impressive man in the council. When he left, taking his horsemen along, it was with an effect of ending a solemn occasion. The New Mexicans, the traders, seemed to shake themselves awake, as though coming out of a spell. The governor wondered if the visitation had been prearranged by the Missourians.

The young trader could hardly help making a comparison between those Indian fighters and the Santa Fe militia four days later when an alarm arrived from downriver country. Navajo Indians had suddenly descended in force upon a group of big river farms, stealing, killing, and burning. The Santa Fe garrison was to ride out to rescue and to punish, and the militia were needed in addition. The trader watched them gather before the palace to be inspected by the governor and the post adjutant before the march was ordered.

"Such a gang of tatterdemalions," he recorded, "I never saw, before or since. They were of all colors, with all kinds of dresses and every species of arms. Some were bareheaded, others were barebacked—some had hats without rims or crowns, and some wore coats without shirts; others again wore coats without sleeves." He was amazed at their weapons in that year of 1822. "Most of them were armed with bows and arrows. A few had guns that looked as if they had been imported by Cortéz, while others had iron hoops fastened to the ends of poles, which passed for lances." The governor inspected the line, followed by his adjutant "in his jacket with red cuffs and collar" and wearing a sword. "He and the little governor seemed big with the fate of New Mexico." At last, when the inspection was done, "the governor sent them forth to the war and himself went to his dinner." The young Missourian gave his enlightened glee full play. "In the meantime where was the enemy—the bloodthirsty Navajos? They had returned in safety to their own country with all their plunder, and were even then far beyond the reach of the governor's troop of scarecrows. . . ."

The traders were done with their business. When they totaled their sales, they found that, owing to the scarcity of actual money, they had been able to take in only two hundred dollars in cash. But they were taking back also many examples of the products of Mexico, and they saw a great future.

The young trader, for his part, knew he would return to Santa Fe, for there was more to see and to record of this unknown country, and much that he could report in his carefully written papers when he should address the historical society at home. Who knew what effect he might have upon the history of his country in its time of expansion? The office of the Superintendent of Indian Affairs at Saint Louis would issue passports to those venturing beyond the Mississippi River into the Indian plains. The road was waiting to be marked by footsteps and wheelturns. Hardly any other effort would be needed to establish "an excellent trail," he was sure. "Few places would require much labor to make them passable." In all the eight hundred miles between Missouri and Santa Fe he could see a need for only thirty miles of mountain travel. The prairies lay open to enterprise; and so—he could not help smiling at their ways—and so did the people of Santa Fe, the old city to which he gave the exhilarating name of the "New Emporium."

iv.

When he came back again, it was with wagons.

Between 1824 and 1844 he made several prairie voyages to the New Emporium, and even beyond. "Voyages," he said, because the great prairie reminded everyone of the sea, with its waves of wind in tall grasses, and its circle of unbroken horizon, and its subjection to the vastly open weather of the sky. The great high wheels of the freighting wagons cut deep ruts in the grasslands, and soon there was a road marked plainly for every traveler to see.

In 1824 a group of citizens from Santa Fe journeyed to Saint Louis to invite trade with the "United States of the

North." Response was so great that it was not long before they had qualms about the energies they had beckoned alive to overwhelm them. For the trade between Santa Fe and various points in Missouri grew fast. The young trader had plenty of opportunity to accompany freighting trains and to describe the ways of the trail and the life of Santa Fe and to make scientific observations of new country along his path in his notebooks of twenty years.

v.

One day in 1824 he met a young fur trapper in the Santa Fe plaza—a tall, fine-looking man from Kentucky wearing the fringed buckskin knee-length jacket, heavy soft cloth hat, and buckskin leggings of his kind. He was freshly shaved, having come to town on important business. His hair was black and his eyes were a lynx yellow. His eyes now shot forth broken gleams from a fiery light deep in the pupil. He was in a rage. His jaw was clenched to hard bone, and the folds of humor about his mouth were white with strain.

He had to talk, and he chose to talk to the trader, whom he offended offhand by ripping forth several strings of oaths. He then moved on to say that any government was an atrocity, and the only place for a man to live was in the wilderness. This was his general view, he said. Then, to be particular, he said that the New Mexican government was the most—and once again he let go with tremendous profanity.

Shocking as it was, his language was not so disturbing to the trader as the intemperate and irrational spirit behind the words, which mocked the ideal of a calm and appraising intelligence. And yet the trader was moved by the richness of a nature capable of such passion, and, when he could, he asked what was the matter?

Well, the governor of New Mexico had refused him a license to trap beaver in the upper New Mexican mountains, that was what was the matter. He had not yet decided just what to do, but he thought it likely that he would first get drunk, and, next, fight any two-armed New Mexican whom he might encounter. After that, he would go out and buy a trapping license from some corrupt Santa Fean, and go hunt beaver anyhow.

No, no, replied the trader, he would be arrested and thrown into the jail at the end of the palace. Everyone knew what that jail was like. He would be put into a mud cell. He would never be allowed to step outdoors, even when the puddle in the center of the room reached to each wall as rain leaked through the roof. He would have to remain on top of the table. He would have no food, no counsel, no visitors. They would give him no firewood to keep himself warm. He would be obliged—the trader had talked to a man who had suffered all these things— obliged "to dig the mud to bury his dung like a cat." And then he might be manacled and made to march to Chihuahua the next time a wagon train went south. There he would be imprisoned once more, and perhaps never be heard of again.

The trapper flared and lifted his head like a powerful young horse. Danger delighted him. He waved away the trader's objections, but he was more cheerful, for having aired his grievance it seemed somewhat to dissipate itself. In a moment or so, with a civil bow, and a yellow-eyed smile, he wandered off.

The Missouri trader put a finger on his lip and watched after him. Some men lived as unconcernedly as animals in nature. It was worthy of remark how many such men were finding their way—and that of their nation—in one or another enterprise to the Great West.

That night at ten o'clock when all windows were dark an alarm sounded from the plaza. The whole city was awakened by the roll of the drum and the voices of fife and French horn—the garrison's field music. Like the rest of the population, the young trader dressed hurriedly and went down to the palace to hear the news. "The frightened women, and the still more fear-stricken men, joined in a full chorus of screams and cries." The word went about in panic that the city was under Indian attack.

All night long the city remained on guard, but in the morning the truth was known. Pecos was the scene of a Comanche raid. The raiders had taken a number of captives, including women, one of whom, returning from a ranch in the country to Santa Fe, was the governor's maiden daughter. Her father was said to be distracted with grief and anger. An avenging party was soon mustered. Four hundred men volunteered to overtake and punish the Comanches and free their captives. The trader had business in the city and was not at liberty to go, but he watched the party assemble. One of the avengers was the Kentucky trapper, who went about his preparations with the large-limbed purposefulness of a man about to exercise his best ability—in this case, to ride a wilderness, find an enemy, kill him, and free a captive.

The great party was back in town again after a week. The Comanches had delivered up their prisoners unharmed. The governor's daughter had been lifted to his saddle by the young Kentucky trapper, who in saving her had suffered an arrow wound. She took him into her father's house and nursed him. She prayed for him every day. Her father came to see him and with tears rolling down his face asked if this was not the same North American who had been refused a trapper's license a while since? Then let him know that upon his complete recovery he would find the license waiting for him at the bureau in the palace, and this at no cost to him, but as an expression of a father's gratitude.

The trapper made his thanks, and retarded his recovery as long as possible. His nurse was slim, pretty, and full of women's unspoken meanings, and he spelled these out for them both when, alone, they were pulled together by their beating blood. The Missouri trader came to see him, and was puzzled by the domesticated effect he made, but he soon heard from him that he was in love with the young woman he had rescued. The trader made some entries in his wallet notebook about the observable effects of "the Gentle Passion."

But the convalescence lasted somewhat too long for the governor's patience, and perhaps for his suspicions. His memory of indebtedness ran out, and when the trapper, fully recovered, presented himself at the palace to receive his license, he found the governor engaged in a business conference with the Missouri trader. The governor received him without dismissing his other caller.

License? said the governor; there was some misunderstanding.

The trapper smiled and then began to scowl.

The governor looked at him with slightly dropped lids and remarked that gratitude was all very well, but there was a limit to what it might proffer. Though he did not mention his daughter's name, her presence was much between the two men. The trapper stood for a moment as rage rose inside him—it seemed to come up in him like smoke, the trader thought—and then he turned and left the palace, and rode out of Santa Fe. The governor's daughter fell ill of melancholy and for a while her life was despaired of. But— the town shrugged—life went on, and she presently recovered to wed a respected elderly rancher who—the town sighed—had seen many strangers come and go at Santa Fe.

vi.

In December of 1825 the mails from Mexico brought word of the fall of Fort San Juan de Ulloa, in the harbor of Veracruz. There, since 1821, the Spanish royalist garrison had held out until now. With its defeat, Mexico came into possession of all her own land. It was the last echo of the campaign of Agustín de Iturbide, who had been crowned emperor in 1822, and who a year later had abdicated, had gone into exile in 1823, and had returned in 1824 only to be executed. Mexico was an independent republic. The Missouri trader, as a rational republican, was well satisfied that this should be so. He witnessed the celebration of the royalist defeat on the evening of December 27.

Just before sundown an artillery salute was given in the Santa Fe plaza, bonfires were lighted before the palace, and a "farm dance" was given in honor of the victory. The dancers "danced and prayed all night." Six days later an official ball—a fandango—was held at the palace "in Compliment to the Recent victory." The Missouri trader did not dance, as such an indulgence lay against his principles, but he mingled and talked with the guests, in order to surprise the interests of their minds. He found only that they talked about the epidemic of measles that was prevalent, and he heard it said that "many persons are ill in Town and this evil is augmented by a Quack Doctor who has recently located here from Kentucky." He was invited to a wedding that was to take place on the next evening "after candlelight," and for the day after that he was engaged to attend the funeral of the oldest child of a family who had befriended him.

There seemed nothing of remark to record about the wedding, but the funeral moved him to notice it in his pages. The child's "corpse was very richly dressed and carried standing upright above the heads of the people. The procession was a very long one chiefly composed of the most respectable inhabitants, many of whom marched in front of the Body carrying lighted torches and wreaths of flowers—The Priest was dressed in his richest robes and the whole moved with a solemn pace—several voices singing and several violins playing. The day was fair and pleasant"—a January day in 1826.

In the same year a public bulletin was posted at the palace which gave the trader another moment of egalitarian satisfaction.

From the Palace of the Federal Government, Mexico:
The President of the United Mexican States to the inhabitants of the Republic, know ye: That the General Congress has decreed the following:

The titles of Count, Marquis, Knight, and all of similar nature, whatever may be their origin, are forever abolished. The Government shall order that the coats of arms and other insignia which recall the ancient dependence upon a relationship of this America with Spain shall be destroyed by the owners of buildings, coaches, and other properties of public use.

But, if republican forms arrived, royal gestures died hard after three centuries of usage. The trader saw a petition submitted to the "Honorable Political and Military Governor of New Mexico" in which the petitioner, anxious before authority, addressed the governor as "Your Majesty."

In the course of his several visits to Santa Fe during the 1830's, nothing seemed more odd to the Missouri trader than the ways of nomadic Indians who came to town. They were permitted to enter the city and were kindly received. Either mounted on their little prairie ponies and peering into windows and doors, or dismounted walking rapidly in groups to follow their curiosity where it might take them, they were, even though never great in numbers, positive enough in style and character to change the atmosphere of the whole city so long as they were there. They were laconic, hard, and direct in their dealings. The citizens were polite to them out of more than habit—they hoped to mollify whatever unpredictable notions might be alive within those striding bodies. The Indians were often half naked, and always carried weapons. They might be Utahs, or Navajos, or Comanches, depending upon which of these peoples might at the moment be officially at peace with the Mexicans.

When nighttime approached, the most curious thing of all took place. The Missourian never ceased to marvel at the simple obedience shown by the visiting savages. For they were never permitted to stay the night in Santa Fe, but had to withdraw to the country outside to make their encampments. Invariably they went without protest. Their little campfires could be seen from the edges of town. On such a night the guard was augmented at the garrison, for a sense of imminent danger wrapped in mystery was in the air. The trader thought much upon the matter.

He wondered if the power of Indians over the imaginations of other people rested in the place like no other in nature which they perhaps occupied—"a place between animal and Man, with all the animal's perfect acclimation to open nature and the use of life even to killing without qualm that which is obstacle or food; and with but a hint of man's Social Enterprise whereby in union with his fellows he may overcome nature with great works." And yet the Indian was human in form and speech. It was a subject to be considered further before its secrets might be yielded up, as to a second Humboldt. One thing was true—Indians inspired some extraordinary statements. A New Mexican, speaking to the trader, said one day in an offhand fashion that Indians had "a high regard for eagles." It was a remark that swept a type of earth-bound mankind up into some striking affinity with the sky.

He had never a voyage in the course of which he did not hear of Indian terrors and their effects upon individuals or the whole government. When Mexicans moved to establish new settlements on the frontiers of New Mexico, the government refused permission. One such movement was answered in 1830: "Until the Territory of New Mexico relies upon an armed force sufficient to curb the invasions of the barbarians, and consequently to protect the new settlements of the frontier, the Most Excellent Commission does not agree to the forming of a single new settlement until conditions meet these requirements." But armies cost money, and neither the local government of Santa Fe nor the central power at Mexico City could provide funds to increase the guard over the Indian frontier. Instead, the Missourian saw families come to the capital with their two-wheeled cottonwood carts to look for work. They were people who had abandoned their holdings in the Indian country. Their neighbors who stayed to face the savage raids and keep the republican settlements alive petitioned the governor that those who fled should lose their grants of land, in justice to those who remained.

The government, through its power of grants, was still the source of all initial wealth. The Missouri trader, in 1832, witnessed a paper in which a countryman of his appealed to the governor for a grant of land on which to establish a sawmill and tannery. It seemed to any North American a legitimate and progressive venture in business. It had its aspects of public value, too, and it seemed advantageous to stress these.

"Wishing to establish a business for the public good, with the just purpose that the citizens of this Territory, generally and individually, shall benefit therefrom," said the petition, it protested that the venture was undertaken "for the benefit of the increase and aggrandizement of this Territory." The petitioner then proceeded to the main interest with a request of the authorities "to be pleased to donate to me for thirty years the place unoccupied, and without owner, known by the name of Old Corral in the center of the sierra of the capital, where I will establish the aforesaid buildings and will only occupy what may be necessary to build a house, some corrals, troughs, a sawmill, and the other things needed for such purpose." He asked for "entire liberty to cut every kind of timber in the mountain," and he made "a solemn promise by this writing to leave for the benefit of the city both buildings with all their chattels, not excepting a single one, at the end of the thirty years of its existence. . . . I sign with two of my countrymen whose honesty is well known, who act as witnesses to my present promise."

The Missourian could not see how his friend could fail to interest the government in an enterprise so potentially valuable. Surely no rational-minded creature could object if in the course of the three decades a foreigner by his enterprise and skill should make a fortune out of the property temporarily granted him from the public lands! But as time passed without action upon the petition, there was a sense of a hand overplayed, advantages too glowingly promised. It was well known that the Government moved slowly; but to have no answer at all?

There were informal channels of inquiry, and the Missourian, out of long experience in the city, knew certain employees at the palace who could be approached not with a coarse bribe but with a friendly donation to be used in any suitable way. He thus discovered that four years earlier, in 1828, the President of Mexico wrote a secret letter to the governor of New Mexico ordering him not to permit colonization by settlers from the United States of the North. "Proceed on this point with the greatest precaution," wrote the President, and mentioned especially "the colonization of points very near the borders of this Republic." As the orders were secret, they could not be invoked openly. The sawmill project, with its attendant Americans in residence, must simply die of inaction.

Weighing the matter objectively, the Missourian had to admit that, from the Mexican point of view, the American nation had already made heavy inroads upon the formerly closed life of Santa Fe. The road from Missouri, the Santa Fe Trail, as it was now called, was in itself literally and physically an "inroad." Moreover, for twenty years the fur trade had been growing, and, though it yielded great returns in tax revenue to the government, it also took great wealth out of the old kingdom, until in the 1830's the demand for beaver pelts began to fall off, and the fur trade began to wither. But at the same time, the overland wagon trade continued to expand, and the summer-long invasions of New Mexico by hundreds of hard-dealing traders—the Missourian could see this—brought an irresistible power from the world outside to unsettle the life of New Mexico which for so long had known little change.

It was the power of commerce, animated by an energy that startled the New Mexicans and made them richer than they had ever been before; but, even as in some ways it delighted them, it also made them fearful. Wagon trains had come creaking out of Mexico for over two hundred

years; but when had any driven into the plaza of Santa Fe
like a wagon train from the North American States?

Even the Missouri trader, with his firmly controlled emotions, was always enlivened by the spectacle of which he was
a part. In the last approaches to Santa Fe, the traders
paused long enough to shave, put on their best clothes,
and smarten up their equipment. As the freight wagons
came down the street toward the plaza, the traders whipped
up their teams and, with cries, charges of dust exploding
with sunlight, the crack of twelve-foot whips, and the rumble
and shriek and quiver of wagonbeds, drove their long train
in a great, rapid spiral about the four sides of the plaza
until at last they came to rest. It was a flourish in the
style of river steamboats back home, which on approaching a landing threw on a handful of pitch-pine to make black
smoke for a spectacular arrival.

A fine crowd awaited the train, and applauded, and
yelled, and waved to old acquaintances among the visitors.
The wagons filled the square. The mountain-locked old
city came alive. The world had come to town. There was
news to hear, and money to be made, and perhaps love,
and fine merchandise to see.

The North Americans dominated the crews of the trains,
but many other nationalities were represented. The trader
made one voyage on which he associated with men of
"seven distinct nations," including Frenchmen, Germans,
and Poles. The company was made up of storekeepers and
hunters, wagoners and handymen, clerks and roustabouts.
They gave a motley appearance in their mixture of dress,
from sober fustian to blue jeans and buckskin and red
flannel and berry-dyed linseys and fancy brocade. They
were heavily armed. Every man had his personal weapons,
and the train sometimes carried small artillery pieces—
"swivels." Mounted on a pair of wheels, these were lashed
to the rear of a wagon. The wagonbeds were somewhat
like American river flatboats mounted on high wheels.
Their square ends curved up at bow and stern, and they

had narrow, high sides, and they rocked over the prairie ruts dipping their great Osnabrück linen hoods that were stretched over hickory bows. Each wagon was pulled by three span of animals—horses, oxen, or mules, and each animal wore a collar of bells to make a fast jingle as the train came trotting into town.

The wagon cargoes changed many aspects of life at Santa Fe. The trader saw how the old Mexican and European and Philippine goods gave way to those from the United States. American clothes gave a new shape to Mexican figures, American calicos and linseys, a new color. American tables, chairs, and chests were mingled with old homebuilt furniture in the rooms of Santa Fe. New foods and spices, medicines, wines, tobacco, tableware, oil lamps and inks and paints were popular. The acts of working and building knew change, as American machines and tools came to the plaza in the wagons. A "well-outfitted lathe" was mentioned in the 1830's in the will of a Santa Fe citizen. It could only have come from the East, and so only could a type of "penknife with twelve blades."

Each wagon brought about five thousand pounds of cargo. On the return trip, it was loaded to only half its capacity, in order to cut the seventy-day journey to one of forty days. Mexican rugs, cloths, hides, furs, and Mexican gold and silver made up the weight going home. The trader saw the business when it started. His first party took home two hundred dollars. He lived to see the annual summer traffic do a business worth almost a million dollars, and he knew of a single train that took home a hundred and fifty thousand in one season.

But the Missourian knew that all the money taken in by his fellows did not reach the States. Santa Fe saw to that, and he made observations on some of its means. There was liquor to be had at high prices—the brandy of El Paso, the whisky of Taos. There were pretty presents to be given to "relentlessly coquettish *mujeres* of Santa Fe," with their faces powdered pale lavender, and their black laces over their cheeks, and their incessant smoking—"the fearsome

vice of employing the *seegarito* to which all females of
the Capital, regardless of age or condition in society, are
subject," and their dovelike curiosity about the strange
North Americans, to which—so the trader thought—they all
too often added "the predations of the Eagle."

And there was, most of all, gambling. The streets near
the Plaza of the Constitution, as the central square was
called in the early time of the Republic, were dotted with
gambling rooms. The Missourian called them "pandemoniums." Night after night he strolled by, musing "tartly"
on human folly, and aridly priding himself on his absten-
tion from the riotous joys of his fellow men. The most
famous gambling house he saw was that located at Number
37, Calle de la Muralla, or Rampart Street. It was run
by a woman of strong temperament and tolerant shrewdness called La Tules.

He saw her many times, never without condemning her
in his thoughts or afterwards in his notes. She seemed like
an animal predator to him. At first she "lived (or rather
roamed) in Taos." She was a female "of very loose habits,"
who "finally extended her wandering to the capital. She
there became a constant attendant upon one of those
pandemoniums where the favorite game of *monte* was dealt
pro bono publico. For some years she spent her days in
lowliness and misery." But her luck changed, she opened a
bank of her own, and "she gradually rose higher and
higher in . . . affluence, until she found herself in possession of a very handsome fortune." In the end, she was
"considered the most expert *monte* dealer in Santa Fe,"
and—he was shocked—she was "openly received in the
first circles of society," calling herself "Señora Doña Gertrudes Barcelo." He could imagine what would be thought
of her "among the gentility and the chivalry" of American
cities. He had an exasperating notion that she would not
care what was thought of her, there, or anywhere, so long
as the money continued to flow across her monte boards
into her black alpaca bags with their stout drawstrings.
On many counts it was always a relief to the Missouri

trader when the train was ready to push on to the second half of its journey, down the Great River to El Paso and thence southward to Chihuahua City.

The trade he had first followed lay between Missouri and Santa Fe; but soon this was extended to the largest Mexican city of the northern states, and the American wagons loaded up not only for Santa Fe, but for the markets of Chihuahua six hundred miles farther south. They pulled out of Santa Fe in early summer and were back again coming northward in the fall. Commerce fell into a more or less ordered pattern, though difficulties with the customs authorities at Santa Fe, El Paso, and Chihuahua, or any point between, might delay the train until a local official could be corrupted with a suitably disguised bribe. If, sometimes, this failed, a whole loaded train might be confiscated on technicalities regarding customs declarations, and the owners would be left with nothing but a disastrous loss to show for all their toil and travel. Then they were glad enough to leave Santa Fe, homeward bound with another enterprise; remarking bitterly upon the "poverty, dilapidation, and filth of the city," and the "ridiculous appearance of the people."

The Missouri trader was more fortunate than most of his fellow voyagers, for he could pursue an interest, even as he traveled, that could never disappoint. Patiently, exactly, he filled notebook after notebook with geographical observations, astronomical readings, and botanical descriptions. He gathered specimens of rock and flower about which he opened a widening correspondence with other scientists of the new frontier. He found a new world beyond the heated interests of men.

Though on his later trips to the New Emporium he could not forbear to gaze at the art of government as practiced in Santa Fe where, all through the 1830's, times were hard—so hard that change had to come, if not through enlightened acts of public responsibility then through violence.

When Mexico became a republic, her internal finances

were soon in a state of crisis. Her farthest provincial capital received less support than ever from the national treasury. "This time of economic depression," said a Santa Fe document of 1826, "that we are experiencing at the present time . . ." The trader heard how the state was so poor that the city council of Santa Fe was forced to complain to the governor about a certain matter of practical need as well as municipal pride. There was, said the council, "no place to hold their sessions for the administration of justice, except a small rented place so small as to be impossible to keep with suitable neatness." There were only "three little rooms, without any ventilation, and so unhealthy and unsanitary that many who go in there in perfect health come out sick." It seemed hard to believe, but the trader was assured that it was true, and, moreover, those who entered on judicial business insisted the council "cannot be distinguished from those imprisoned, including criminals, and it is necessary to keep them in the same room, and this contrary to the spirit of the law." The council asked that a better courthouse be provided, "in the name of the Mexican Nation to which we have the honor to belong."

Not only the form but the substance of justice made a poor impression upon the trader at times. He was told by a petitioner, who repeatedly went to his alcalde to ask for justice in a land claim, that the alcalde said, "he would place on me a pair of shackles, and never again to speak to him of the subject."

It was enough to make a Jeffersonian citizen's blood boil. What had the petitioner done about it? wondered the Missourian.

Well, replied the man, "seeing so much rigor, I retired in great haste."

In 1836 the council received "a petition from the jail warden, demanding his back salary." In the absence of funds, the councilmen took the matter "under advisement." On another occasion, when the public treasury was empty, the council discussed the need for "fetters to bind criminal offenders—five pairs of irons and six shackles." Even if these could not be at once paid for, the councilmen thought that "there would certainly be some persons who, because of the reliability of its Excellency the Council, would furnish sufficient iron for the purpose, and who could be paid the value thereof when sufficient funds are available." Everywhere he looked, it seemed to the Missouri trader that he saw poverty of matter and of spirit.

Though even then the old city tried to make little gestures of style. In 1835 the presiding officer of the city council "proposed to its Excellency that, in so far as it is possible, it should try to adopt a uniform style of dress, according to the means of each one of the Mister Members, the coat and trousers to be always black." The measure was approved, and so was another in the same year stating that "several musicians had requested that they play at municipal obligatory services, lending their talent to the church and whatever public functions might occur."

Character, of a sort, thought the Missouri trader, was most fully illustrated in the echo heard in Santa Fe of the Texan War of Independence of 1836. At the end of May, the city council enjoyed a letter from the departmental military chief "regarding the fortunate success which our unconquerable president Don Antonio López de Santa Anna had with the Texans." But other news soon followed; for by the third week of April the new Republic of Mexico had already lost forever her immense Texan province, and President Santa Anna was a Texan prisoner disgraced by ignominious capture and contemptuous release.

As Spain had lost Mexico, so Mexico lost Texas.

Revolt was a contagion.

It spread even to New Mexico, and the Missourian on his summer voyage of 1838 gazed upon its most noticeable local result: This was the new governor, Manuel Armijo, who kept his office longer than any other whom the Missouri trader met at Santa Fe.

vii.

"Style," thought the Missouri trader with a proper republican contempt.

First came the split sound of a trumpet, trapped between the close earthen walls of Santa Fe streets. At the sound, he, and all others, turned to see what came, though all knew. Through a haze of dust and scattering infants and squalling chickens and shrieking dogs and suddenly activated old men and women came a squad of outriders with blown hats and flying serapes, followed closely by a heavy coach drawn at their best speed by four mules. The coach was really just a long, plain wagon without springs, mounted on massive axles. But its front glittered with carved gilt work, and its air of state was genially supported by its occasion, who rode within.

This was a large man with a swarthy face so full that it sagged with every bump of the road. His smile, though constant as he gazed out upon the people amid whom his passing brought havoc, was given a flickering effect by the rough ride. His eyes were large and expressive—vivid lamps of an ardent temperament. Over his brow waved a white plume fixed in his gold-laced cocked hat. He wore a general's blue uniform with a scarlet shoulder sash. One full hand rested under his chin upon his sword hilt, and the other showed its plump knuckles to the populace in greeting, as if to acknowledge cheers, of which there were none. The Missourian caught a greeting intended personally for him. Glaring, he bowed slightly, and stared after the coach while all about him, children, chickens, dogs, and old people, closed in its wake upon their interrupted concerns, and the dust fell back to its source in the street. It was the governor who had gone by.

The trader never heard of any other governor at Santa Fe who gave himself such airs and privileges. On the other hand, he would have to admit that he had never encountered a public man so candid in private discourse. He came to know Manuel Armijo well, profited in a business way by his favor, and even felt his spell of heavy flattery. The governor saw at a glance that the trader was a severe man, shy of convivial appetites; and therefore regaled him often with lusty anecdotes as though the trader were his own kind of man, greedy, sensual, and not overscrupulous in matters of honor if gain could be united to immunity.

The governor had served a term in his office under a previous appointment in 1827, and now he was back again in the palace on the heels of a revolt that swept New Mexico in 1837. He changed sides twice in the course of it, acted the coward in battle, betrayed justice in dealing out sentences of death, and, far from having at heart the public good, engaged in the whole campaign to protect his own property and even improve it. But his brimming smile and stout nudge indicated that, if this was the way he had come to power, then surely it must always be so with anybody else with ambition, an eye for opportunity, and a man's joy in the good things of life.

The Missouri trader thought him voracious as a baby, though not so innocent, and thoroughly contemptible in his ethical views; and yet—it was unsettling to a man of principle—he almost liked him. If the governor was a remorseless rascal, yet he loved life, and, if he took advantage of his position, well, after all, it was his, he was the governor, and anybody else would do the same. This was what his expression seemed to say. His heavy dark eyebrows were usually arched high, giving him the look of one falsely accused, even while his slightly dropped lids and heavy lips shining with the moisture of desire or interest confessed and invited any manner of shady indulgence.

He was rich, and founded his fortune on stealing sheep, and didn't mind telling about it with a wheeze of fellow feeling when a handful of real men came together for a drink. His country was critically poor and his people were badly fed and ignorant and ill. Between 1837 and 1840 there were epidemics of typhoid fever and smallpox. The governor accepted these conditions as visitations like those of the weather, and gave his best thought to his own affairs. He was always glad to see callers, made them handsome speeches, and all but admitted that, if he was a great man, it was a matter of luck, which might not hold forever. Times were changing, and a wise man watched them change, perhaps seeing everything a little bit sooner than his neighbor, and taking advantage of what he saw.

The Missouri trader always felt warmed by the governor's heavy good cheer, and once or twice wished he might be a little bit like him. As this was impossible, he despised him, and frowned at him in ironic politeness. How could the people of the old capital and of the old kingdom accept such a man? he wondered.

And then he must remember that the people did not elect their leaders, but received them by appointment from the central government in Mexico. Power could be seized by force of arms. It could not flow from the peaceable will of the governed at Santa Fe. And yet all about the world, the trader reflected, whole peoples were being freed by the example of successful new republics. Why not Mexico, and New Mexico? The governor was perfectly frank in stating that it was the policy of his national and local government to exclude learning "lest the lights of civil and religious liberty should reach" the New Mexicans. He was only sorry that they knew of the success of the Texans two years ago in their war of independence. Actually, a year ago in Santa Fe, the New Mexican rebels of the north had talked of calling for the Texas Republic to aid them in their schemes. It was Governor Armijo's candid opinion that in putting down the New Mexican revolt he had prevented the loss of New Mexico as a Mexican province.

But this was only a statement in his bravura manner, and he knew it. In the Texan affair there was no parallel with the case of New Mexico. The Texan revolt and subsequent independence arose from the presence in Texas of many thousand settlers from North America who had refused to accept the centralist policies of the Mexican government and who had gone to battle to gain self-government. No such group of North Americans lived in New Mexico. Only three were registered as permanent residents of Santa Fe. The rest were, like the Missouri trader, merely visitors. They would best be kept so, in the governor's opinion. The trade was profitable. Relations were pleasant.

A man could make a good thing out of smoothing the way for visiting businessmen, if he knew how.

And then, after all, if the North Americans should ever work toward a New Mexican conquest, why, there were always the regular army and the militia to throw against them. The governor was a general officer, you see.

The trader was almost dizzied by the fatuity of such a sentiment, for he knew in 1840 that the regular New Mexican troops, few enough in number, were armed only with bow and arrow, lance, and English muskets; while the militia were "still largely using the *escopeta*—the firelock gun of the Spanish sixteenth century."

In 1840 the Missouri trader was dismayed to learn on his arrival at Santa Fe that a new decree of the governor would prevent his continuing his journey to its terminus at Chihuahua. He presented himself at the palace to ask why, and was shown a ledger of decrees including the one that affected him and his associates. The government at Chihuahua City had notified Santa Fe that some of the New Mexican traders were in collusion with Apaches "when they make their incursions and even share in the plunder." Until the practice could be ended, all trade to the south was halted. It was useless for a train to push on in hopes of slipping past the customs depots on the southern road, for the document stated that "This decree shall be circulated in the Prefectures and the offices of the rural inspectors in order that they may take care of its execution."

For the moment, he amused himself by leafing through other decrees which reflected the accent of life in Santa Fe and the temperament of the governor.

A resident of the country made a petition to be delivered of imprisonment. The governor replied, "This Government, realizing that the petitioner is insignificant in every way, orders merely for the sake of humanity that the Justice of the Peace . . . shall give him absolute liberty." It seemed to the Missouri republican an offensive reason for restoring the dignity of freedom to a man.

But the governor seemed not to hold his people in very

high regard. In another paper he indicated that he considered most New Mexicans thieves. He forbade travel by the "upper road for the Californias, because nearly all who have left have gone with the intention of robbery . . . a known habit their elders have had since they first set foot in New Mexico." In an accent of tireless nobility, the governor added that his "government is obliged, and furthermore has determined, to sacrifice itself" to put a stop to the thievery.

In another familiar interest of the New Mexican, a petitioner made a request for a gambling privilege. The reply was suggestive of the governor with all his virtue turned on, as the trader thought. "Let the petitioner understand that the Government would be degraded by even considering matters pertaining to gambling, and therefore it shall be understood that he shall never again in any way bring up subjects of like nature."—This, mused the Missourian, when he was almost certain that the governor took profits from the revenue of gambling halls, and was in any case known to be a heavy gambler himself.

In his state papers, the governor seemed to sigh over the complexity and willfulness of human nature, which he as an official father must deal with to his distraction. Even a public disturbance between two "courtesans," as the Missouri trader primly styled them, had to be adjudicated. If Dolores had not given Juana provocation, and if Juana had behaved so outrageously to Dolores, then Juana must be "corrected according to the laws." Wearily, the great man wrote in his decree, "The thing that is happening here at every step is conceivable: that the public women think they have a right to insult each other without holding the respect due to the public." A pair of sparring cats, hissing and spitting at one another through the streets? The trader had seen such. He thought the governor's conclusion mild. "The guilty party should be punished in some way if they do not agree to a reconciliation." But then the governor had a weakness for women, and if necessary used his position to have his way with them. The Missourian snapped the ledger shut. It was high time to do so when such concerns intruded themselves into official affairs.

But in his driftings about the city he could not but observe how warmly and frankly the inhabitants dealt with what in other connotations he had called "the Gentle Passion." He made a note on the dancing of the Santa Feans, and sent it to *Niles's National Register,* where it was published in 1841. "The fandango is a lascivious dance, partaking in part of the waltz, cotillion, and many amorous movements, and"—he used a worldly tone—"is certainly handsome and amusing. It is the national dance. In this the governor and most humble citizen move together, and in this consists all their republican boast."

In the same year, though not for publication, he noted a strange communication shown to him by a man to whom it had come from a prominent citizen of Taos. The letter said, "I send to Scolly one vial elexer of Love—tell the old Gentleman not to interfear with the arrangements of yourself and other young men, for no doubt he will be able by the use of a little of this, to raise him-self very high in the estemation of the lady's . . ." The Missourian looked up from the wrinkled page into the face of his Mexican informant. Was this meant seriously? He saw the answer in the fixed and dreaming face of the other.

Perfectly, it said.

The trader sharply shook his head and walked away. What a city, so willing to make such a reputation. He walked over to the plaza and brought order into his thoughts by examining the condition of the garrison headquarters, which needed repairs. But this, he recognized, was nothing new. The defenses of the old capital had always been poor.

viii.

In that summer of 1841 they were put to a strange test.

In a sudden cooling of relations with the governor and his people at the palace, the trader and his associates felt the first hint of what was coming. North Americans at Santa Fe were made to feel unwelcome. They were being watched. Natives who consorted with them were warned to desist and, if they continued, were arrested. Many men were jailed otherwise for no apparent reason. The North American traders held meetings to consider their situation and the safety of their goods and indeed their persons.

Finally the reason for all such oppressive behavior was exposed. The governor let it be known that a large expedition was marching from the Republic of Texas for Santa Fe. He had been warned of it by the central Mexican government. All resistance would be offered here. He knew all, and he told what he knew. A plot was afoot among his own people. Some were said to have written a letter from Santa Fe encouraging the Texan invaders, promising them immediate overturn of the regime as soon as they arrived. A scheme was being hatched in Taos to assassinate the governor and thus aid the enemy. The Texans would try to make good their claim, to which they had held since 1836, that their boundaries extended all the way up the Rio Grande to its source country, taking in Santa Fe. They would rape, pillage, and murder. They would, of course, said the governor, abolish the holy religion of the people. In this month of August, 1841, he was prepared to destroy the invasion and save his province, but to do so he must have the support of all loyal New Mexicans. The North Americans in their midst could be expected to sympathize with the Texan enemy.

It took little of such officially inspired opinion to release an atmosphere of hostility against the traders, though on August 6 there was a slight lessening of tension, when an application to travel to "the Californias" was approved at the palace, with the notation, "in the opinion of this Government the news received regarding the Texans is exaggerated and even suppositious." But this was a mood that did not last, and for good reason.

For in early September, a New Mexican detachment hurried into Santa Fe from the southeast plains bringing three prisoners. The city was at once alive with conjecture and emotion. The three were from the Texan forces. They were "commissioners" traveling in advance of the main body. They said they were men of peace, and only desired to share the benefits of commercial intercourse with the Santa Feans. But with them they had brought hundreds of copies of a proclamation addressed to the New Mexicans by President Mirabeau Buonaparte Lamar of Texas which in itself was enough to convict them. The document referred to the Rio Grande as the "natural and convenient boundary" of Texas territory: the old menacing claim again. It said that Texas would "take great pleasure in hailing" New Mexicans "as fellow-citizens, members of our young Republic, and co-aspirants with us for all the glory of establishing a new and happy and free nation"—quite as if taking for granted the annexation of New Mexico. President Lamar declared that his proposals were made in "kindness and sincerity," and concluded by hoping for "the perfect union and identity of Santa Fe and Texas."

But Santa Fe did not in the least desire "union and identity" with Texas. The governor raised troops. The imprisoned commissioners were interrogated—until a few days after their capture they escaped from the muddy jail in the palace. Overtaken, they were recaptured and one of them was killed. The other two were lodged in confinement at San Miguel del Vado, on the Pecos River, to await the governor's disposition, which would be their death. He was now readying his field forces to march out against the main body of the Texas invaders, whom he promised to destroy. He made this promise in a proclamation to his citizens, offering forgiveness to any who "seduced with or deceived by coaxing words" may have considered supporting the Texans on their arrival.

He took another precaution which the Missouri trader soon heard about, for along with all other North Americans the trader was summoned to the office of the United States consul on September 16 and shown a letter from the governor. It read:

As Commanding General of this department, and, in the name of the Mexican nation I warn you, as Consul of the United States of the North, that neither yourself nor any one of the strangers staying or dwelling in this Capital leave it under any pretext or motive; that you all must remain in the city till my return. . . . Acknowledge to me at once the receipt of this precept. God and Liberty, Santa Fe, September 16th, 1841.

It was a sober moment. The Missouri trader understood his situation well enough without having to learn from what followed. The city was in an uproar of feeling as the governor, riding a huge mule and wrapped in a magnificent serape of blue wool studded with gold and silver bullion lace, led his forces out on the trail eastward. Almost immediately afterward the trader heard a commotion in front of the consul's house, and then heard the door crash open, and saw a New Mexican officer with a squad of soldiers erupt into the office. Beyond in the street was an eager mob. The officer went to the consul and struck him in the face and insulted him with words. It was like a nightmare, to be suddenly treated with hatred in a town that for all its outlandishness had come to seem like another home during the past twenty years. Someone broke forward from the street crowd—a responsible citizen—and persuaded the soldiers to quit and go. They went, promising to return after the triumph against the Texans was completed, "and destroy all of us, the strangers," as the aliens wrote in a letter that same day to United States Secretary of State Daniel Webster.

At the time, it did not seem like an idle threat. The trader and the others wrote of the "extreme excitement and danger" in which they, "a few isolated American citizens, together with a few other citizens of other nations," found themselves. "It has been learned here," they wrote, "that an invading expedition of 325 men from Texas is approaching this Territory; on that account, all the inhabitants and all the officials of the government have become so exasper-

ated against all strangers in this place that we deem our-
selves in danger of our lives and destruction of our property; there is danger imminent; and we fear that before
this reaches Washington we shall have been robbed and
murdered. . . ."

The consul sent a letter also to the governor protesting
the abuse he had suffered from the soldiers, and their
threats against the other strangers. From the line of march
the governor returned a note assuring him that the foreigners would be protected in their rights if they conducted
themselves properly. They could only wait at Santa Fe for
news from the Pecos River valley where the enemy must be
found.

The Texan force was powerful—six military companies
with a cannon, ten merchants with their goods train and
wagoners, a doctor, a little company of observers and ven-
turesome travelers, all commanded by a Texan brigadier-
general. If the Texans prevailed, would they reach Santa Fe
in time to save the other foreigners from enraged citizens?
The Missouri trader knew the condition of Santa Fe arms.
He could not imagine how they could defeat an army from
Texas, where all men were famous fighters and deadly
riflemen. Or, if the New Mexicans gained the victory and,
returning to Santa Fe in high spirits, decided to finish off
the other aliens according to various threats, what might
save the trader and his friends?

He reviewed every possibility but that which turned out
to be astounding fact.

For, in a very few days, word came to the city from the
governor's field forces that he had indeed found the Texans.
Their great body was divided into several parts, and it was
hard to say which was the more miserable. The Texans
were in rags, starving, thirsting, only hoping to be rescued.
Badly organized, their supply had given out weeks before.
They lost their way on the oceanic plains. Too weak of
body and will to carry them, many of them threw away
their weapons. They numbered a turncoat among their
company who was an early captive of the now glorious
governor, and this man had led the New Mexicans to the

camps of his exhausted comrades. It was but a moment's work to promise the Texans safety and immunity if they would discard their remaining weapons. When this was managed, the governor's officers then stripped them of any of their garments that remained whole, tied them together as prisoners, and organized them into parties to be marched south along the Great River to the jails of Chihuahua. They were not brought through Santa Fe, which was regretted by many citizens ready for a spectacle.

But the victory was complete anyhow, and the march to the south was conducted, by the governor's own command, with satisfactory strictness. His order was quoted and enjoyed: if any of the Texans so much as *"pretends* to be sick or tired on the road," he said to the officer in charge of the captives, *"shoot him down and bring me his ears! Go!"* In time, five pairs of Texan ears reached His Excellency and were tacked on the walls of his chamber in the palace, alongside many other such trophies of vigilance in office.

By the time it was all over, autumn was in possession of the land. The Missouri trader went home with his train. Few North Americans remained at Santa Fe. He did not return until two years later, and then for the last time. For in the summer of 1843, President Santa Anna ordered shut the customs houses at Taos, El Paso, and Presidio del Norte. The wagon trade of the Missouri-Chihuahua Trail by way of Santa Fe was suspended.

ix.

He closed out his business in Santa Fe, but, when it seemed time for him to go home again, he lingered, even into the winter months.

The trees were like sticks of bare gold in the sunshine and the blue mountains had robes of white. The city was calm and quiet, and he thought it must be much like its old self, of the time before the years of American trade. He was content there, even though he could specify all that was wrong with the place.

It was not his view alone that judged the old kingdom.

He heard a petition presented to the governor—once again his friend with all the old nudges of willing complicity—in which two New Mexicans tried to justify their application for a land grant by promising their skill, care, and industry, in contrast to the state of society as they saw it in January, 1844.

> "Of all departments of the Republic, with the exception of the Californias, New Mexico is one of the most backward in intelligence, industry, manufactures, etc., and surely few others present the natural advantages to be found therein, not only on account of water, forests, wood and useful timber, but also on account of the fertility of the soil, containing within its bosom rich and precious metals."

But, said the petitioners, nobody exploited all such wonderful resources, but, instead, many men gave way to idleness, and

> "Idleness, the mother of vice, is the cause of the increase of crimes which are daily being committed, not withstanding the severity of the laws and their rigid execution."

The Missouri trader recognized a flattering obeisance to Governor Armijo in this statement. But to make a case for their own probity, the petitioners proceeded with their description of their country's life.

> "The towns are overrun with thieves and murderers who, by this means alone, procure their subsistence. We think it a difficult task to reform the present generation, accustomed to idleness and hardened vice. But the rising one, receiving new impressions, will easily be guided by the principles of purer morality."

The petitioners stood ready to provide such new impression for the oncoming generations, and signed themselves, and dated their paper "Santa Fe, January 8, 1844."

The Missourian could not but admit that much of what they cited was true, and as offensive to him as to anyone. And yet—he could not quite say how—the old capital benighted by ignorance and an absence of ethical standards held him a while longer. In his last weeks there, he formed a resolve that gave him deep satisfaction and even, if he dared but admit it, excitement. He nurtured it in silence, as was his way, and would speak of it only when he felt sure of its value.

Meanwhile, he was witness to one more act of the florid politics of Santa Fe. A new governor, appointed by the central government, arrived from the City of Mexico and displaced Governor Manuel Armijo, who relinquished the palace calmly enough. When the day came for the Missouri trader to leave Santa Fe for the last time, he went to look for his old friend ex-Governor Armijo and was told that he had gone to the palace to see his successor, Governor Martínez de Lejanza, with whom he was on genial terms. At the palace, the trader was indifferently waved toward an inner room where the two governors were conversing. He was about to enter there when the nature of their conversation made him pause irresolute out of sight but within earshot.

Why, asked Governor Armijo, why had President Santa Anna relieved him of office?

Governor Martínez de Lejanza had to shrug. He did not really know. But anybody in high office was subject to sudden acts of unfair discrimination from those still higher up. Meanwhile, a man had to work his selfish advantages while he could; and he, for one, would admit that he had done so, in his time.

Governor Armijo had a man after his own heart there; and, in his turn, richly confessed to his own successful uses of public office for his personal ends.

The Missouri trader had heard enough. Pursing his lips over his old friend, he withdrew without saying good-by.

x.

A year later his great resolve was about to bear its fruit. In Philadelphia, he saw the last press work on a book he had written out of his many little pocket-wallet pages. It was the work which he called *The Prairie Voyager, or,*

Observations, Social, Geographical, Zoological and Botanical, of Twenty Years in the Chihuahua Trade, by A Missouri Trader. It was to be issued in two volumes, tall octavo, with bindings of pressed black silk stamped in gold designs of Victorian Gothic style. He could not say that he had written a classic work about Santa Fe and the prairies. All he could claim was that he had given himself wholly to his material. Most privately he knew this was just; for the raw stuff of his book had given him life.

BOOK THREE:

UNDER THE
UNITED STATES

VII

The United States Lieutenant: 1846

i.

THE LIEUTENANT, a small, stocky, black-eyed man riding a bright bay horse, gazed ahead, refusing in assumed disdain to see the conquered city. He was young and had never before taken part in a conquest. He carried his saber drawn, like all other soldiers who were so armed. It was still raining—it had rained all day—and in the narrow streets lay great puddles white with sky and rimmed with mud. The army's horses splashing through them cast fans of spray over the mud houses on either side. No residents were visible, but the lieutenant could hear sounds of grief within some of the houses. He supposed these appropriate to a fallen city.

Santa Fe was captured. The day was August 18, 1846.

The lieutenant was a member of the conquering general's staff. He was conscious of his place in history, even though no one would ever hear of him. The army of which he was an officer, the Army of the West, as it was officially styled, commanded by Brigadier General Stephen Watts Kearny, had taken New Mexico without a battle. It was the second great success of arms in the War with Mexico, for three months ago, near the mouth of the Rio Grande, General Zachary Taylor's command had won two famous battles to drive the Mexican army out of Texas. Wherever Mexican territory could be reached, the United States in the prosecution of the war was reaching for it. The movement against Santa Fe was the first of a series directed against northern Mexico through Chihuahua, and against California.

The lieutenant was exhilarated by the power and glory of his country, of which he felt like the sole representative. Long later he saw a description of the Army's entry that day, and it recalled to him the feeling he had at the time. It said the American soldiers marched into Santa Fe with "drawn sabers and daggers in every look." He was hungry, for he had marched ever since five in the morning without any food, and, in some ways, the mystifying failure of the New Mexicans to give battle for their city was more exhausting than the real thing. But he made a virtue out of his endurance, and saw everything as twice its real size, including his own part in the conquest. He did not know it then, but he was running a fever.

His part of the entering column of troops reached the plaza at about a quarter of five o'clock. The rain stopped. More troops marched in, and then, at five, moving at a mild walk, the general, mounted, appeared and rode up to the palace. The lieutenant, as was his duty, went to join him.

In the deep long porch of the palace stood the provisional government of Santa Fe, waiting to receive the general. When General Kearny dismounted and walked to the acting governor to shake his hand, the sky opened and the sun broke through with blinding shafts of light that struck sparkling rays off all the dripping trees and the army's arms. The United States artillery passed through the plaza and gained the top of the fine hill north of it and, in a few minutes, fired a thirteen-gun salute, while the general officially assumed the powers of governor, and the flag of the United States was run up over the palace. In a letter home, the lieutenant later wrote that "there was not the least

show . . . of resistance in any way." He intended to discover why, for he was still amazed by the fact.

The staff accompanied General Kearny into the palace,
where they were given El Paso wine to drink, and presently
were led to dine at the house of a Mexican officer. The
lieutenant was glad to eat, and said the meal was "very
much after the manner of a French dinner, one dish suc-
ceeding another in endless variety." He talked with a
Santa Fe officer who had learned English during the years
of the North American commerce, and who told him that the
New Mexicans had failed to defend their city because the
governor after neglecting to prepare a proper defense, had
run away yesterday morning. This was General Manuel
Armijo, who only last year had returned to the palace for
his third governorship.

But why had the governor acted so? wondered the lieutenant.

The Mexican officer shrugged. He was a man of pride,
and he suffered for the conduct of his runaway commander
in chief. He could not bring himself to say that Armijo
was a greedy coward, but in the hard light that came into
his eye he expressed the feeling of this opinion, and the
lieutenant was suddenly abashed, almost sorry to be one of
the conquerors. He glanced about to see General Kearny,
and took heart, and manner, from the example he saw.

The general's courtesy was real and perfect. He could
put himself in the place of others. The men he was talking
to had surrendered their city and their province to him,
yet he made them feel like his hosts. He was at ease, and
so were they. Ever afterward the mountain air over the
city would be colored by the stripes and the stars of his
flag. It was the greatest change that ever had come to Santa
Fe. He worked to make it the easiest for all.

General Kearny was small of figure and trim. He was
fifty-two years old. His eyes were gray, large, and set in
wrinkles of humor that showed pale against his prairie tan
when he was not smiling. He wore his dress frock coat of
blue with gold epaulettes, gold pipings, and gold buttons.

His belt and saber were laid aside, but when dinner was done he called for them and strapped them on, saying he and his people were tired after the day's long march. He returned to the palace, where he showed his officers through the empty rooms. In his office they saw dried human ears tacked on the wall, and the lieutenant had an impression of Governor Armijo. There was a long ballroom with a packed earthen floor. Some of the inner doors were covered in buffalo hide painted to resemble grained wood. The lieutenant noted everything for his next letter home, including the "state of decay" of the old building, where General Kearny spent his first night "sleeping on the floor."

Before going to sleep on his own piece of floor in the palace, the United States lieutenant at last heard from a senior staff officer the final facts behind today's "bloodless possession" of the city.

By the end of June—six weeks ago—Santa Fe knew of Taylor's victories at the Gulf of Mexico, but apparently few citizens were concerned. It was chiefly Governor Armijo who was exercised by the news, with its implications of historical irony. For if the Texans had failed five years ago to take Santa Fe as their own, they now, with their border claims against Mexico, gave the United States its whole pretext to make war, and so to threaten Santa Fe. The annexation of Texas brought with it more than the vast rich Texan lands; it brought with it all Texan problems, of which relations with Mexico presented the most acute difficulties.

Armijo, said the colonel, was no fool, though he was evidently a poltroon. He could see the dangers of the war, for himself if not for his countrymen, and when he heard that a force of United States troops was ordered to march overland against Santa Fe, he saw that he was about to be put into a trap. For he had little with which to defend his capital, and yet, if it fell, he, as the responsible officer, would be blamed. He had often been likened to President Santa Anna—a comparison which, in Mexican lands, was a compliment. Now it would have been a happy solution for him if, like Santa Anna when his country was suffering a crisis, he could have retired to his country estate, there to ride out the storm and be ready to return to reap the benefits of the objective view.

But as this course was not possible, the governor adopted one which had its philosophical aspects, whatever else might be said of it.

And what was that? asked the lieutenant.

The governor sold himself and his state—yes, really. General Kearny sent two men to see Armijo in secret six days ago. One was a Kentucky trader, James Magoffin, long familiar with Santa Fe and the governor; the other was Captain Philip St. George Cooke of the Army. They entered Santa Fe, dined with the governor, with whom they got along like a house afire, and before the evening was over had his pledge to put up no resistance to the Army's entry. The colonel heard that Mr. Magoffin had arranged a payment of up to $50,000 as the governor's bribe. The whole scheme had been hatched months ago in Washington by President Polk, the Secretary of War Mr. Marcy, and Senator Benton.

In consequence, as the Army approached, the governor, for the sake of appearance at home, made warlike preparations, but without any intention of fighting when the time came. He mobilized 4,000 men, armed mostly with bows and arrows and obsolete Spanish firearms, and he took one fieldpiece to Apache Canyon, placing it not as a plug in the mouth of the bottleneck, where it could well have done damage to any force approaching through the pass, but out in the open a couple of hundred yards from the mouth, where it could easily be surrounded and captured. As everyone knew by now, he scattered his forces before the Army came into view and without warning his people ran off himself, a richer, if lesser, man. In fairness to him, concluded the staff colonel, he was quoted as saying that with the resources at his disposal, "it would have been . . . sheer foolishness on his part to oppose the Americans." On the other hand, it was hard to work up any sympathy for a man who had often given as his motto the statement that "it is better to be taken for a brave man than to be one."

And where was he now?

Hurrying south somewhere along the Rio Grande highway with all the riches he had been able to load.

Nothing in that summer of strange experience was stranger to the lieutenant than the story of the governor, with its odd mingling of tones—squalid betrayal and cheerful realism.

The lieutenant was a young man with little knowledge of the world. His judgments were simple and his trust in people great. His heritage was decent. The world he knew was that of a small town in Ohio—an image of white picket fences, white wooden steeples, and gray clapboard houses, all set, a life of fixed innocence, in billows of green wooded hills. A volunteer officer, he had an ache in his heart to see something new, a fragment of his future, sought out by his own will.

Santa Fe filled him with excitement, even in that first weary night. Was it the mountain altitude? The foreign quality of the people? The soldierly triumph of his Army in which he shared? He did not separate the causes of his feeling, but let it course through him like a fever. For this it was. Late at night he awoke in a sweat, though the clear starry air of August was cold. He was overwhelmed by strangeness, a sense, heavy with prophecy, of a lost self. But in the morning he felt clearheaded again, and went to see the city.

ii.

Like many others before him, he thought it looked "like a very extensive brick-yard indeed." The palace was merely an elongated shed, with its raw wood overhang all along the front, supported by rough planks. The plaza was "level, unpaved, and rather sandy," with an irrigation ditch on each of its four sides feeding rows of young cottonwood trees. All around the plaza in front of the shops and dwellings and the governor's house was a continuous covered walk. There were no street lamps. Near one corner was a market where he bought peaches, grapes, melons, and apples. He was thirsty and his head rang. In a saloon he found a place to sit, eat, drink, and meditate. Gaming tables— poker and monte—were already at work in midmorning.

When he resumed his walk he realized that he saw no gardens, but only cornfields encroaching upon the houses. But when presently he ventured through a wooden doorway in an earthen wall he found himself in a patio, and there in abundance were flowers, vines, plants, and children, and a parrot, a dog, a cat, and an old man napping in the sun. The place was spotlessly clean, full of color in painted plaster and woven hangings, with dense shadow beyond deep doorways where he saw movement. He was oddly stirred by a glimpse of life alien and inviting. It was a scene typical of most houses in Santa Fe.

He moved on and in a walled court behind the palace came upon an odd contraption. "Armijo left in such a hurry," he noted, "that his state coach fell into our hands and is still here, a curious specimen of Mexican taste and workmanship." He described its heavy construction and its gilded front, and added, "as to going out in it, no one in his senses would risk his neck in such a clumsy and crazy affair."

The city had five churches, though one of these facing the palace across the plaza was not finished. He looked inside the other four and saw the altars with bright paper flowers, lace, painted wooden panels, gilt candlesticks, and the coarse native statuary hung with votive gifts of rosaries, jewels, and little objects in silver. On the walls were time-smudged paintings of Christ's way of sorrows. He thought the general effect "rich and even barbaric." The exteriors, he thought, were like those of barns, if a barn could be built of unfired clay. And he wrote, "they are loaded with bells, as many as five being on the main church"—the parish church of Saint Francis which stood at the east end of the oblong plaza. The bells rang, he insisted, "all day long, and half the night." The natives seemed to know what the bells were saying.

He watched the men and women of Santa Fe, those whom the Army regarded as foreigners, and among them he felt himself to be the alien, not they. He was stirred by a wish to be accepted among them. It was a wish which he concealed. He could not imagine what was the matter with him. He felt like someone in love, but not with anybody or anything he could name. His blood was hot and powerful, and at other moments he felt chilled and listless. Scowling to conceal his feelings, he did his work with the staff, and in the evening ranged with the officers through the dance halls, where they announced "phandangoes almost every night." He put down an opinion in order to mask an acute desire: "Women not handsome, rather more intelligent than the men." How the women of Santa Fe looked at him and the other soldiers. There seemed no end to the depth of their dark eyes, and to the question, and the promise, that smoldered there.

iii.

Her name was Luz. She was twenty-two years old, married to a Mexican sheep rancher who lived almost all the time on his lands thirty-five miles east of the city. She was small and exquisitely shaped. Her face was palely swarthy, and her eyes were so dark with such thick lashes that from a little way away they looked like cloves. Her mouth was made by nature to rest in a hazy smile. The lieutenant never saw another expression on her lips, even in moments of extreme passion or even asleep. She was poor in money and he gave her what he had, which she accepted without noticing how much or acknowledging what for. She had little to say, but it was always amiable, and her darkling eyes sparkled at him with fondness and wonder which he took for love.

He was in love as never before in his life. The fever

that drove him, his excitement over Santa Fe, were merged and delivered through his love for her. She was a dream made flesh. Perhaps he had carried in his head some long-projected image of her which he must cross the world to find; and now he had found it.

He wanted to marry her.

She shrugged. She already had a husband.

Divorce him.

She was a Catholic; it was impossible.

Run away with him.

Where, how? He was an officer, how could he run away from an Army? No, things were better as they were, just as with all the other soldiers who lived with women in Santa Fe.

It did not satisfy him. He longed to regularize a relationship which to him was so obsessively sweet that in it he imagined a scheme for his whole life. And yet he hesitated to press her for fear she might grow impatient and think him ungrateful for what already was theirs together. He was with her every night and as much of every day as he could take from duties.

Ohio looked over his shoulder and gave him a pang now and then; but if Luz touched him, or murmured against his cheek, or sprang like a young cat into a movement for no reason, he lost all thoughts and sensations but those of her. He was made immensely a man, and yet now and then his happiness made him tremble in his bones with weakness like a reminder of illness, age, and death. He wondered if his brother officers who had taken up with women in town knew such extremes of feeling. He decided that they did not, and, further, that nobody suspected him of taking so seriously a conventional affair between a conquering soldier and a woman of the conquered territory.

Luz, he would think, and translate her name, which meant "light." She seemed to fill him with light. He gave it forth upon others. Associates began to see him as if for the first time. He looked brilliant, charming, and either feverish or alight with extraordinary energy. Someone laughingly said he was like someone under a spell. It was true. He was hungrily so.

iv.

His duties with the general made him a part, if a small one, of many important acts in the following weeks. The general struck precisely the right note with the residents of Santa Fe. He publicly promised them the integrity of their civil and religious rights, and kept his word. He even had a wise and kindly thought for the future of Governor Armijo.

"His power is departed," he said, "but he will return and be as one of you. When he shall return you are not to molest him . . . I am your governor—henceforth look to me for protection."

In reply, speaking for his fellow citizens, New Mexico's last Mexican lieutenant-governor, Juan Bautista Vigil y Alarid, gave New Mexico over to the sovereignty of the United States with grave nobility. "To us," he said, "the power of the Mexican republic is dead. What child will not shed abundant tears at the tomb of his parents? I might indicate some of the causes for her misfortunes, but domestic troubles should not be made public. It is sufficient to say that civil war is the cursed source of that deadly poison which has spread over one of the grandest and greatest countries that has ever been created. . . ."

The general received the allegiance of the Pueblo chiefs, and of the clergy, and even a message from Governor Armijo "asking," from a safe distance, "on what terms he would be received" if he should decide to come back. But the general was through with Armijo and moved on to more productive work.

He ordered the construction of Fort Marcy on the north hill overlooking the city, where volunteer and regular troops built a classic fortification of earth, with star-pointed revetments enclosing artillery pieces. Disposing of the boundary question, he revealed on August 27 that the old Texas claim of Mexican territory all the way up the east bank of the Rio Grande to its source country was now superseded. The United States annexed the whole province of New Mexico, even beyond the Great River all the way to California.

The news was received quietly, but in secret it enraged a group of New Mexicans, most prominent among whom was Colonel Diego Archuleta, who had been Armijo's second in command of the Mexican military forces. He had been promised his rewards in turn by James Magoffin if he would but remain neutral in the sellout of Santa Fe. Among these suggested rewards was the lordship of all New Mexico lying across the Rio Grande. The lieutenant was present when Magoffin reminded the general of this proposal. Archuleta must have something—either an empire of his own, or a position of authority under the new government. The general was busy, and did not send for Colonel Archuleta, who for his part suffered in silence. It was evidently not an idle silence, for the lieutenant heard that he was at work with friends, creating unfavorable public opinion against the occupying forces.

But there were more immediate things to do, it seemed, than mollify a displaced Mexican commander, and the staff, the lieutenant, attended to the details. There was a ball to be arranged in late August at the palace for "all the officers and to citizens generally." The lieutenant saw it as "a political or conciliatory affair, and we put the best face on it." He dwelled on a certain aspect of it. Now he saw that "the women are comely—remarkable for smallness of hands and feet," he observed. Women of all classes attended. Nobody inquired about the nature of relations between officers and those whom they escorted. Absorbed in his own infatuation, he felt that he and Luz were exempt from all notice, and, quite like a man already married and respectable, judged the women of other officers by remarking that "nowhere else is chastity less valued or expected."

In the same vein he described the ball. "There was an

attempt at cotillions, but the natives are very Germans for waltzing. There were men present in colored cotton trousers secured by leather belts, and jackets, but they danced well. The American merchants"—many of whom had once again entered the city in the wake of the Army—"were, of course, very genteelly represented. There were twenty or thirty of them. The supper was good, particularly in cake. The fiddlers accompanied their music at times, by verses, sung in high nasal key. . . . The ball went off harmoniously, and quite pleasantly, considering the extravagent variety of its make-up. But we did not feel particular—out here." Again not seeing himself truly in his surrender to life in Santa Fe, he patronized it with an Ohioan's view.

But on other evenings, when dusk crept up the eastern mountains, he was pierced by impressions that moved him with a kind of nostalgia for the present, and gave, as in his love, a bittersweet flavor to every moment, if soon, in the movement of the Army to California which must come, he must leave what he had found. The artillery band played every evening at tattoo—"a clear calm evening"—and afterwards the city stirred to life, with the music of distant "phandangoes," and the clatter of the gaming rooms, and lovers talking along the leafy river. At ten o'clock the curfew gun sounded and he heard steps running away to privacy and darkness, like that which he enjoyed in Luz's room, and then the only sounds were those of "the tread of the sentinels, the rattling of their arms, or the reliefs going on post," or a sentry calling a challenge to some late walker —all the ways of the Army which was his itinerant home, and which he loved, as he loved everything then in the high city on its mountain-lofted plain.

v.

But duty returned with daylight, and it was a daytime purpose, firm and ordered, that took him away with the general and a contingent of 700 soldiers on a reconnaissance to the Great River. They left on September 2 with their "banners flying to the breeze." The women of Santa Fe watched them from the housetops as they marched out. He looked for and found her. Her half smile cast a hazy shadow upon her face and he waved to her, quite certain that all the promises he felt in his breast would be plain to her through his hand raised in the air. My strange darling, he said urgently and silently, it is pain to leave you, but only wait till I come back, and we shall make it up to each other in our very own way. A placid happiness came upon him as the column wound away from the city and down La Bajada toward the river. He was already imagining his return to her.

The march was a success. The downriver population gave welcome, and hundreds fell in behind the Army and followed along through the countryside. Indians at Santo Domingo gave a magnificent sham battle to entertain the general. In the valley towns, soldiers bought everything they could find, using their uniform buttons for money. The general was looking for Governor Armijo, or signs of an insurrection in his favor, but found none, only meeting Mrs. Armijo at Albuquerque. She was alone. The lieutenant thought her "good looking . . . and rather cheerful." Her husband was still hurrying southward toward Mexico. For the Americans, the people gave plays, fireworks displays, and balls. At Tomé the volunteers in the Army grew restive, and the general sent the lieutenant with a platoon to quiet them with extra duty.

Sandstorms came up in the last days of the tour, and, during one of these, the lieutenant seemed to lose his breath. He was forced to halt, lie down, then sit up, hauling on deep drafts of the dust-bitter air to keep life going in him. He coughed until he made blood on his kerchief. It was an hour or two before he felt well enough to remount and ride on to overtake the column. He knew now that all his strong and strange impressions of the past weeks had taken their character from fever. He was feverish now, and again all things seemed especially near to him and vivid, but not pleasantly so. He hurried in his mind to return to Santa Fe. Once there, her hand on his face would cool him and restore him.

On September 11 the reconnaissance party re-entered the capital. In even those nine days while they had been gone much seemed to have happened there, and the soldiers, after visiting in Mexican towns below, were struck by what they called the "United States look" of the place. On its hill, Fort Marcy was built up enough so that it began "to show itself to the town." In the streets were throngs of blue-uniformed soldiers—the garrison that had been left behind. The Army's well-ordered rows of tents in the fields below Marcy looked like an American colony. Little Mexican boys hailed the troops with Americanisms, and the American merchants, at last sure of the protection they had needed for thirty years, were running their emporiums full blast, giving to the plaza a new character. There were trophies, too, in the plaza: Governor Armijo's artillery, which he had abandoned in the countryside. "It has been found and brought to the city," observed the lieutenant. "There are nine pieces; one is marked 'Barcelona, 1778.'"

One of the disadvantages of staff duties was that, when troops were dismissed in formation, all personnel but the staff were free to go at will. But the lieutenant must follow the general into the palace, and work the rest of the day on a draft of the official report of the reconnaissances. It was long after nightfall when he was dismissed by the general.

He went at once to the straggling earthen house at one end of which Luz occupied a single room which she rented from her brother-in-law. The room was dark. His heart rose and beat, for she often awaited him in the dark. He lifted the door latch, but it was locked. He called her name into the crack of the doorframe. He rattled the latch. At once a vomit of fury sounded in the room—it was a dog, barking in throat-raking menace. In another moment the door was opened a little, and a man stood there, hushing the dog and asking who came?

The United States lieutenant was unable to speak. It was an unspeakable thing that he had found.

Well? asked the man inside impatiently, and was answered by her voice in the dark, telling him to shut the door and return to bed, for it must be only one of those drunken North American soldiers, who went about after dark beating on anybody's door, looking for any woman.

The man said yes, yes, she must be right, and told the lieutenant to go or he would set his sheep dog upon him. He slammed the door and locked it against the cold night which was alive with unwelcome visitors.

The lieutenant walked back to the creek and crossed it. He shook with chill. His jaws rattled against each other. It was impossible and yet it was true. She was with another man. To think of it was enough to drive him out of his head. How could she have done this. He had thought of nothing but her during his absence. He had longed for nothing but his return to her. His head cleared and a bitter ray of hope entered it. Perhaps it was her husband, the sheep rancher; yes, he had a sheep dog; it was her husband who had returned. No doubt he had overcome her with his rights, and, when she could, she would come to him and explain, perhaps begging his protection against her husband whom she must now detest. The lieutenant all night long made a future out of this notion, and, when morning came, he returned in caution to her house.

The door of her room was open. He approached. A woman with her head tied in a dustcloth came out shaking a scrap of woven rug. He spoke to her, seeing beyond her that the room had been emptied of personal belongings.

Yes, said the woman, her sister Luz had left early that morning with her husband to go to live on their sheep ranch south of Galisteo. The room was vacant and for rent, if he knew of any soldier who needed a nice room with all comforts, very cheap. As she spoke in Spanish, he required several repetitions of all or parts of this news before he was sure of what she said.

Against his will, then, he finally understood and believed her.

On the following Friday during work at the palace headquarters he was obliged to ask permission of his staff colonel to return to barracks, as he felt ill. It was granted. An hour later, lying on his bunk, he began to choke and cough on a long stream of blood flowing from his lungs. An orderly was by and helped to ease him until the seizure was over, and then went to fetch the regimental surgeon. After an examination, which included many questions as to his sensations during the previous weeks, the lieutenant was told that he was a victim of tuberculosis of the lungs. The disease had undoubtedly been contracted before his departure from Fort Leavenworth, said the surgeon, and any undue excitement or—he gazed levelly into the lieutenant's young face—or indulgence would not only have been characteristic of the disease but also aggravating to it. He must remain in bed for a few days, and his condition would be closely watched.

On the following Sunday, September 20, General Kearny, in fine spirits, whimsical, fatherly, and confident, came to see him during the morning. He shook hands with his young staff officer, told him to lie down, and behave himself, and said he would no doubt be himself again in a jiffy. But the surgeon had made it clear that he must not expect to march with the Army for California five days from now.

The United States lieutenant rolled upward on his elbow to protest. Once he had wanted never to leave Santa Fe. Now he could not bear to stay.

No, said the general, he must stay and get his strength back, and, if he did it soon enough, he might be able to march south to Mexico with Colonel Doniphan and the Missouri Volunteers when time came for their departure. Meanwhile, the general added, things in the staff were in an almighty mess without him, and, if he felt up to it and if the surgeon said so, he must please come to help before the California contingent went on its way.

Anyhow, as of that morning, it was another beautiful

day, and he was not at all worried, said the general, about
the invalid, who he wished had been with him just now,
for as a gesture of courtesy to Santa Fe he had attended
mass at Saint Francis's Church, and he was moved by the
service, and amused to note that the music, on three violins
and a horn, was exactly the same as that played for the
dances around town!

He talked nonsense for another five minutes, but he
looked closely at his young subordinate, and he knew that
spitting blood was all very well, and familiar enough, and
ominous, but that, whatever it was, there was more to this
case than that. The lieutenant saw that the general had
this knowledge of him, and this gave him comfort. After
the general left he slept well for the first time since his
trouble burst forth.

vi.

General Kearny came to see him every day, though he
himself was unwell with a local type of dysentery for which
the surgeon had been dosing him. On the next Sunday
the general said he was committed to a dinner party given
by an important Mexican citizen, and thought he felt well
enough again to risk the fiery diet of Santa Fe. He wondered
if the lieutenant might feel up to going along as his aide.
He had had a favorable report from the surgeon about the
lieutenant's improvement in health—physical health, he
meant. With quizzical candor, he raised the question
whether the lieutenant might not be ready now for a little
diversion for his spirits, which for one or another reason
seemed rather low. They would go at two o'clock, and by
six he should be safely home in bed again, and, in any
case, should he feel tired, he would be at liberty to leave
the entertainment at any time.

The lieutenant went. He and the general were received
at the double door of the street wall of the house by their
hostess and her two sisters. Crossing a large patio, they
were conducted directly to the dining room, where on one
side of a long table several Mexican gentlemen were seated

on cushioned benches. Facing them were their ladies. Food was being brought to the table by four young Indian maid-servants. After greetings, the guest of honor and his aide' were seated on either side of their host on the men's side of the table.

First they were served a thin soup with fine noodles, followed by another soup, thick with meat and vegetables. A dish of boiled rice, dressed with butter and salt and covered with slices of hard-boiled egg, came next. The main dishes followed one at each course—roast meat, boiled meat, and chopped meat stewed with a broth of hot red peppers. The officers welcomed the champagne which was poured then. Leaning to his host, the general asked permission to propose a toast, which was granted with solemn courtesy. The general put down his napkin, rose, lifted his glass, and said,

"The United States and Mexico—they are now united, may no one ever think of separating."

All stood, and drank, and the Mexican gentleman cried out, "*Viva, viva!*" and no one mentioned that, way to the south in Mexico, Americans and Mexicans were far from united. General Taylor was moving toward Saltillo and Monterrey in battle trim, and General Santa Anna had returned to Mexico from Cuba to enter the field against him, after the overthrow of President Paredes.

The desserts were brought—a boiled custard seasoned with cinnamon and nutmeg, and a cake pudding, and "fine cool grapes." When after three hours dinner was over, the ladies withdrew, and the gentlemen stayed at table for more champagne. Presently they joined the ladies in the long sitting room, which was furnished "with cushions, no chairs, two steamboat sofas, tables, a bed, and other little fixtures." Everybody took seegaritos and the air was soon blue with smoke. The general made a point of having a word with each guest and, after half an hour, rose, nodded to his aide, and returned to the palace. He was reasonably well satisfied with his experiment in bringing the lieutenant "back into the land of the living."

Two nights later he took him to another party, this time to the house temporarily occupied by a trader and his wife who were on their way to Chihuahua. They were Samuel and Susan Magoffin, brother and sister-in-law to James Magoffin. It was a gathering mostly of American soldiers and merchants. Mrs. Magoffin was the only woman but for an elderly Mexican lady whose single remark of the evening was directed to her. She complimented Susan Magoffin on her cape which she had seen her wear. She admired it because it was *"high in the neck,"* and asked for the pattern. She said she disliked to go into the plaza where there were "so many *Americanos,* and her neck exposed."

The officers talked shop. For weeks a section of the staff had been at work on drawing up "an organic law," a legal code, for the new Territory of New Mexico, and the general was about to publish it before his departure for California two days from now. It would bring the administration of Santa Fe and the territory into harmony with the prevailing laws of the United States, without, the general hoped, doing violence to any of the cherished customs of the New Mexicans. Certainly with a reformed code of laws, and an orderly administration of them, the population, hitherto so disadvantaged by looseness of government, would have a better chance than ever before to lay the foundations of prosperity. The Americans had never seen poverty so great as that at Santa Fe. In this connection, one of the officers mentioned with amusement the intelligence lately come to headquarters in a New York paper dated July 3 of that summer of 1846. He could quote it, and did so, to the delight of all present but the elderly Mexican lady, who preserved the tactful fiction that she did not understand it.

" 'In the capture of Santa Fe,' " recited the officer relishing the difference between the report and the reality, " 'it is estimated that, if the movement is prompt and efficient, at least fifteen millions in specie and gold dust will be captured.' "

In the midst of the laughter that followed, the general made a sudden "very unceremonious jump, and an inquiring glance around to know the meaning" of what had just happened to him. He was spattered with rain water. It was raining, a hard thunderstorm, and the roof leaked. It was soon "leaking all around, the mud roof coming with the water." Mrs. Magoffin moved them all to another room. Someone began to discuss the qualities of two local race horses, Night-Shade and Bright Eye.

The United States lieutenant moved to sit with his hostess. She made a complimentary remark about General Kearny: how agreeable he was in conversation and manners, conducted himself with such ease, could "receive and return compliments." He had said a most gallant thing to her; she would never forget it. He said as he was now the governor she must come under his government, and, at the same time, he placed himself at *her* command, and to serve her when she wished would be his pleasure, and so on. "This," she said, "I am sure is quite flattering, *United States General Number One* entirely at my disposal, ready, and will feel himself flattered, to be my servant." At the same time she cast a fond look across the room at her husband. She was a recent bride. And now, she asked, what did the Army think of their commander? Surely he was the admired of all?

To conceal his feeling, the lieutenant looked at her severely and replied with formality.

"The Army of the West," he said, lifting the subject away from vanity and prattle into serious professional values which he felt it deserved, "marched from Bent's Fort with only rations calculated to last, by uninterrupted and most rapid marches, until it should arrive at Santa Fe. Is this war? Tested by the rules of science, this expedition is anomalous, not to say quixotic. A colonel's command, called an army, marches 800 miles beyond its base, its communication liable to be cut off by the slightest effort of the enemy —mostly through a desert—the whole distance always destitute of resources, to conquer a territory of 250,000 square miles; without a military chest, the people of this territory are declared citizens of the United States, and the invaders are thus debarred the right to seize needful supplies; they arrive without food before the capital—a city 240 years old, habitually garrisoned by regular troops." His voice was unsteadied by passionate admiration and spots burned in his cheeks as he answered her question. "I much doubt if any officer of rank but Stephen W. Kearny would have undertaken the enterprise, or, if induced to do so, would have accomplished it successfully.

"This is the art of war as practiced in New Mexico," he concluded.

Mrs. Magoffin was a little dismayed not by what he had said but by his manner. From across the room, the general caught the effect of the lieutenant's hectic animation. He had no idea what the young man was het up about, but he thought it was time to take him home. The thunderstorm had gone west toward the Great River valley. They could hear its grand broadsides receding.

The lieutenant was ordered to bed. The general reminded him of what the surgeon had told them both—that his disease could only be controlled through a sustained, perhaps even a lengthy, regime of rest and wholesome, light recreation. An avoidance of undue excitement was recommended. It was the last time his commander spoke with him. Had he been offered a precept for a lifetime?

The next night there was a grand ball at the palace in farewell to the general and his officers. The merchants of Santa Fe gave the party. A chill wind was up, for snow had fallen that day and the mountains were "covered." It was decided that the lieutenant should not venture out into the cold night. In his barracks he could hear now and then a scrap of merriment from the direction of the palace— the wiry music of a violin, the clang of a guitar. He was reminded of much. With sad gratitude he felt sleep coming.

He was out the next noontime—September 25, 1846— to watch the troops march for California. The general was taking 400 men and a battery of two howitzers. Colonel

Doniphan and the Missouri regiment would remain at Santa Fe until relieved by Colonel Price and another volunteer regiment coming overland from the east.

General Kearny had been much occupied all morning with many matters to settle at the last minute before leaving. The lieutenant was reluctant to take any of his time. He went to the plaza and from the crowd watched the formation as it fell in before the palace. A great throng of Santa Fe was gathered. On the rooftops, mostly women, shaded by their black head shawls; in the covered walks, men; and at the edges, giving stir and sparkle, little boys playing like wavelets along a placid shore. Presently the crowd quickened. The staff came out of the palace. Colonel Doniphan saw the general to his charger. The general mounted. He took the plaza with a smiling sweep of his eyes; nodded for the command to be given, "At a walk, forward, march"; and the regulars of the Army of the West moved out of Santa Fe for California. They were going down the Rio Grande to turn westward near Socorro. The United States lieutenant with his weak lungs, his uncertain future, and his betrayed heart was left behind.

Nine days later, on October 3, Colonel Sterling Price arrived at Santa Fe with another regiment of Missouri volunteers. The lieutenant saw the Army's work as if from a distance. He was not yet strong enough to be assigned to duty. A battalion of Mormons who had accompanied Kearny's march from the east moved on to California on October 15 and 16. Three hundred of the general's regulars returned to Santa Fe. He had sent them back, for on October 6, at Valverde mesa on the Rio Grande, he had encountered the scout Kit Carson returning from California with news of American victory there. The general would not need a battle force now on the West Coast. Colonel Doniphan and his men left for Chihuahua on October 26.

Again the lieutenant was left behind, for the surgeons had again decided that in his condition he would be only an encumbrance to an army in the field. In due time, Colonel Price had an interview with him and advised him to be mustered out of the Army. The only question was whether he should return to Fort Leavenworth for his discharge or accept it in Santa Fe. On the whole, with winter not far off on the plains, it seemed most sensible to stay in Santa Fe and recover his health in a climate ideally suited to the cure of consumption. His pay would be forthcoming later. Right now, said the colonel, though the U.S. Army paymaster had lately arrived in town, he had brought no money.

The lieutenant could manage for a while, which was lucky, for, in writing home for small regular payments to keep him while he found his health, he noted that "the quartermaster's department remains without a dollar." He found a small room in a house near the plaza. He took his meals for a dollar a day at the Fonda Hotel in San Francisco Street. He found himself learning to speak Spanish. Cautiously he took short rides on a horse which he bought and stabled at the edge of town with a family who were kind to him. He went to mass and to other services and, like the Santa Feans but for different reasons, for he was not a Catholic, he came to regard the events in the churches as the most important of the week. He simply wanted something to do.

He thought about life for the first time in his young career. Up to now, in health and youth, he had lived heedlessly. Now he wanted to know why he held his opinions. Feeling an intimation of returning strength, he came slowly to a sense of judgment and an awareness of values in his own terms. To go west with the Army, to find and lose love in Santa Fe, and to break down in health were the first moral experiences of his life.

vii.

As autumn changed into early winter, he began to feel a change in the human climate. The New Mexicans were bored with the American invaders, and then they became quarrelsome, and showed their dislike in mockery and petty annoyances, such as thefts and defacement of Army equipment. The Santa Feans said the Americans were overbearing bullies. Even Pueblo Indians changed their manner and, though not long ago they had hailed the Americans as their deliverers from Spanish and Mexican bondage, they now felt "outraged" by the American occupation. The Americans should just wait—they would see—all was not over yet; such sentiments were muttered about town, and, when the United States lieutenant spoke of them to the Mexican who kept his horse for him, all he got for an answer from a man whom he had held as a friend was a silent shrugging of the lips. Something was coming, there seemed no doubt of that.

But even so, the lieutenant was amazed when one day just before Christmas the Army's artillery was wheeled into the plaza, commanding all entrances, and sentries were posted all over town. At the same time, fifteen prominent Mexican citizens were arrested for plotting a revolution which was to break forth everywhere in New Mexico on Christmas Eve, when every North American in the territory was to be murdered or held prisoner. The lieutenant heard that the plot had been exposed to the authorities by Doña Gertrudes Barcelo, La Tules, who would have had much opportunity to hear it discussed in her gambling rooms in Rampart Street. The leader was supposed to be Diego Archuleta, but he was not among those captured by order of Governor Charles Bent, whom the general had appointed to rule the territory. Colonel Archuleta was still in hiding somewhere. It remained to be seen whether his revolt had been effectively stopped.

After a day or so, the city was again free. The sentries were withdrawn, and the artillery went to armory shops to be prepared for delivery down the river to Colonel Doniphan, who was waiting at El Paso for the batteries which he must take with him into Mexico. "The clanking of the anvil is incessant," as the lieutenant heard it. "Caissons and gun carriages are strewn around the forges." But the feeling of uneasiness was still so strong that he wondered whether the cannons ought not to be held at Santa

Fe for the safety of American citizens there. But Colonel Price had heard by courier of a great victory over Mexican troops won by Colonel Doniphan on Christmas Day on the Rio Grande forty miles north of El Paso, and, not to delay him further, sent him the artillery on January 8.

Against those who would undermine faith in the promises of the new American government, the governor published a proclamation in early January. Charles Bent was a resident of Taos, a man whom the lieutenant admired for his simplicity and honesty.

"You are now governed by new statutory laws," Governor Bent told the New Mexicans, "and you also have the free government promised to you. Do not abuse the great liberty which is vouchsafed to you by it, so you may gather the abundant fruits which await you in the future. Those who are blindly opposed . . . also those persons who dream that mankind should bow to their whims, have become satisfied that they cannot find employment in the offices which are usually given to men of probity and honesty, exasperated have come forth as leaders of revolution against the present government. . . . Their treason was discovered in time and smothered at its birth. Now they are wandering about and hiding from people, but their doctrines are scattered broadcast among the people, thereby causing uneasiness, and they still hold to their ruinous plans. . . ."

The governor took cognizance also of unsettling rumors of a movement of Mexican troops from Chihuahua to recapture Santa Fe and dismissed it. He asked his citizens to get back to their tasks and keep the peace.

With the United States district attorney, the governor left to spend a while in Taos, even though he was warned that he might be in danger there. For Taos was a hotbed of some of Archuleta's most fanatical followers. The Indians of Taos pueblos were said to be in the forefront of the revolution, and so was the pastor of Taos, Father Antonio José Martínez. The lieutenant wondered if these troubles would have broken out if General Kearny had been able to remain in Santa Fe. He noted that they had all come about after the general's departure. In any case, he hoped they had run their course.

But on January 20, 1847, a Taos Indian loyal to the American government hurried into Santa Fe to bring disastrous news to Colonel Price. Two days before, all day long, throngs of Indians from the pueblo had crowded into the Mexican village at Taos. There they gathered together to drink Taos "lightning" whisky. As their uproar grew, Governor Bent was advised to leave for his own safety. He refused to do so. Before dawn the next morning the Indian mob, with some Mexican malcontents, went to the governor's house, shot him with arrows, scalped him, and left him to die. They then moved to all the other houses where Americans were staying, turned them out, tortured, and killed them, including the United States district attorney. North of Taos, at Arroyo Hondo, and eastward, at Red River, other Americans were destroyed. In all, twelve were massacred. Now the Taos rebels, sure of success, were planning to march on Santa Fe, take the capital, and inflame the whole territory to rebel. Colonel Price at once ordered full mobilization. In a short while everyone in town knew the story.

The United States lieutenant now wished he were still in the Army. He offered his services, but they were not accepted, as he could hardly go as a civilian volunteer, and there was no time to accomplish the paper work required to make him a soldier again. He had to wait in Santa Fe with all the other citizens when Colonel Price marched out to the north on January 23 with 350 men and four brass twelve-pound mountain howitzers. Snow covered the ground, making the road hard to follow.

For almost two weeks Santa Fe waited to hear the outcome of the punitive expedition. But, at last, couriers from Taos brought word of battles in Taos Canyon, where the rebels met the Army, and at Taos Pueblo, where the Indians were besieged and defeated. In the dark before morning on February 5 the Taos chiefs surrendered to Colonel

Price, who demanded the delivery of the Indian leaders of the revolt. They were yielded up to him, and put in jail to await trial. Ten United States soldiers had been killed, and fifty-two wounded, of whom several died afterward. A hundred fifty Indian and Mexican revolutionists were killed, and many more than that number wounded. The revolt was now at an end. In a few more weeks the rebel leaders, Indian and Mexican, were hanged at Taos, after a brief and barely formal trial.

Santa Fe and its new government seemed now to be safe from further threat of overthrow, but Colonel Price reported to Washington that "it is certain that the New Mexicans entertain deadly hatred against the Americans." The lieutenant would have to agree that this was a true report. It was not until the autumn of 1847, when the surrender of all Mexico was certain and when new troops arrived at Santa Fe from the east, bringing the total garrisoned there to 3,000, that the course of the future seemed sure. "And then," recorded the lieutenant, "New Mexico surrendered."

By then, he was well enough to return to Ohio, if he wanted to. But he did not want to, though he could not satisfy his family at home with reasons why. He mentioned "opportunity," and "salubrious climate," and "prospects" which he was "looking into," all of which were true enough. Yet there was a further truth which he could not speak because he was not entirely aware of it. But where he had shared in glory, known joy and misery, danger and excitement, and found health —there he must stay.

viii.

Once he had made up his mind to live in Santa Fe, events moved rapidly for him. Within two years he was married, and the father of an infant son, and a partner in a sheep-ranching and wool-production business which had already started him well on the way to founding a fortune.

It was a matter of unending and amusing interest to him that his destiny had all developed from the purchase of a horse and the stabling of it in the care of a Mexican family on the edge of town. As native bitterness against the American conquest wore off, the Mexican householder once again became his friend, in time introduced him to his family, and revealed details of his personal business.

He had a young and appealing daughter. He owned a sheep ranch where he wished he could work out some plan of a twofold operation. It would be good if one part of his time could be spent at overseeing the raising of sheep and the shearing of wool, while another part could be devoted to the operation of a wool warehouse in town from which bulk sales and shipment could be made eastward, now that trade with the other American states was really established and growing. But the rancher was not so young as he used to be, and it took another kind of head than his to run a commercial business. He was at home on the mesas where the flocks moved under the shadows of sailing clouds. He was no man to handle those Yanqui traders who came and sat in the Fonda Hotel or the United States Hotel on the plaza and bought and sold things so fast that a man sometimes did not understand what was going on.

The United States ex-lieutenant asked if he might not, for a modest commission, undertake to sell the next season's wool crop to the American traders. If he managed the transaction well, perhaps some continuing business relationship might be established.

It was tried, and he found that he could deal with his countrymen in their own shrewd terms. He was able to make over to his employer a return substantially better than any ever before earned by the wool crop. The Mexican rancher found his American friend to be imaginative, enthusiastic, and honest. He engaged him as his permanent agent. He was gravely pleased when the young man asked to marry his daughter, and consented provided the parish priest gave his approval of a mixed marriage. No obstacles were presented, and the wedding took place. The bride was secretly proud to bear an American name, and to be called Missus instead of Señora. This was how the future was going to be in Santa Fe. She was one of the first to reach for the new ways. On the birth of her first son, her father expressed his joy and his faith in the future by taking his son-in-law as a full partner, and coupling their two names, one Mexican and one Anglo-American, in the name of the new corporation they founded together, which prospered from the beginning.

In 1849 trade was active both to the east and south. Caravans of from twenty to forty wagons moved along the old trails from Missouri to Chihuahua. They were escorted by United States troops to protect them from attacks by horse Indians. Many a wagon in such a train carried wool from the crop of the newly established wholesale wool dealer. Where he had once looked at life in Santa Fe as an outsider, he was now helping to make it as one who belonged there.

He still kept up his friendship with the Army garrison. There were 280 soldiers stationed in Santa Fe in 1849. Sometimes the commanding officer called upon him to handle privately some matter of delicate relations that might come up between the military and the native residents. He was trusted by both elements of the population.

As he prospered he acquired confidence in himself. He grew a trifle portly. He impressed people as a substantial citizen. He never gave his opinion hastily, but always made a point of hearing what anybody had to say, and of considering his own conclusions in silence and clouds of smoke from expensive imported seegars. Sometimes people had to wait almost unbearably long to hear his reaction to their solicitations, or offers, or views. When at last he would speak, it was like hearing a judgment at law. Having found himself, he matured rapidly. His Mexican friends gave the honorable prefix of *Don* to his first name. Because of his marriage to a Mexican-born lady, his American friends took up the habit of using the title in addressing him. He accepted it calmly. It seemed to him suitable to the position of a leading younger citizen of Santa Fe. It was difficult to remember when he had ever been anyone else. A change toward happiness obliterated much, and even dulled the critical sense of a fresh eye.

ix.

Some measure of how much he had changed was presented to him one day at the United States Hotel. He sat in the lobby turning over in his mind how different the place looked today, remembering the rainy afternoon in 1846 when he had marched in with the Army. Trade was not only booming now, but overland travel to the California gold fields had suddenly come upon the city in 1849, and all hotels and roominghouses, eating rooms, saloons, and gaming halls were thriving wildly. Presently the ex-lieutenant was seized in conversation by a tall, thin man with sidewhiskers and rubbery lips which were never still. He took the next chair, and, recognizing another eastern American, broke into talk as if resuming a monologue lately interrupted in the middle of a sentence.

". . . and can't seem to hang on together and git up and git for California the way we meant to do. So today we dissolved it and let me tell you, that's no easy thing to—"

As he droned on in a high whining tone which seemed to bring him proof of his own inexhaustible excellence, it gradually became clear that he was a member of the "New York Knickerbocker Association," which had been incorporated as a company to drive overland to the California gold fields. Members bought shares. All had work to do on the trail. According to his investment, each had a guarantee of a percentage of profits which must come if only they could reach the fields. Now think of it: after all those meetings in New York, and those months of travel, the association on arriving at Santa Fe fell to pieces, because some members were sick of the wear and tear of the trip, and of each other, and others had heard that the gold discoveries were not all they were supposed to be, while the rest would hear of nothing but pushing on and making a fortune. But did he know something? This was a fact, that unless *everybody* wanted to go, why, the old association was not what it was supposed to be, and, of course, *nobody had* to go, and everybody knew it, and so today they held their last meeting, and the shares were offered for sale all over again, and those who were for going on bought them along with the equipment of those who wanted to go home. He for one was going on to California, and he for one couldn't get out of Santa Fee too fast to suit him.

"It's the greatest place *I* ever saw," he said in mockery which he assumed must be shared by his listener, who said nothing, but only rolled his cigar slowly and watched its smoke flutter upward and listened.

The New Yorker said he walked up to Fort Marcy and looked back, and from there the houses of Santa Fe presented the appearance of "a vast quantity of pig styes." It was his view that the population was "composed of scapegoats from every nation of the earth." He declared he "never heard such profanity or saw so much vice in two days." He understood a gambling license cost $3,000, and he believed a single table often took in $100 a night. The territorial governor was Colonel Washington, whom he had met, "a very mild and fine man," but—the New Yorker had to laugh—the governor had not "the nerve for such a place."

He never really in all his born days saw such a place. He arrived in town late one night with an advance group of his party and went straight to this hotel. There he saw a great number of men gambling at a long table with piles of dollars heaped up. The landlord managed for supper and a drink, and then sent him to bed on the billiard table with some other guests, while still others slept on the floor under it.

Well, sir—and as he went on talking his unwilling listener uneasily but with humor had to recognize many of his own first opinions and impressions of Santa Fe—well, sir, he wandered about town—a "poor and miserable-looking place"—and noticed the artillery park in the plaza, and called at several private houses which despite their unpromising exteriors were "splendidly fitted up and furnished" within, and ended up dining at the officers' mess at Fort Marcy, where he had himself a fine meal. Kit Carson was there for dinner, and the Army's chief muleteer. These two, with the New Yorker himself, were named, he said, the "Lions of the Day."

If the ex-lieutenant thought the talker was out of breath he was wrong.

Half-closing his eyes the better to enjoy his own visions, the New Yorker made a certain point about local society. He had been to a fandango. The party was given by merchants and officers all of whom brought their Mexican women, who were dressed fit to kill—grand clothes and Christmas tree jewelry. Those women—why, he never saw "more genteel and better behaved ladies," and yet, he said, they were "all concubines." Still, he stated, opening his eyes wide, they were "much before the men in refinement, intelligence and knowledge of the useful arts." He slapped his spider-like leg and added that everybody went direct from the fandango to early morning services at the parish church, which in itself was a caution to see, with all its tinsel and mirrors and "most miserable paintings."

The New Yorker paused and yawned comfortably. Then he drew out a dog-leg stogie from his inner pocket and a box of locofoco matches. Striking a match, he said,

"See that? You ought to have seen an Indian when I struck a locofoco in front of him. He turned and he skedaddled." He laughed at the memory. Well, he said, with all of it, he wasn't sorry he came. Some folks were fussing and crying if they weren't accommodated on a Palace Drawing Room Steamer on the water or riding in the steamcars on the land, but he managed well enough wherever he was with whatever he had. He was going on to California in the morning, and that suited him just fine. When, he asked, was the gentleman with whom he was having such an interesting conversation, when was he going to get out of Santa Fee?

The ex-lieutenant stood up and shook hands with him.

"Never," he said, and walked away.

VIII

The German Bride: 1870

i.

HOLDING THE NEWSPAPER up before her eyes, her hands trembled as she read what it said about her wedding. She tried to pretend unconcern, but the warmth of her welcome through the daily *New Mexican* of Santa Fe for a certain date in 1870 moved her more than she wanted even her husband to see.

She had married him—how did the paper know so much about it?—in the Hauptsynagoge of Nürnburg at twelve noon, in the company of all his relatives who had stayed in Germany when he and his brothers left home for America many years before. Her family were there, too, and it was a matter of pride to see how substantial they all were, how well dressed, what fine clothes the gentlemen had, what valuable jewels the ladies, how lavish the decorations. The wedding feast took place at two o'clock in the Hotel zum Rothen Ross, with the best wines, which naturally led to many toasts, merry and sad, honoring both happiness and separation so far away across the sea—for she was to leave immediately with her bridegroom for America, and the West, and Santa Fe, where he and his brothers conducted their thriving mercantile business. In a few short years they had made their fortunes, and had attained for themselves positions of respect and influence in the old city.

It was but fitting, therefore, declared the newspaper that brought hidden tears of pride to her eyes, that the happy couple should be welcomed home, and that the editor, speaking for the community, should offer a salute to her personally as a "gifted and charming lady in whom our society will appreciate a valuable acquisition." The article ended by announcing that the bride and groom were at home to their friends at their house in Palace Avenue.

To her it seemed like the end of an amazing journey which had begun, really, three generations ago when under the sorrowful conventions of the ghettos of Germany the ancestors of her husband and herself had still been denied the dignity of surnames. But her husband's great-grandfather was a man of such goodness of nature and such skill in his craft as a goldsmith that after the Code Napoléon had taken effect, he received the bestowal of a surname from a certain patron of his, a baron, who said he was proud to share his name with such a man, under a procedure which the new laws made possible. Ever since, the family had honored their name by diligence in work, honor in character, and cultivation of the higher tastes in life.

When the four brothers of this generation emigrated to America and settled in New Mexico, they brought to the commercial ways of town and prairie a new style. Their manners and the taste of their minds echoed the comfortable culture of middle-class Europe, even while their business sense was as sharp as that of the established American traders of the prairie trail.

Returning to find a bride in the Germany he had left, her husband, the youngest of the brothers, was already an American. He was fluent in both the American language and in the New Mexican language. He was handsomely dressed. His portmanteaux were full of clothes bought in

New York. About his manner there was a new spaciousness. To his German family—and hers, after they had met —he seemed like an image of the United States. There seemed little doubt that already he could afford the best in life. And if he could—why not have it? Their journey home to Santa Fe was done in the highest style possible.

They sailed from Bremen on the United States ocean steamer *Commodore Vanderbilt*. In New York they took a suite at the Fifth Avenue Hotel and went to concerts at Castle Garden. From New York to Saint Louis they traveled by Pullman Palace Cars, and at Saint Louis they took a veranda cabin in a Palace Steam Pacquet Boat on the Missouri River as far as Kansas City. There a prairie wagon train loaded with goods for the family firm at Santa Fe awaited them. They joined the mule train and for seventy days the German bride lived with her husband on the trail which he had crossed so many times through adventure and peril.

Everyone's first impression of her was of how small she was, and then they forgot this, and saw the proud carriage of her head, and the inclusive sweep of her darting glances. She was dark-eyed. Her mouth was often set in a smile with its corners downward which left the way open for a teasing mockery or a tirade of opinion, depending on her mood. She made something of a point of her moods, even if she recognized their existence as a habit, when they ceased to be entirely convincing. Her sense of fun was acute, and behind her airs of a grand lady it always threatened to break forth in some minor indiscretion of which she later spoke as an "outrage" which she had committed. She blushed easily and often. Her skin was white. Her clothes were beautifully made in the highest of fashion. She animated them with something of the effect of a small girl dressed up playing queen. She could make everybody smile simply on meeting them. Wait till she played the piano for them, and then she would make them sigh, or even weep. Her Mendelssohn—they would never believe it. *Lieder ohne Worte. Unglaublich.*

As the consort of so much temperament, her husband was lucky in owning a calm nature with a deep unspoken resonance in it somewhere. He was considered the most dignified of the four brothers, and also the best-looking. He was almost tall, his hair was black, and he wore a beard and mustaches trimmed like those of Prince Henry of Prussia, whom he had once seen. When he was dressed up he wore a black frock coat and vest, with light gray trousers that had gaiter straps under his thin black kid boots. His face was ruddy and his cheeks were high, pushing ridges of silent glee up under his gray eyes. His dark brows cast strong shadow over his eyes, and the light in his eyes came straight out of the shadow like a beam. He had only to look at anyone to be believed, and he deserved to be, in so far as he could know the truth. More than his brothers, he had a thoughtful cast of mind, but, just as much as they, he loved the strange and often dangerous experience of crossing great wildernesses to carry out their business as merchants. He enjoyed the physical life, and was happy that his work required him to be so much in the open air.

On their first journey westward together over the plains, he spent hours telling his bride of his experiences. She could not hear enough of his tales, about which she wrote in copious letters to her older sister Charlotte who lived at Wiesbaden, where his family also had connections. He talked to her in Spanish, for he wanted her to be able to speak to their Mexican friends in their own tongue when she should first encounter them. She was a willing pupil. Any challenge to her mind and character she rose to meet with a little shrug of scorn which said that of course she could do it—whatever it might be.

Ordinarily, he said, when he went on his commercial enterprises he traveled with the well-protected freight wagon train operated by his firm out of Santa Fe. But once he had to go on a quick trip without escort to Saint Louis on behalf of the firm to attend an important auction of wholesale dry goods thrown on the market in a bankruptcy case.

Speed of travel was necessary. With a friend who, like him, was a crack shot with a rifle, he crossed the plains in a buggy drawn by two government mules borrowed from Fort Marcy.

But how could he carry enough supplies in just a little buggy for such a long trip? she asked.

Ah. There was the sport of it. They shot buffalo, butchered the meat and jerked it by hanging it from the buggy top, and ate it just like that, dried raw.

But why didn't they cook it? She wished she had been with them—she would have cooked them something marvelous out of it.

No, he said, they traveled at night, and avoided building any campfires, for just one reason. She could guess, perhaps, what that was?

She shuddered satisfactorily and said, Indians!

Seguramente.

Please, what did *Seguramente* mean?

He smiled and replied that it meant *gewiss*.

Well: one dark night on that buggy trip they lost their way, and passed within a few miles of an Indian camp, but thank God escaped detection, though they were so near they could hear the barking of Indian dogs. Farther along, after sixteen hours of steady traveling, they spread their blankets and went to sleep for a few hours in the darkness. When they woke up, the sun was shining brightly, and she could not guess what they saw to their horror and surprise: the wreckage of an ox team and wagon was scattered all about them, and nearby were the bodies of two teamsters who had been scalped. A little bit away they saw the ashes of another teamster who had been tied to a tree and burned to death. The buggy travelers had camped on the site of a recent massacre. They gathered what identification they could find and did their best in utmost haste to bury the poor wagoners, and resumed their own travel even though it was daytime. They looked back over their shoulders more than ahead, he could tell her. But they made it to Saint Louis safely.

She clicked her tongue and drew many short breaths of horror and relief. She was a good audience. She was also practical, for she asked: And the auction?

He smiled with pleasure in her respect for business, and told her that he had arrived in time to attend, and had outbid the field to acquire the entire stock. The brothers cleared over $60,000 on this one deal alone in the course of a few years.

Sitting next to him in the rut-borne wagon, she straightened up, lifted her head several times, and silently nodded to the world how right she had been to marry such a clever, brave, and handsome man. As he was meant to, he saw these gestures of opinion from the corner of his eye and was content.

He had another story for her. One time a traveling circus was stranded at Santa Fe. He heard that the proprietor needed to raise money. He went to see what might be for sale, and made an offer for the biggest and most golden and showy wagon in the circus train. It was accepted. Then began the wonderful experiment of the roving emporium. He fitted up the interior of the golden wagon with shelves to display a full stock of merchandise. He carried dry goods, clothing, hats, caps, bacon, ham, jewelry, watches, shoes, rifles, pistols, powder and bullets, and candy and jew's-harps and rhinestones and ladies' kid gloves. She could imagine the effect of this chariot, with all its gilded angels with trumpets, and fancy carving studded with hundreds of small mirrors, and scarlet paint amidst the giltwork. He took the wagon to the Indian towns and Mexican villages down the Great River road. In the clear air and bright sunshine, they could see the wagon coming from thirty miles away, because the sun reflected in the mirrors flashed and sparkled plainly visible at that distance. Crowds always met the shining wagon wherever it went.

She was delighted with the story. Where was the wagon now?

He opened his hands apart in comic resignation. It had

been swallowed up by quicksand while fording the Rio Grande below Albuquerque on a return trip a couple of years ago. Fortunately, the stock was all but sold out. He had managed to save the mules—and himself.

Himself? Was it that dangerous?

Assuredly. She would soon learn that this was country in which anything could happen.

ii.

When she came to the end of their first journey together, she found a good house of adobe all ready for her, newly furnished, lacking only a piano. She took charge at once, rearranged all the contents, and asked if she might use her father's wedding present in money to buy a square Steinway piano, assuming it could be shipped across the plains. Her husband agreed, and also told her, now that they were home, that if all went well he intended within a very few years to build a new house—a mansion—of brick, with scroll-saw woodwork and a cupola, surrounded by a garden, with a fountain in front, and a carriage house in back bearing a gilded weathervane aloft a little steeple. It would be the first house in Santa Fe to be built in any style but that of the old days of Spain and Mexico among Indians. He was neither Spanish nor Mexican. He had been a German; he was now an American—a successful one. His house must reflect that.

What a good man, she thought. No wonder the daily newspaper went out of its way to welcome him home. For her part, she would begin at once to take her place in Santa Fe by showing interest in everyone and everything there, however outlandish. More than most people, she liked to be liked.

One of her first duties, as she saw it, was to inspect the family store on the plaza. It was one of several stores and she noted with satisfaction that it was the largest. Among the clerks were a couple of young German cousins who had come to the States to make their fortunes and were beginning under the family wing. Other clerks were Mexicans. It delighted her when she heard them murmur her husband's nickname—"*El Bonito*," "The Handsome."

The salesrooms were two long, deep rooms that grew dark in their ends away from the plaza. She was not prepared for the profusion and variety of merchandise on the shelves and counters. She said there was anything there anybody could want—groceries, plain and fancy, including delicacies imported from Europe; drugs; baked goods; dry goods ranging from muslin to velvet; books; building materials; pots and pans; furniture; even a line of iron stoves. The stock was worth several hundred thousand dollars, and, but for a few local items like Indian rugs and Mexican embroideries, every item had been hauled over the plains to Santa Fe. The place had a thriving air. On some mornings, she heard, people were waiting on the covered sidewalk in front of the store before the doors were opened. The business day was started with an air of circumstance when one of the young cousins from Wiesbaden unchained the doors, unlocked the padlocks and big bolts, and slowly swung open the gates of commerce.

Her three brothers-in-law were on duty in the store with her husband, for the days had passed when personally they had to take turns commanding the prairie trains. They employed men whom they had trained for the job. She made her husband's brothers know her strong family feeling for them all. If she had a keen, realistic view of them, they knew too that she would love and defend them all if the need should arise. They shook their heads complacently over that youngest brother. Everything he did was a success, even to finding a wife on a trip to Germany undertaken for that very purpose. He had an eye for quality. She could even talk a little Spanish, and tried it out on the Mexicans in the store. Also, she missed nothing.

What, she asked her husband, what were those pieces of paper money hanging framed over the cashier's desk?

"Shinplasters," he told her. During the Civil War, when times were hard, and ready money was scarce, and ship-

ments of specie and currency over the trail was full of risks
owing to disturbed conditions of the United States, the
store itself issued script which was circulated among its
customers, and even honored by other business houses in
town. Each note was worth fifty cents if presented in
amounts totaling five dollars. Actually, for that war inter-
lude, the family firm had gone into banking. When the
war was over, the script had all been redeemed in good
hard United States money.

And there, above the safe, that saber hanging on the
wall? What was that?

It was a saber, as she saw, but not just a meaningless
relic. It was the saber worn by her husband during the
war when he served, with the rank of captain, as adjutant
to Colonel Canby, who commanded the Federal troops in
New Mexico. She was stirred. He had not told her that
he was also a soldier. Did the war, then, reach Santa Fe?

There was much of interest to discover about the war
years, if she wanted to know how things were before she
came. With animation she entered into all the life of her
new home, even to aspects of its past, which she learned
from anyone who would tell her.

iii.

It was a shock to the city when, in the spring of 1861,
the commander of United States troops in the Territory of
New Mexico left his post and went to join the Confederate
Army. He was succeeded by Colonel Edward R. S. Canby,
who began to organize defenses against invasion, if once
again the Texans, now in the Confederacy, should reach
for New Mexico. It was not long until the invasion came.

In July a Texan force took Fort Bliss at El Paso, and
marched up the Rio Grande to seize Fort Fillmore. The
Texan commander organized southern New Mexico and all
of Arizona as a Confederate territory with himself as military governor. Only Fort Craig, near Socorro, and the garrison at Albuquerque stood between the invaders and
Santa Fe, the capital. Governor Henry Connelly called for

the mobilization of the New Mexico militia in September, 1861:

> This Territory is now invaded by an armed force from the State of Texas which has taken possession of two Forts within the limits of the Territory, has seized and appropriated to its own use other property of the General government and has established military rule over the part already invaded; and . . . there is every reason to believe it is the intention of the said force to pursue its aggression further and establish the same military rule over the balance of the Territory and subject us to the dominion and laws of the Government of Texas. . . .

The militia turned out—but in woeful condition. It totaled 1,000 men. They were mostly of Mexican ancestry, poorly armed, and untrained. Colonel Canby recruited five regiments of volunteers. He gave the colonelcies to Kit Carson and other prominent New Mexicans. His adjutant had heavy work in the organization of the defense forces. The stakes were great. Not only the freedom of Santa Fe and the rest of the territory was at issue. The federal government at Washington saw that, if the Texans could capture New Mexico, the way would lie open to Colorado; and if Colorado fell, next would fall California, and with them both, their gold fields. These were what President Lincoln called "the life-blood of our financial credit." If they were lost, the nation would lose a great part of its power to meet the cost of war. And not only that: the whole mountain west in enemy hands might give the Confederacy opportunity to purchase or conquer a vast new empire embracing the states of northern Mexico, adding open seaports on the Pacific to the Confederacy's Atlantic harbors closed by Union blockade. New Mexico was the gateway to the whole enterprise. If it were forced open, the whole Union cause would be in grave peril.

Seeing how much depended upon the poor resources of New Mexico, Colonel Canby appealed to the governor of Colorado to send troops to help in the defense of the federal west. Two companies from Colorado arrived in time to join the union garrison at Fort Craig in February, 1862. Santa Fe breathed easier. But not for long.

On February 20 and 21 a newly raised Texan brigade brought battle to the federal forces of Fort Craig and defeated them. Fort Craig was the biggest post in New Mexico except Fort Union, the army headquarters near Las Vegas. Albuquerque was the next objective of the invaders. If it fell, they would surely move for Santa Fe, with its small garrison and its prestige as the capital. The northern cities had word of the calamity from Colonel Canby with firm orders to destroy all public property "and particularly provisions" rather than let these fall into enemy hands. Canby and his surviving troops were now hurrying north to Fort Union, which must be the rock of final defense.

But even at the expense of the cities of Albuquerque and Santa Fe?

Even so. It was a hard necessity, but a proper one, in military terms, no matter what might be threatened—a great mercantile establishment, for example. Men rode out of Santa Fe toward the river road to see what might be seen, and on March 2 saw a great pillar of smoke rising above Albuquerque, and knew that the Army there was destroying its stores. Later in the day, Union soldiers from the Albuquerque garrison appeared on the road to Santa Fe. Albuquerque was abandoned without a fight. Santa Fe was only sixty miles farther north. The war was coming near. The retreating troops told how the militia had all but melted away. The volunteers were deserting too. The hopes of all once again rested in help from Colorado, for more volunteers from the Colorado gold and silver fields were already on the way.

With her lively imagination supported by her sense of sympathy, the German bride could imagine how people felt in Santa Fe then. In only a few days more, the Texans were marching up from Albuquerque. The federal troops in Santa Fe went to work burning supplies, and, when that work was done, they marched away eastward to join the concentration of forces at Fort Union. Santa Fe was open before the enemy. Nobody knew what must come. The city seemed to hold its breath. At last the Texans would have what they had reached for so many times—possession of New Mexico. The road they must follow coming into Santa Fe passed by the Convent of the Sisters of Loretto, which was between the Santa Fe creek and the plaza. The German bride found an early friend in the superior of the Convent, Mother Mary Magdalen, who had vivid recollections of the war period.

How bitterly the Santa Feans awaited the Texans! They regarded the invaders as their hereditary enemies, and were now about to succumb to them. Mother Mary Magdalen considered that the worst had come when the Confederate troops, marching into the capital, halted on the road before her convent, and presently established their camp in the fields along the creek just opposite her main door. Lent had begun. Evidently it was to continue as a season of peril as well as penitence. Mother Mary Magdalen dismissed her students from all classes and attendance at the convent until further notice.

Already the invading soldiers were behaving with impertinence. They climbed up on the convent wall and ranged over the outbuildings and spied on the courtyard whenever they could. Dreadful rumors came to the convent. The Texan general was going to make allies of the Apaches and turn them loose on the inhabitants. He was also planning to have the Mormons of Utah join forces with him, and expend their old resentment against the United States by launching attacks from an unexpected quarter. It must be only a question of days until the Texans completed their preparations for a movement eastward through Apache Canyon and a massive assault upon Fort Union. Three fresh regiments from Texas arrived in Santa Fe during March. The New Mexican government had fled to establish a temporary capital at Las Vegas. Texas soldiers were saying, "Fort Union is ours already." If that should be true, there seemed little hope for New Mexico.

"The whole time the Texans remained here," said the

reverend mother, "we were in continual distress of mind. We hid many of our provisions for fear they would pay us a visit when they found no more in other places. We spent the whole of Lent in fear because of this war. We made many novenas."

The whole city knew it when on March 22 a force of 600 Texan soldiers moved out on the Santa Fe Trail toward Apache Canyon. It was the beginning of the end. The Texans were leaving to blockade the canyon against any use of it by Union forces. The main body of the Confederate army was at Galisteo twenty miles to the southeast. Santa Fe was cut off from Fort Union and her own nation. It was a time of heavy hearts.

It could the better be imagined, then, what emotions broke free a week later when first one, then another, party of wounded and broken Texans arrived in Santa Fe from Apache Canyon with news of their total defeat in a two-day battle. They had been overwhelmed by the United States troops from Fort Union. Most of these were the volunteer soldiers of the First Colorado regiment, who had arrived at Fort Union two weeks earlier. Coloradoans ranged along the rocks of the canyon walls "like mountain sheep," said the Texans. They beat the Texans back to the canyon mouth and, when the Texans tried to rally themselves there, drove right into them and scattered them.

Two days later the Texan main force came up from Galisteo and reopened the fight against more troops from Fort Union. Again the canyon saw battle, this time at Glorieta Pass, and once again the enemy was beaten. For though there were now enough Texan soldiers to fight through to victory, they were lost when a Union detachment came around to their rear and destroyed their supply train. The Coloradoans burned 85 Texan supply wagons and bayoneted 600 horses and mules. The Confederates were done. They ran away to Santa Fe, bringing their wounded.

And now Santa Fe, and Albuquerque, the two biggest towns of the territory, had little left, after the burning of government stores and supplies, on which the invaders could live. They were obliged to retreat from New Mexico. The reverend mother remembered well how the encampment opposite her shuttered convent was broken up, and how the enemy soldiers took themselves off the way they had come, and how not long later the city was free. She and her community had continued the offices of their novenas.

"The last was to Our Lady of Prompt Succor," she related, "and the day it ended, which was our most solemn feast, that is, the feast of the Seven Dolors, April 11, our troops entered and thus our good God granted us peace once more."

The Texans retreating down the Rio Grande were chased all the way by Colonel Canby and the Union troops, until finally all of New Mexico was again free. The Civil War, so far as fighting went, was over in the territory. But still there was no peace.

No peace? How was this?

No, for, after the battles between the armies, the Indians broke forth anew and everywhere created extreme horrors and sufferings. And it was not only Indians—white men, too, it seemed, caused terror with their crimes. Human nature was awry. Apaches and Navajos made life difficult if not impossible for outlying settlements and lonely ranches and travelers on the roads, and renegade killers of the white race terrorized citizens in their towns, killing for the pleasure of it. Right there in Santa Fe innocent men had been shot down in the street. The Army had more work to do when the wartime battles were done with.

Colonel Canby was called to a command in the East. He was succeeded by General James H. Carleton, who marched into New Mexico with a column of crack troops from California. He found conditions in such a turmoil that he and the governor resolved on a continuance of martial law. And for the first time, the Indian problem was approached with energy and firmness. For some time the government had considered the segregation of hostile Indian nations upon reservations under federal control. Now General Carleton actually did round up the Apaches and the Navajos and took them away from their homelands in mountain and desert, and established them at Fort Sumner, on the Pecos River, in the wilderness of southeastern New Mexico. At the same time, he patrolled the towns with his troops, and quieted to a great degree the lawlessness which had cost so many lives. When the war was over everywhere, there really seemed to be a chance for peace to prevail at last.

And so it must have, for when she had come to Santa Fe to live, the German bride surely had found a thriving community where business was good and social life was active.

But all did not move so smoothly as might be hoped, and, if the people were safe from the Indians for a while, it was true that the Indians on their reservations at Fort Sumner were in miserable circumstances. It was all very well to say that they deserved to be, but they were human beings, and could suffer, and feel homesick, and grieve for the heritage lost to their children. Conditions at Fort Sumner were viewed by a Santa Fean whom everyone believed and loved. His reports were unhappy.

Who was he, then?

He was Bishop Juan Bautista Lamy, who went with General Carleton on a trip of inspection to the Indian reservation. He realized all that was needed for the Indians to relieve their hunger and privation. But he was a poor man, and his church was poor, and he could offer little in this respect. But he saw also 3,000 Indian children growing up in utmost ignorance like small animals—detached from their own tribal traditions and places, and provided with no education or training by their custodians. One thing, then, the bishop could offer: he could offer to find teachers to send to those Indian children. For reasons of policy, the Army, the government did not accept his offer. In any case, within five years the reservation was abandoned. The Indians went home, the Apaches to their mountains, from which they went raiding again; the Navajos to their deserts, where for the most part they kept the peace.

And the bishop?

She would find in him a friend. He had long been an intimate of her husband's family.

iv.

And why not, as she would agree, if she listened to this story.

One summer in the early fifties, 1852, exactly, the family firm had a train of twenty-five wagons outward bound for home from Saint Louis. Her husband, then a very young man, was making his second trip on the prairies, learning the business. He learned by ordeal; for he was in charge of the expedition. As his brothers said, it was "sink or swim." For the first few days of the journey he felt well —powerful and clever; and then one day he was shaken with a sudden attack of terrible weakness and a flux of the bowels so violent that he thought he must die of it. At nightfall the train came to a halt on the prairie near a sod house belonging to a trapper. It was the only habitation in hundreds of miles. He was hardly aware of what was happening to him when a squad of his Mexican teamsters carried him into the sod house, which was empty. At the same time a single wagon overtook the merchant train, and from it a tall man came forward to see what was amiss with him who was being carried into the shallow prairie hut.

"Who is this?" he asked. "What is the difficulty?"

The teamsters replied, giving his name, and explaining in terror that he had cholera morbus, which was deathly contagious. They could not keep him with them or they must all fall ill and die. They would put him down and drive on. It was the only wise thing to do.

The stranger did not agree with them. He went to the sick man at once, leaned over him, and said,

"My good friend, we willingly make room for you in our covered wagon and will nurse you until you regain your strength, for we could not think of leaving you here in this lonely prairie cabin. We do not believe you have cholera, and even if you have it we are not afraid of contagion."

He spoke with simple dignity. He sounded like a prince
and like a saint. It was the Bishop of Santa Fe. He ordered
the bearers to carry the invalid to his covered wagon at the
end of the train. When the train moved ahead the next
morning, the bishop's wagon moved with it. Traveling
with him were several young priests whom he had summoned from France, his native land, to return with him to
Santa Fe, where so much work waited to be done for God
and man. They all nursed the sick man, who recovered in
a week. The prairie voyage lasted for another two months.
The bishop was one of the best horsemen the young merchant ever knew. He could also handle a rifle. Hardship
and inconvenience alike seemed to mean nothing to him.
He was strong and gentle. He never seemed to think of
himself at all, and in consequence his manners were beautiful. By the time the wagons reached Santa Fe he and the
young merchant were great friends. What did she think of
a man like that?

She was so moved that she seemed almost angry at the
question. She told her husband not to be such a great
booby as to ask a thing like that. Anybody who had saved
his life, and who had done it so selflessly, so unquestion-
ingly, was to have her undying gratitude.

He laughed and told her not to snap his head off so.

Soon afterward they called on the bishop in his little
adobe house which was set deep in the large garden south
of the cathedral. He received them in a square room with
whitewashed walls. There were books about, and he used
a red velvet armchair. Her husband shook hands with
him, but when she was introduced she had a sudden idea
of what to do. She was still European enough to remember
all about Catholics. Without in any thought betraying her
proud allegiance to her Jewish faith, she made a curtsy
and kissed the bishop's ring. It was a large amethyst en-
circled by small pearls. She then looked up, winking away
tears of emotion as she remembered what this man had done
for her husband—and for her life.

The bishop was tall and sparely built. He stood very

straight. His cassock was black, piped in violet, with violet silk buttons all down its front. He wore a violet silk skull-cap, and a wide sash of heavy silk of the same color. His forehead was open and broad, and the bony structure showed in his head and face. His brows, cheeks, and jaw were all marked with sharp shadow made by the thinly fleshed bones of his skull. In repose his face was grave and almost sad, with a falling line to his broad mouth. But when he smiled, the effect was one of light. His eyes kindled, his cheeks rose, his lips made a challenge to copy his radiant good feeling. From many years in the open weather, he was deeply, and it seemed permanently, tanned. He spoke both English and Spanish with a French accent, for he was a Frenchman, from the Auvergne, a land which he had left thirty-one years before to come to America as a young priest.

The call ended as a success. With reassuring promptness the bishop returned it at their house in Palace Avenue. She was not insensible to the further prestige brought upon her household by his continued and increasingly easy friendship. Without any doubt he was the first citizen of Santa Fe, and was regarded as an intimate friend by everyone from the poorest beggar in the plaza to the foremost figures of society—those who believed in conventional amenity for its own sake. He had been there for twenty years now in 1870, and his adventures and his achievements were matters of conversation. He could be induced to reminisce upon occasion, and she begged him to do so whenever the moment seemed right. From him and from many others she gathered his history, which had so great an effect upon Santa Fe and the whole of the Southwest.

v.

He came to Santa Fe in August, 1851, to assume control over the affairs of the Church in New Mexico.

That vast empire had come to the United States under the Mexican War treaty, and the Mexican Bishop of Durango was therefore no longer the prelate to whom

Santa Fe must turn in ecclesiastical affairs. And what affairs: the Church, the faith of the people, even the integrity of the clergy, had fallen upon evil days. In the 1830's the Franciscans had been sent out of New Mexico leaving secular priests to administer the parishes and missions. Mexico, independent of Spain, had even less support to give the far-flung colonial church than the mother country. The bishop at Durango was too far away to give proper supervision to his people in the north. Nevertheless, temperamentally and historically, they needed the Church in every aspect of their daily lives. But by 1850 there were only nine priests in the great territory, and not all of these were faithful and devoted. The churches were falling apart in ruins. The mission schools were long since abandoned, and the Catholic Indians were left to their mixed memories of Christ and the earth gods of their ancestors. There was ignorance everywhere.

These conditions were examined by the Plenary Council of American Bishops who met at Baltimore in 1849. They petitioned Pope Pius IX to establish New Mexico as a vicariate apostolic separate from the see of Durango, and they nominated Father Jean Baptiste Lamy, a young French priest working as a missioner in Kentucky, to be appointed administrator. In the next year the appointment was made. Father Lamy was consecrated as bishop in November 1850 at Cincinnati and soon afterward started West. He went by way of New Orleans and the Gulf of Mexico, sailing for Galveston on a steamer in poor repair, which was wrecked on the coast of Texas in freezing weather. He and the other passengers were lucky to come ashore in safety. All his belongings were lost or ruined, including his vestments, his books, and "a fine wagon which he bought at New Orleans for the trip over the plains to Santa Fe."

He made his way to San Antonio, where further delays followed. For one thing, he suffered a painful injury when forced to jump from a new wagon which he had bought for the remainder of his journey. It was May before he left with an army train for El Paso. With him were his old friend and new vicar general, Father Joseph P. Macheboeuf, and two priests who joined him at San Antonio. In how he asked Father Macheboeuf to go with him into the unknown the bishop revealed both his humor and his modesty. "They wish," he told his friend, "that I should be a Vicar Apostolic, and I wish you to be my Vicar General, and from these two vicars we shall try to make one good pastor."

At El Paso he discovered that his predecessor, the Bishop of Durango, had lately passed by there on a round trip to New Mexico quite as though New Mexico did not already have a new bishop. No one seemed to know of Bishop Lamy's appointment. To prepare Santa Fe for his coming he sent letters ahead from El Paso to the church authorities. When he proceeded up the Great River in midsummer, the people received him everywhere with enthusiasm. But not the clergy. The priests, wrote Father Macheboeuf, "do not want the bishop." And why? "They dread a reform in their morals, or a change in their selfish relations with their parishioners."

At Santa Fe on August 8 the new bishop was received by the population, who came out in procession to meet him. The weather was hot and dry—there had been an extended drought. He entered the city amid crowds of citizens and accompanied by 8,000 Catholic Indians who animated the triumph with sham battles and dances. The cannon of Fort Marcy fired salutes. A *Te Deum* was sung in the parish church of Saint Francis. A state dinner followed at the house of the resident vicar, Father Ortiz. The day was crowned by a good omen: rain fell in torrents. Everything indicated a good beginning for the bishop.

But it was too soon to rejoice, for from an unexpected quarter a hard difficulty arose. The local clergy had received no official word of the bishop's appointment. The Bishop of Durango had not mentioned it. They had no authority to place themselves under a new prelate. In vain Bishop Lamy displayed his letters of appointment from the Vatican, the Papal bulls creating his office. Father Ortiz and the clergy under him refused to recognize the authority of

the vicar apostolic. Bishop Lamy reviewed various solutions of the problem, and necessarily came to the one that
was hardest. He must go on another long journey, to secure
recognition of his office from the Bishop of Durango, 1,500
miles away in Mexico. Leaving Father Macheboeuf in
Santa Fe as his representative, he rode off in September on
a mule, accompanied by a guide and Father Ortiz, who
must in person hear the decision of Durango.

The arduous journey was worth while. By Christmas
the bishop was back in Santa Fe, bringing with him official
documents in which the Bishop of Durango renounced all
claim to ecclesiastical jurisdiction over New Mexico. Durango had submitted to Rome.

And now the new bishop was free at last to go to work.
Without any further delay the city, the territory felt the
power and the grace of his energy. His resident priests
either reformed or departed. Missions were reopened when
new priests came to join him from the seminaries of his
native province in France. He established a school in which
English was taught in Santa Fe for the first time. In 1853
he went to Rome to make a report and returning brought
with him six nuns of the Lorettine order to found a convent
school for girls. In the same year New Mexico was given
the status of a diocese with Santa Fe as its see, and Lamy
as its first bishop. A college for young men was opened in
Santa Fe—Saint Michael's, next door to the old church
of San Miguel which had suffered the Pueblo Rebellion
of 1680.

The bishop and his vicar were seen everywhere in the
diocese, riding into remote pueblos, calling at hidden
ranches, enlivening mountain villages with their contagious
sense of what people deserved in the way of a good life.
If any of the clergy harbored the old emotions of destructive
independence—and several did, notably in Albuquerque,
Taos, and Arroyo Hondo—they were asked again and
again to follow the bishop's example of probity and hu-
mility; and, when they refused, they were removed from
authority and excommunicated. He was patient—but he

was strong, and growth in all good things followed where he went.

He was a true frontiersman. His fellow citizens were proud of this. In spite of rather delicate health, he was able to show remarkable endurance. He rode to Arizona on a visit to the scattered Catholics there. It took him six months and he went 3,000 miles. Often he slept "under the moon." Sometimes he went nearly a hundred miles without water. He walked his horse to rest him. Colorado needed him, and he rode there three times. He went to Indians, and with them once had to eat meat from a dead dog out of politeness. Mexican families offered him tortillas which he could not digest, but happily they also provided chili con carne which he enjoyed, even if the meat was often over a month old, "dried in the sun, of course," as he said. For the rest, he lived "on the fat of the land," by which he meant *el bendito frijole y el santo atole,* "the blessed bean and the holy porridge." When he could remember to do so, he took in his saddlebag a little bread, some crackers, and a few hard-boiled eggs.

Like any other frontiersman, he knew from experience what danger from Indians was like. In 1867 he crossed the plains going west with his party of twenty-five, who included priests, lay brothers, and nuns. They attached themselves to a large wagon train. At the Arkansas River the caravan was attacked by 300 Comanche Indians. For three hours the men of the train fought off the attack. Among them, the bishop handled a rifle. On the same trip the company was visited by an epidemic of cholera. Several died, including two of the bishop's people.

All his work and his far-flung travel showed results. Arizona and Colorado were added to his diocese and, in time, were given diocesan stature on their own. In his province he presently had forty-one priests where he had come to find nine. The eroding churches were repaired, and 85 new ones were built, until in all he presided over 135 in active use. Three schools flourished in Santa Fe. The Indian mission schools were revived. The children were taught "English, Spanish, reading, writing, geography, history, and arithmetic." The sisters of Loretto maintained five convents and academies in the diocese where none had been before. In 1866 the first hospital and the first orphanage of New Mexico were opened in the same building on New Year's Day. The building was the bishop's own house, which he gave up to the purpose. It served people of all creeds. Help and enlightenment, through the charity of God, must belong to all. He worked for the passage of legislation to provide free public schools. When it was passed into law, he was appointed a member of the commission, along with the territorial governor and the secretary of state, to administer the act. A new breath of life seemed to bring Santa Fe into the ways of the civilized world. It was his example that did it, and the gentle, persistent replanting here of the traditions and values he had brought with him.

The new cathedral of Saint Francis was a solid illustration of this. In 1869 he oversaw the start of construction of a stone building to take the place of the old adobe parish church of Saint Francis which he had used as his cathedral since 1850. The new building was being built as a shell around the old and, when it was finished, workmen would take away from within it the stones and earthen bricks of the old church, leaving only the transepts and sanctuary to serve as parts of the new structure. For the style of the new cathedral the bishop referred to the romanesque churches of his boyhood in the Auvergne. His architects came from France. So the massive new church rose— slowly, for money was scarce—in the thick pillars and heavy arches of his earliest Auvergnat memory. The stone was brought from a volcanic deposit twelve miles from Santa Fe.

Of course, the work at the cathedral was one of the first things the German bride noticed when she came to Santa Fe, for to go to her house in Palace Avenue she had to pass the building. One of the most enlivening things she heard about the cathedral was the story of the cornerstone, which gratified her taste for the sensational. On July 14, 1869, the year before her arrival, the cornerstone had been laid with all suitable ceremony, sacred and civil. The stone was engraved with the names of President Ulysses S. Grant and of leading New Mexicans. It had a hollow place where coins of gold, silver, and copper and documents and newspapers were enclosed. And then what? It was enough to make an ardent listener gasp with fascination and shock: soon after it had been placed with all those speeches and blessings, the cornerstone was stolen, with all its contents, and was never found.

But work continued on the building and, though it would take years to finish it, it was not long before its style was evident. The dusty golden stone, rising in plain wall and pillared arch, brought a new character to Santa Fe. Looking about, the German bride saw that the whole town was of earthen construction—except for those buildings erected under the hand of the bishop. Saint Michael's College was a three-story building with a mansard roof, a cupola, ranks of tall narrow windows, and balconies along the ends and front. It was like many a European church property she could think of. Inside, the corridors were paneled in narrow ribs of wood, and the light fell infrequent and pallid from high transoms. Nothing could be less like the long, low, blind native buildings of Santa Fe, which in both materials and manner resembled the houses built for centuries by Mexicans and, for centuries before them, Pueblo Indians. The convent of the Loretto sisters was another foreign house, and the plans for their chapel to Our Lady of Light called for a gothic imitation of the Sainte-Chapelle of Paris. The sisters' hospital and orphanage was the bishop's old house, which had once belonged to Vicar Ortiz. But the one that would replace it would follow an eastern American institution style, two-storied, with second-floor galleries on the outside, and gabled roof. What she saw was that the expression in architecture of Bishop Lamy's energetic belief in faith, mercy, and enlightenment was changing the face of the old city.

As all of this indicated progress, she was .proud of it. One day, visiting the work at the cathedral, she saw a new detail above the main doorway. It was a Hebrew word—the word for God, Yahweh—enclosed in a triangle. Her heart kindled at this, for she liked to think that the bishop had placed the inscription there as a kindly gesture toward his close friends among the German Jews of Santa Fe—though later she learned that the inscription over the cathedral door was a traditional symbol used by the Church to indicate the Holy Trinity.

She always enjoyed her little exchanges with the bishop, and made almost a comic conspiracy of them, to give them a special flavor, unlike that of any of his friendships in Santa Fe with the native New Mexicans, for example. She felt that they were both Europeans of a quite distinct sophistication. He had brought a French culture with him and, though he was a good American, his heritage could not help expressing itself in all that he did. Her education was excellent, and she spoke a social kind of French, so that when they met she engaged the bishop in his own early language. He replied in kind, amused to speak the language in which he still realized much of his thought. And as they conversed in a tongue foreign to Santa Fe, she could never resist a little flaring glance about at the rest of the company, to discover if her special accomplishment in relation to the great bishop were observed, appreciated—and perhaps envied.

vi.

For she was always alive to the social tone wherever she was. As her local acquaintance widened in her early years in Santa Fe, she established a weekly day at home when in the afternoon she received callers, and gave them tea and coffee and cakes in the yellow-silk drawing room of her new house in Palace Avenue.

It was one of the first brick structures in town. It had three stories and an attic, topped by the cupola her husband had promised her. There was much ornamental iron work on its roof ridges. The woodwork throughout was massive. Doors and windows had fluted frames with curved tops, set in plaster moldings with decorative edges of leaves and clusters of grapes. The social rooms were large and high-ceilinged. Their effect was doubled by a number of floor-length mirrors framed in gold leaf. Everything in the house came "from the East," and was meant to reflect the richest taste and best style. It was a style with a long history of travel behind it—from Prince Albert's Germany to the England of his married life, and from the England of his widow to the Atlantic United States, and from there across the country, until by wagon train it reached even to Santa Fe.

Her piano was installed in the bay window of the red sitting room. It was a square Steinway of ebony, with panels of cutwork revealing red velvet above the keyboard. She practiced faithfully in order not to lose her "touch," for which she admitted she was famous. When asked, she would play generously, first removing her rings, an act which harmlessly called attention to them. She played works of Schubert, Chopin, Anton Rubinstein, and Liszt, but those of Mendelssohn were her favorites. His animation and art-less spirit called forth her sentiment and her guileless energy.

In addition to prominent local families, Mexican and "Anglo," her callers included the officers of Fort Marcy and their wives, who lived in government quarters along the new street below the north hill on which the earth fortress had been built by General Kearny's troops in 1846. The old fort was now abandoned. There was no further need for artillery emplacements above the city. But the garrison establishment was still spoken of as Fort Marcy, and, with cotillions and riding parties, the military resident gave a certain dash to society, which she entered into with gaiety. At her parties she liked to see the officers in their uniforms, with epaulettes, sword belts, and white gloves. She served with their wives on committees and paid calls on them, driving out in her varnished black open carriage to leave her calling cards, which were made for her by Tiffany's of New York. Sometimes she drove as far as the bishop's country house at Tesuque, four miles north of town. There he had a modest lodge which he called the Villa Pintoresca. It consisted of a few rooms built around a small private chapel where he said his daily mass when he retreated from town to spend a little while in rest and meditation.

Her family grew rapidly until she had four children, two boys and two girls. One son died as a baby after an illness of several weeks. During that ordeal her hair prematurely turned white. If anybody thought she was perhaps frivolous with her busy social occupations, this change in her appearance—and its occasion—proved that to her duties as a wife and mother she gave herself most of all. She seemed to have time and strength for whatever the children needed of her, and yet more for the active life which she shared with her husband in society.

She took pride in her cooking, and taught her Mexican and Indian servants how to prepare a great variety of German and French dishes. Her dinners were always formal, in many courses, served by two uniformed maids at a table set for a large company with European china, cut glass, silver, lace, and linen. Her husband saw to the wines, served in Bavarian glasses of the proper sizes and shapes, decorated with painted medallions and gold. Before dinner the children were brought into the yellow drawing room by their nurse to learn how to say how do you do and shake hands, or make their k'nicks for the company. After dinner there were Havana cigars for the gentlemen, and later, coffee, brandy, music, and conversation in the red room. Along with gossip of local interest, they talked about the affairs of the world, for, since the telegraph had come to Santa Fe in 1868, the *New Mexican* newspaper was published every day, with telegraphic dispatches bringing the latest news from everywhere within twenty-four hours.

Sometimes in the evening her husband left her to join his business friends at a recently opened resort which served the city as a men's club, though it was not privately organized. She read of it in the *New Mexican,* when the editor published a news item.

We have of late paid several visits to The Beer Brewery of our enterprising fellow citizens, Messrs. Carl and Brien, situated about ten minutes walk from the Fonda, on the Fort Union Road. A more delicious mug of beer we have never drank in any city than we have found there. Having an ice-house of immense capacity, well stored with that summer luxury, the beer is kept in bottles, on the ice, and is brought to the guest at once foaming with vim and freezing with cold. It is truly a delightful evening resort.

The army garrison could be counted on to provide evenings of theatrical entertainment. There were always enthusiastic actors and singers among the officers and enlisted men and their families who came and went according to the army's orders. They gave plays, variety bills, and even, sometimes, an opera. The German housewife often took part in such productions, either as an actress much admired in farce, or as an accompanist at the piano for musical turns. Any soldier with a specialty was encouraged to come forward and give it. There was never a lack of spirit or talent for the evenings of theater, which were usually given for the benefit of a worthy local cause. It was not much spoken of, but many people, as they watched the intensely earnest performances of the soldier comedians, were moved to think of the other work that often enough called the troops away from Santa Fe to the dangerous lands where untamed Indians or renegade cattlemen killed and pillaged among scattered settlements or along lonely highways.

And sometimes theater came to town with professional pretensions. A handbill of 1866 addressed to the public in Spanish announced the kind of performance that was still given in the early years of the German housewife's life at Santa Fe. The theater was the patio of a large house near the plaza. Admission cost a dollar. The show began at ten o'clock in the evening. The audience sat on rough wooden benches under a roof of stretched muslin, and several bedspreads stretched on a line served as the front stage curtain, operated by an old man who was visible throughout the performance. The stage was lighted by a few candles set out in a row. In front sat an orchestra largely made up of players upon brass instruments.

When the curtains parted the audience murmured with pleasure, for the scenery was of painted canvas representing some splendid background of life remote from the experience of Santa Fe, and magical so in its power to transport those who watched—a palace hall with marble pillars or a terrace with heroic statuary framing a vista of garden, fountain, and lake. The traveling company usually gave two plays on a bill. One was a tragedy of the lives of kings, turning on elaborate legal dilemmas, and the more elevated it was in tone, language, and sentiment, the more it delighted the audience, so far removed from all the associations of the play. The other was a farce.

The audience smoked cigarettes, and there was often present the "usual American drunken rowdy" who flourished a pistol and promised to "whip any damned greaser" he chose. The playbill proclaimed: *"Teatro Mejicano! Gran funcion para la noche del Domingo 5 de Agosto de 1866."* She was able to translate the rest. "The representation given tonight is one of those dramas in which everything breathes life, youth, and enthusiasm. Its author is the eminent Victor Hugo, who, like another Lord Byron, has centered upon himself the attention of his own country and all of Europe. People rush in crowds to witness his pieces when presented in the theaters, his countrymen honor him, and he is called by them the Father of the French Romantic School."

If there was no organized, rehearsed drama to observe, the climate of Santa Fe was always there to provide positive experience. In summer the rains came late every afternoon, with thunder and lightning. After the shower the very light of the sky was an event, so open, shafted with such pure glory. In winter the snow came thick and dazzling, and ice froze on edges, and in sunlight or moonlight shone with fresh purity. The mountains in snow seemed to stand near, and looked so new and strange that people drove out on the country roads to see them in wonder. Even seasonal promises of all such weather were sometimes improved with surprise. On August 22, 1872, in the middle of a quiet afternoon something happened that moved the *New Mexican* to report on the following day:

> The severest crash of thunder that we have had for years broke on us yesterday afternoon in the midst of a dead calm. It came so suddenly, and so unexpectedly, and was so terrifically loud—causing houses to jar until the very pebbles jumped from the roof—that nearly everybody rushed outside in terror to see what had happened, and no one cared to hear it repeated. At first we thought the comet had come and knocked the brains out of "Old Baldy."

The event took on even stranger character when it was known on the following day that "the lightning accompanying the terrible crash of thunder yesterday instantly killed a woman living in the west end of town. She was a young woman by the name of Matiana." The German matron knew her, and was sad to know that she was "near her confinement" at the time of her death.

The air was sometimes so still and clear over the city at night that the sounds of life would carry everywhere and keep whole households from falling asleep. The couple in Palace Avenue laughed over a report given by the newspaper of such a night in the summer of 1872, for it brought up a picture of many familiar elements of life in town.

> What came over the serenity of Santa Fe last night? It came like a huge concert saloon—a bloated bagpipe of music. From one quarter came the blasts of horns, the beat of drums, and the clash of cymbals; from another the sweet notes of the harp and guitar; from another the screech of the violin and the pick of the banjo, while from every direction, like a crossfire of discordance, came the "pawing" of ivory, the unwinding of lungs, the mewing of cats, the barking of dogs, and the braying of jacks. Later in the evening the dogs, as usual, had the best of it and kept the canine chorus up till joined by the crowing of cocks and the bellowing of cattle.

At such a time all life, human and animal, seemed to be spun about by a spirit of unrest so general that some people, making a wise look, spoke of occult influence, to which they believed Santa Fe was particularly subject. Anything, they said, could happen in Santa Fe—"and often did," they added, with an accent of indirect pride.

Such notions were foreign to the active and practical nature of the German housewife. It was her impulse to suggest that oddities might better be controlled than indulgently explained away. There was plenty to engage the attention of anyone interested in keeping public order. In 1872 she was offended by the hogs that ran at large in the city streets. Moreover, the plaza was filthy from refuse, feed, and barnyard droppings from the wagon trains that came to rest there as in a harbor. For days at a time the heavy wagons with their hoods like great sunbonnets clogged the streets while their cargoes were unloaded. Like everyone else, she often went to see them, for they represented the city's most important source of prosperity, of which her family earned a large share, through hard work, sound judgment, and imagination exercised within the limits of the actual.

These were qualities, she must conclude, which many a man preferred not to trouble himself with. Too many people, it seemed to her, came West in order to get rich the easy way. And yet she could not really blame those who were gullible. It was true that the gold fields of California and Colorado had already yielded immense wealth. Even now, after 300 years, people remembered what mountains of gold and silver the New World had given up to the Spaniards. Few people were skeptical in Santa Fe during the summer and fall of 1872 when the city was the center of new excitement over dazzling reports of vast wealth that lay on the ground only waiting to be had for the taking.

This time the word was diamonds. Parties were coming from the East, via Denver and Pueblo, to pass through Santa Fe on their way to western New Mexico and Eastern Arizona where they expected to find "the diamond fields." In New

York a group of quiet, sober businessmen had exhibited "the great pink diamond of Arizona—102 carats—a mountain of light" with reports that many more of its kind were to be had from the same source. The gentlemen had formed a company to sell shares, which were being taken up fast. Private parties hurried west, and in late August, 1872, were "passing through Santa Fe every day," according to the *New Mexican*. Local citizens caught the fever and made up their own expeditions. Diamonds were the topic of the day. The daily paper gave a running report on developments, and the German housewife followed them with eagerness and a touch of shrewd, self-protective doubt.

She had some support for her skeptical views. The newspaper quoted a story from New York which said that "Tiffany and Company, of New York, stated to a reporter of the *Tribune* that they had examined a number of stones purporting to come from Arizona, and believed they were diamonds, but that the largest did not exceed $700 in value. Whether the stones really did come from Arizona or London, as suspected, they could not say." But she kept her opinion to herself, for the *New Mexican* said in September that "parties are quietly leaving here every day or two" and "as soon as mining begins, wonderful developments will no doubt be made," adding that "some shrewed men in our midst" were full of quiet belief in the reality of the diamond fields. Who would believe her if she spoke out?

Public evidence was longingly cited—even when it referred to everything but diamonds. A man from Santa Fe had "several trophies from the diamond lands in the shape of opals, garnets, and topaz. In addition to these he exhibited one piece of black carbon." He said he got them at Fort Defiance, and that they were "as common as the sand there!" However, "the real sparklers he didn't produce." Again, soldiers returning from duty in Arizona "had pockets full, and bags, of precious stones (so called). . . . They said they knew where they could find *them by the bushel,* but refused to give us any hint of the locality. They were very anxious to know what was thought about the

Arizona diamonds in the States. . . ." Real proof seemed elusive, and a further note of restraint was sounded by the *New Mexican* in October. "We would advise diamond hunters to get into some other business, as in a few months the market will be so overstocked that they will not be worth ten cents a peck." Behind this sardonic advice was a report in an eastern paper that "there is a diamond factory running day and night in New York City, and capable of turning out any amount. It is reported that fifty pounds have already been manufactured and disposed of for the sum of two and a half millions of dollars."

Nevertheless, the diamond excitement was "getting hotter and hotter every day," said the Santa Fe paper. Business in town was excellent as the prospectors kept coming. "We in Santa Fe are already beginning to feel the benefit of the 'rush,' " reported the editor, "and"—he felt obliged to add a qualifying word—"as far as facts will sustain us, we say, 'pile in.' " But if he was pressed for evidence on behalf of the eager public faith in a new source of prosperity, his newspaper, in its honesty, must resort either to ambiguity: "we saw some stones brought in by Mr. Macallen from the diamond regions, and if many of them are not pure diamonds, their brilliancy, perfect transparency, hardness, and prismatic beauty are found in other stones equally valuable as jewels and ornaments"; or to comedy: "a large and not very brilliant quartz diamond was laid on our table by Col. Lambert, found, as he asserts, in the vicinity of this city. This really beautiful specimen can be seen by calling at our office. The Colonel was very much excited; his eyes were distended, his nostrils dilated, his eloquence, always fine, was now superb, and nothing short of a drink could in any way calm his excitement. The Colonel thinks his fortune made. We hope so."

By early November, mining parties from New York, Salt Lake City, Prescott, and San Francisco were at work in five different locations, all radial to Fort Defiance at distances up to a hundred miles. As the month went by, reports came that the "diamond excitement" was "on the increase in

Denver," where several companies had "been organized to explore the southwestern portion of Colorado," which now was "believed to be the best and richest locality." One new company was incorporated for $5,000,000, offering 50,000 shares for sale, said the *New Mexican* on November 25.

But within a week the same paper was publishing daily installments of the disheartening truth about "the great diamond fraud." The news broke in San Francisco, where investors in the diamond stocks brought charges against the syndicate whose shares they had bought. The swindlers had shown real diamonds—$150,000 worth at Tiffany's, in New York, for example—but it was at last clear enough that none of the jewels came from "fields" in the West. One of the chief purposes of the swindle was to establish credibility in a "diamond mine" called the Burro, and sell it to "English capitalists." The diamond rush was finished in a matter of days, and, when it was discussed over afternoon coffee in the yellow-silk drawing room in Palace Avenue, the hostess was able to say lightly and honestly that she could have predicted the outcome months ago. It was a satisfying position to hold with respect to the whole affair. The *New Mexican* went back to reporting more familiar if less exciting events of a local nature: "There was a single fiddle baile last night. . . ."

The Spanish word *baile,* as she knew, was pronounced to rhyme more or less with the English word "highly." It meant a dance. From her husband she learned something about the various degrees of respectability it could represent. There were four degrees, to accord with the women who attended. First, and lowest, was that frequented by "whores" —her husband used the word and, though she agreed that a husband could say anything to his wife in private, she caught a sharp breath in shock, which gratified him. The second was for women who held themselves "exclusive for a term of months or years" for their men. The third was for "American attachments—Judge A's, Mr. B's, Captain C's, woman," and so forth. The last was for wholly respectable society.

The only time she lent her presence to such a party occurred one night in 1873 in a mountain village near Santa Fe. She had gone with her husband on a little business trip to see the storekeeper there. They were invited to attend a fandango given in the village store after supper. She could not refuse without impoliteness, and, furthermore, she wanted to attend.

Whole families came to the dance. A gallon of whisky was provided for the men, and five pounds of raisins for the women and children. The orchestra "consisted of a young and active fiddler" from a nearby town. The master of ceremonies was "a gentleman in buckskins." She thought the party very "tame," a "melancholy affair." The figures of the dance were so "slow and monotonous" that she was reminded of "a pair of old turkey gobblers fighting." The old mayor of the village fell down drunk, and was "laid out on the floor covered with a newspaper." The guests capered around him staging a mock funeral. They put candles on the floor by his side, and another old man "scattered whisky over him as if it were holy water, and pronounced the last blessing." She hoped the blasphemy was excused by the fact that its perpetrators were simple creatures too full of whisky who had few occasions for merriment in their lost mountain life.

How different it was from the social events in her own house, where over the years she and her husband had for their guests such visitors as President and Mrs. Rutherford B. Hayes, and many army generals, including Pope, Logan, Miles, Sheridan, and Sherman, and the bishop, along with certain prelates who came to see him, and, once, the notorious philosopher Robert G. Ingersoll.

vii.

In the mid-seventies she helped to celebrate, a year apart, two occasions of glory in Santa Fe.

The first fell on Wednesday, June 16, 1875. Preparations were made for several weeks. She was a member of a women's committee on arrangements. The occasion was one which the entire city took to its breast, for it was one which brought honors to Bishop Lamy, and thus to all his fellow citizens. On that day by order of the Holy See he was to be raised to the rank of archbishop, and his vast diocese was to become an archdiocese. In only a quarter of a century the bishop had put new spirit into an old civilization to such a degree that his work was given extraordinary recognition at Rome. To show their pride and their love for the bishop, the people of all faiths united to do him honor on that day.

At daybreak cannonading sounded over the city in salute from the guns of the garrison. Little boys ran in the streets, which were decorated with evergreens, and set off firecrackers, while the bells of the churches rang out in the fine early air. Shortly afterward the students' band from Saint Michael's College entered the bishop's garden to serenade him.

Even the new cathedral, almost finished, was too small to take in all who would attend the ceremonies of investiture. Accordingly an altar was ready in the rear courtyard of Saint Michael's College. It stood on a platform against a background of massed American flags. Another American flag hung over the new archbishop's dais. His devoted feeling toward the United States was well known.

At nine o'clock a procession was formed at the cathedral to move toward the college. Bands played. Banners walked in the air, marking the sodalities that took part. A great throng, including the German housewife and her husband, marched with the religious. There were twenty priests who would assist at mass. At the end of the procession moved a large purple canopy borne by honored laymen, and under it advanced at the slow rocking pace of procession three mitered prelates. These were the archbishop-designate and two of his closest old friends—Joseph Macheboeuf, who was now apostolic delegate of Colorado, and John Baptist Salpointe, another recruit from the Auvergne, who was apostolic delegate of Arizona. Bishop Salpointe carried the pallium which had come from Rome, and which later on behalf of Pope Pius IX he would place over the shoulders of Bishop Lamy.

Four thousand people were massed in the college patio when at ten o'clock Bishop Macheboeuf with his deacons and assistants began the pontifical high mass, during which the choir of Saint Michael's sang "with good effect." Sermons were delivered by Father Eguillon, the vicar general, who spoke in Spanish, and by Bishop Macheboeuf, in English. And then came the solemn moment of investiture. At the foot of the altar, Bishop Lamy knelt before Bishop Salpointe, who read aloud in Latin, Spanish, and English the papal decree creating the new archbishop. He then lowered the pallium over the shoulders of the kneeling archbishop, who responded by speaking in Latin the oath of his new estate. Archbishop Lamy then rose to face the people of Santa Fe.

His face was white with strain. They could see how moved he was, and, accustomed to his usual calm presence and easy manner, they were stirred as they felt his emotion. His old friend the German housewife felt tears in her eyes, which she winked away trying not to be a fool. Quite as though she were responsible for his well-being and his acquittal of himself with credit in this moment, her heart beat fast as he began to speak.

He did not speak long. He was humbled by the act of new dignity that had just been done upon him. His words were plain and extraordinarily moving. He cited the blessings that had come to him in life and gave thanks for them. These were the loyalty and aid of his colleagues, the faithfulness of the people, and the "free republican institutions" of the United States. He gave his pontifical benediction to his hearers. The liturgical rites were completed.

The procession was formed again, and now moved off at a joyful pace toward the archbishop's garden, where a luncheon banquet for a hundred guests was waiting. The German housewife accompanied her husband to their places at the board. It was now noon, and the brilliant open light of the sky shone down through the trees and shrubberies of the garden, where a fountain played, and a sundial stood on a pedestal of Santa Fe marble, and aisles of trees, plants, and arbors reached away. As lunch progressed, the Eighth Cavalry Band played lively airs among the trees. Presently the acting governor of New Mexico Territory, William G. Ritch, was seen to rise with a manuscript in hand. Silence fell. The governor was about to speak for all of them who loved the archbishop. He spoke at length, in measured eloquence. Most to be remembered were those words in which he gave credit to Archbishop Lamy for the remarkable changes he had brought about toward the improvement of life in Santa Fe.

"It will not, I am quite certain," said the governor, "be regarded as undue commendation when I say that the reforms, the general elevation of the moral tone, and the general progress that has been effected since the American occupation, are very largely, and in some cases entirely, due to the judicious ecclesiastical administration and to the wholesome precepts and examples which have shone forth upon this people from the living presence of the Archbishop of Santa Fe, whom we all know, and know only to admire and respect." And again, he said, "I tender the thanks of the people of this territory to His Holiness, Pope Pius IX, for the honor—for the eminent consideration that has been, by his authority, bestowed upon one so worthy to receive; and for so substantial a recognition of the worthiness of this people, from the supreme head of the oldest and most numerous of Christian denominations. . . ."

When he was done, the guests sprang to their feet with cheers. The archbishop responded with thanks, and offered toasts to the health of the pontiff, and to the distinguished guests present in the garden, many of whom had the impression that he had caught their eyes. The lunch party broke up in the middle of the afternoon, and the celebrations were resumed and finished during the evening in the plaza. Eminent citizens appeared on the bandstand to make speeches in Spanish and English. A band concert was given by the Fort Marcy musicians. Bonfires lined the streets. A program of fireworks was presented, followed by a balloon ascension. Stretched in the air were illuminated transparencies of the Pope, the archbishop, and the two visiting bishops from Arizona and Colorado. Late at night all ended with a torchlight procession. It was an exhausting day, and as such, and for its occasion, entirely satisfying to the German housewife. For it was one of the strong expressions of her spirit that she loved to join with other people in full-hearted celebrations of any reason for public pride and joy.

Her next opportunity to do so came on July 4, 1876, when the city observed the one hundredth anniversary of the Independence of the United States. One of her best accomplishments was called on to contribute to the arrangements, for during her girlhood in Germany she had been trained in fine needlework; and for many days and much of many nights she worked to make costumes for some of the young women, chosen for their beauty and popularity, who were to appear in the leading feature of the day's parade. She was sorry that her own daughters were too young to be included in that select group.

The famous day was greeted with a thirteen-gun salute from a twelve-pound brass cannon at Fort Marcy. Flags broke out all over town. Early in the morning crowds began to gather in the plaza, and over them sounded the bells of Santa Fe, for the archbishop had ordered masses said in all parishes of the archdiocese to give thanks for the birth and growth of the nation. It was a clear and sunny day.

The parade began to form at half-past eight in front of the palace, and, when it moved out on the line of march, applause and cheers rose up to greet the creation which exhibited the theme of the day. It was a "Car of Independence," constructed upon "a large government ambulance tastefully and appropriately prepared." The ambulance was hidden by a pyramid with a wide base projecting over the wheels. Around the base sat the chosen thirty-nine young beauties of Santa Fe, who represented all the states of the Union and the Territory of New Mexico. They were dressed in white, with sashes and shoulder rosettes of red, white, and blue satin, and wreaths of flowers on their heads. Each held a little banner carrying the name of the state she represented. The German housewife peered critically at the costumes she had made for the group, and found them magnificent. From the top of the pyramid rose a flagpole cut from a thin white aspen trunk brought from the mountains. From it flew the national flag, and about it stood three symbolic characters. These were the Goddess of Liberty in white, with a red sash across her breast, and on her head a blue tiara showing the word "Liberty"; Brother Jonathan, impersonated by a citizen six feet six inches tall, wearing a stovepipe hat wrapped around with ribbons, a swallow-tailed coat and strap-breeches of red, white, and blue homespun; and a boy in a brown and yellow suit, with a straw hat, a flag, and a streamer which bore the name "Young America." The whole was drawn by "six tremendous black mules with a groom at the head of each."

General Edward Hatch, commanding the Department of New Mexico, rode his charger at the head of his staff, followed by Company I, Fifteenth United States Infantry. Three bands of music played the step at different points of the parade—those of the Ninth Cavalry, Saint Michael's College, and the City of Santa Fe. One hundred Pueblo Indians in paint, feathers, silver jewels, pine branches, fox and rabbit fur, ceremonial sashes and kilts, and white buckskin leggings and moccasins, danced their way along. A swarm of boys in the uniforms of a volunteer fire brigade—red shirts, black caps, and blue and white trousers—drew a miniature fire engine steamer and a hook and ladder apparatus. Their juvenile leader "carried the trumpet" of fire captain. To make the crowd laugh a donkey brigade trotted by "at random" without bridles, carrying sabers and wearing masks above their motley costumes.

Of the many floats three were particularly popular. One of these was presented by a local cigar factory. Workers on the car made cigars in view of all and gave them away to the crowd as fast as they were made. Another showed the saloon of the Bank Exchange Hotel with its bar. Another was a float offered by the brewery, "in full blast, fireplace and all," manufacturing lager beer, drawn by a vehicle resembling "a huge locomotive with smoke rolling from the stack."

After the parade the crowd broke from the sidewalks and gathered around the bandstand in the plaza to hear speeches. The Declaration of Independence was read in English and Spanish, followed by an oration "in elegant Castilian" by a judge, and another in English by an ex-governor of the territory, who concluded his remarks with an original verse:

> Santa Fe, the oldest born
> Of Columbia's cherished towns,
> Yet as fresh as glorious morn
> Life from every nook resounds,
> Old yet new, grown gray yet strong,
> Jubilant for right, but death to wrong.

A band concert followed, and at four in the afternoon, in the style of a proper outing, a contest on a greased pole, and sack races, which "created rivulets of laughter." Fireworks at nine o'clock in the evening ended the tremendous day. Exhausted with pleasure, families went home. If all were proud that day, the newest Americans, such as the German housewife, were among the most ardent in their patriotism.

viii.

She could not help thinking now and then that she was making her life in a strange place—that city where much that was ancient was mixed with many new and incongruous elements. But she saw that this was a great part of its appeal to visitors, and to herself. In her letters to her sister Charlotte in Wiesbaden she tried to capture the scenes and flavors of the town she had come to love even as she worked to educate it by example in superior social usages. She found that, when she went to the effort of describing the life around her, its details became more vivid to her as she set them down on paper.

In 1876 she told how people during the warm summer

nights slept out of doors, some of the poorer ones right in the street. The black shawls of the Mexican women as they went to mass made her think of "crows' wings." The plaza presented a lively spectacle day and evening. She saw people of all sorts there in an "active throng," composed of "fashionably dressed civilians, military officers in blue and gold, rough-looking soldiers, weatherbeaten emigrants, broad-hatted teamsters with rawhide whips that they crack like a pistol" over an "eight-bull wagon team." It was a matter of love and pride, too, that among the children out for a walk in the plaza, "handsome and tastefully dressed," with "very natty nursemaids in attendance," were her own little girls with their nurse. What was there to see in the plaza? The only ornament on the whole face of the four sides of the square was a barber pole. No, people went there to see each other. The gentlemen found occasion to drop into a saloon, like the Bank Exchange Hotel Bar, which she understood was remarkably decorated—"ruffled over with tissue-paper frills" which covered "ceiling, walls, and bars."

The officers' quarters at Fort Marcy below the north hill were always pleasing to visit. They stood in a "row of pretty little cottages set in gardens among trees, their wide porticoes walled with a bowery wall of trailing plants—top and bottom —flowers of every color and many shapes." The windows were curtained with damask and lace, and she found the interiors furnished "with a degree of luxury and taste." The Regular Army, she felt, knew how to do things. In the evenings, the cavalry band played serenades, and the army ladies engaged in croquet, and when she drove by she would hear "the beat of mallets and the strain of the music." She did not see, but she heard of, the troubles that came in 1876 when the Sixth Cavalry relieved the Ninth at Santa Fe. In the routine of the relief of one such unit by another, horses were exchanged, and fights broke out between enlisted men of both regiments over the quality of the horses involved.

She often saw religious processions in the streets, and always stopped to watch, enchanted by the sparkle and shimmer of gold and silver embroideries and paper flowers and sculptured tin that proceeded through the brilliant air from banners, vestments, sacred vessels, candelabra, and images. The faith of the marchers always touched her, for it was the breath of their life made visible in the old earthen streets of Santa Fe. They marched from the cathedral and down San Francisco Street, and turned back to the plaza, and along their way they paused many times at shrines placed before private doorways where the occupants asked the marchers to pause and rest and sing and pray. The men and women in procession were for the most part dressed in black, and, when at the end of the procession the archbishop came robed in red violet and white lace, he made a note of splendor. She always made him a deep curtsy as he went by, and he would respond by making the sign of his blessing toward her.

She must marvel at how much the archbishop achieved without ever giving an impression of being too busy for his friends. She enjoyed calling on him in his garden, and evidently he enjoyed showing her about. It was a fine model of what could be done to achieve green shade and brilliant blossoms in a land mostly arid and rocky. Water was a precious ornament there. The archbishop had not only a fountain, but a lake covering half an acre made from a dammed-up spring. Little bridges led to small islands in the lake, one of which had a miniature chalet with a thatched roof. Water lilies grew and among them stared and fled the archbishop's little school of trout which he liked to feed. Water flowed in ditches from the lake to the flower beds and the aisles of trees. He grew fruit and berries and vegetables, and worked lovingly over a great variety of trees whose saplings or seeds he had brought to town, sometimes with great difficulty, as when he brought the seeds for his horse chestnut trees in a pail of water all the way from Ohio. Much of the original stock for his plantings came from his boyhood homeland of the Auvergne. Nothing pleased him more than to share his prize cherries, strawberries, apples, grapes, peaches, cabbages, and turnips with his friends.

Above all, she would never forget the day when he came to her house in Palace Avenue and knocked on the door to explain his mission. He carried a spade and held a bundle of damp newspapers wrapped around two slim saplings. He had come to plant these as a gift to her household. While she watched with brimming feelings, he dug two holes, one on each side of the front gate, and planted two young willow trees. When he was done, he put aside his spade and blessed the trees. She hardly knew how to thank him. But he had not come for thanks but to make something grow. It was another act of friendship in a long series that had started years before on the prairies when he had saved the life of the man she was to marry.

In 1878 her family made new friends. These were Major General Lew Wallace, the new governor of the territory, and his wife. Governor Wallace had been persuaded to quit his private library in Indiana, where he wrote popular historical novels, to go to Santa Fe, where he must assert the power of the federal government to put down the cattle war in Lincoln County, a great area of southeastern New Mexico newly populated. The chief troublemaker was a youthful gunman named William Bonney, called Billy the Kid, who had many murders against his name. He was soon heard to brag that he would ride up to the palace and put a bullet through Lew Wallace. The governor was patient with him, and granted him an interview under safe conduct, but this resulted only in further acts of murderous insolence; and Susan Wallace, for one, was relieved when the sheriff of Lincoln County shot the outlaw to death one night at Fort Sumner.

When Mrs. Wallace took her place as first lady of New Mexico, a new period of high official style began. The Wallaces lived according to the grace and amplitude possible to a family of means. They found the palace interesting for its native architecture and violent history, even if its comforts were primitive and its condition, as ever, dilapidated. But they made it the center of good entertaining, and both husband and wife found it a sympathetic place in

which to write. The governor had a long novel to complete
—*Ben Hur, a Tale of the Christ.* The room in which he
worked was ideal for an author. "The retirement," he said,
"impenetrable to incoming sound was as profound as a
cavern's." Susan Wallace was busy with prose sketches of
Indian and Mexican life for the *Atlantic Monthly.*

As a matter of course the Wallaces exchanged invitations
with the family in Palace Avenue, and General Wallace,
who not only wrote well but drew delightfully, showed his
drawings. The German housewife, with her instinct for the
authentic in matters of taste, took much pleasure from
turning over the leaves of his portfolio. The governor made
drawings of the views and objects that caught his eye by
their local picturesqueness. He drew the façade of the
palace and saw its impressive appeal under all its plainness.
Other drawings that recalled the society and the land he had
come to govern showed a variety of subjects:

A buffalo under a mesquite tree.

A plains Indian, dead, with yucca plants nearby and
mountains beyond.

A Mexican rancher standing in a tall adobe doorway. He
wore a hide vest over naked belly and arms, and a kilt of
rawhide. His dog sat beside him.

A group of carters asleep in a patio, with their two-
wheeled cottonwood carts beside them.

Two children riding goats while they practiced lassoing
a goose in front of adobe houses.

A shepherd and his sheep in a desert landscape.

A study of quail, mesquite, and yucca.

A romantically handsome native boy, known as a guide,
riding a burro past a cactus plant.

Mexican riders in a party.

A ranch house built like a *jacal* with a curious round room
at the end of the adobe front.

A hacienda.

A *mozo* "in breeches of rusty leather" and a sombrero,
with, as Mrs. Wallace wrote, "a swagger so easygoing yet so
perfect as an emphasized insolence." Many of the drawings

were made as illustrations of her magazine pieces. The time-less sights of New Mexico were still of great interest to cultivated newcomers, who, whether they came to visit or to stay, brought the modern world with them.

In 1879 the transcontinental tracks of the Atchison, To-peka and Santa Fe Railroad were advancing slowly into New Mexico from its northeast corner. It was a shock to Santa Fe when the railroad company let it be known that the track would not reach the city, but would by-pass it seventeen miles away. The hills below Santa Fe presented engineering difficulties which would cost more to solve than the line would pay. The city's leading citizen—it was of course Archbishop Lamy—refused to lose the convenience and advantage of rail connections with the nation. If the main line would not come to Santa Fe, then Santa Fe must go to the main line. A branch must be built connecting the two. If the railroad would not pay for it, then perhaps the citizens would. The archbishop headed a petition asking for the territorial government to authorize a bond issue election calling for an appropriation of $150,000 for the branch line. How exactly like him! thought the German housewife—that refusal to be daunted, that energetic action on behalf of his fellow creatures, that recourse to the ways of democracy. If he could ride 10,000 miles on a mule over desert and mountain, she reflected, he could also build a railroad.

The election was held, the bond issue was carried by a three-to-one vote, and construction was ordered. On Feb-ruary 9, 1880, to cheers and the music of Saint Michael's College band, Governor Wallace drove the last spike in the branch line. The junction point on the main line was named Lamy, after the archbishop. Though in any reference to him his name was always given its French pronunciation, the name of his little railroad town was pronounced after the American fashion by most people—but not by his Ger-man friend in Palace Avenue. She continued to follow the foreign usage for both man and town. If anyone chose to think her affected in this, let them think so. Time and maturity had brought her to the edge of being old-fashioned, however greatly she might approve the signs of modern progress. She knew this, and laughed over it, and said that everyone had better watch out; when the time came, she was going to be a perfectly dreadful old lady, imperious, a tyrant, a holy terror, thumping the floor with a cane and wearing a lace cap. Nobody believed this, least of all herself, and with good reason. Her fulfillment in character came from working for and with other people.

She was gratified in a sense of municipal patriotism when in 1880 the first steam machines were set up in town to motivate various industries, and when gas for lighting was installed. The streets of the plaza now had lamps—tall standards with four-sided glass lanterns on top that cast a greenish yellow radiance all about in little islands of light. The darkness of a night without moon in Santa Fe had always been black beyond description, and up the by-streets and lanes the night could still be dark as fear. In her house she promptly hung new chandeliers to burn gas inside of etched globes from which depended prisms of Baccarat glass.

In the light of these fixtures, her household treasures took on new brilliance when guests were present at night. From a recent business trip in Mexico her husband had promised to bring her "something fine" he had heard about in Mexico City. When the gift came, she was delighted by its beauty and moved by its history. It was a set of twelve silver service plates, heavy and shiny as water, bearing the crowned monogram of the Emperor Maximilian of Mexico, who had been shot to death at Querétaro by a firing squad only a few years before her arrival in Santa Fe. These plates had been used at his own dinner table. She resolved to set them out only on the grandest of occasions. The story of the last Mexican empire appealed to her romantic sense and, with the plates as a beginning, she undertook to collect other mementoes of the Mexican reign of Maximilian and Carlota.

In her affections the emperor's plates were second only to a painting which she bought in New York when she went east with her husband on "a combined business and pleasure trip," as the newspaper said. This was a small oval portrait of a plump young woman with powdered hair in which strings of pearls were looped. Her face was rose white and rose pink. Her eyes, the color of sherry wine, glowed with reflected light. Her lips were parted in a breath of a smile over small teeth in an even row. The neck of her blue satin dress was wide and low, showing her powdered bosom on which a garland of diamonds rested like little leaves and branches on a white velvet cushion. The portrait was a small monument to the luxury, taste, and charm of the eighteenth century. The painting was signed; the artist was Nattier. On the back of the ornate gold frame a label gave the title: Portrait de Mme. la Marquise de R———.

Its owner in Santa Fe loved it because it was a portrait of her secret self, though she did not explicitly admit this in her thoughts. In admissible values, she liked it for its artistic qualities of skill and style; and for the fact that, so far as she knew and judged, it was the only work of art of any distinction in Santa Fe. Pioneer—it was a word frequently used by people around her to describe their forbears on the westward journey of the United States. Well: she bridled with humorous indignation in her mind: in her own way, she was something of a pioneer, too.

ix.

In the 1880's one of the four family brothers went to Wiesbaden to visit relatives and take the waters, and there died suddenly. His death, so far from home, summoned up old feelings and old images of Germany to the survivors at Santa Fe.

But Europe was only a memory now. Real life was rooted here in the mountain city at the end of a journey begun generations ago in darkness.

To her as to anyone who took up the hazard of making life out of love and work came all the usual trials and worries of a family. But these did not overcome her world. She revealed her temperamental outlook when frequently she played a piano transcription of an overture by her favorite composer. It was Mendelssohn's *Calm Sea and Prosperous Voyage.* The music perfectly fulfilled the title, and the title exactly expressed her vision of life's journey—that confident vision which as a German bride she had brought to Santa Fe, and which, ever since, had illumined her heart.

IX

The Doctor of Medicine: 1883

i.

IN ACCORD WITH his touch upon the little brass focusing wheel, the microscopic field of vision suddenly cleared and stood forth, a silver disk of light, faintly mottled by familiar blurs, so that he thought as always of a full moon standing forth in darkness.

It was an allegory of knowledge dispelling ignorance which brought a smile to his mind even when, as in this particular night of 1883, he identified the tubercle bacilli floating, with all their promise of suffering and perhaps fatality, in the smear on the glass slide under his lenses.

The night over Santa Fe was dark, late, and still. The small adobe room which he used as library and laboratory was lighted only by a brass oil lamp—a student lamp with a green glass shade about its yellow flame. The lamp could be lowered or raised on its upright stem. Now it was lowered almost to the desk top to let light pour upon the tilted reflecting mirror in the microscope while the green shade protected his eyes from glare. His concentration was like an island of thought and light in the intimate darkness of the room, and in the greater darkness outside. Beyond the huddle of the quiet city reached the vast land with its emptiness broken, he knew, by only a handful of railroad or highway towns, and those Indian towns of the Great River where human prehistory still lived.

He was in his early thirties, a doctor of medicine with a degree in surgery. During his first years of study he had intended to prepare himself for general practice in his home town in Massachusetts, but he became interested in the pathology of pulmonary tuberculosis, and he resolved to devote himself to special study of it on completing his regular curriculum. Throughout his internship in Boston he worked whenever possible among tubercular patients, and later returned to medical school for advanced work under a professor who was an authority on tuberculosis.

This was an old man who had exchanged observations for years with Robert Koch of Berlin, and who on various visits to Germany had followed Koch's approach to the identification and demonstration of the tubercle bacillus in the microscope, which had just been achieved in 1882. Though Koch had not yet published a monograph on his discovery, his American visitor made notes on his technique, and in turn shared these with his young protégé, in whom he saw much promise. In Germany, the old teacher had studied also the theories of Brehmer and Dettweiler about modern sanatorium methods, and to these he added observations of his own from data he had gathered on the effect of various climates on the disease.

He told the young doctor that in his own youth he had marched as a surgeon with the Army of the West on its way to Mexico through Santa Fe in 1846. In his view, the climate of upper New Mexico was the most promising he had ever seen for the treatment of lung affections, and he wondered if his student might consider going there in pursuit of the new theory of treatment in high altitudes with a minimum of humidity. There was not, thought the old gentleman, much of anything but climate out there, as the town, the society, the facilities were primitive—at least in his time. But if the young doctor should settle there for a while, he would send him patients from the east, and perhaps from such a beginning significant strides might be taken toward establishing a systematic regimen of treatment which could contribute materially to the conquest of one of mankind's worst enemies.

The young man, like anyone who loved his vocation, was an idealist in relation to his work. He decided to act upon his teacher's suggestion. He had saved a little money, and, with the dutiful agreement of his wife, he moved to Santa Fe early in 1883, bringing all the clinical equipment he could buy for cash or credit and, above all, his superb microscope. This was a gift from his old professor, who had bought it from Zeiss in Jena. The gesture was not only generous; it was, to a man with the young doctor's nature, inspiring—the handing on of a beautiful and powerful weapon from an old warrior to a young one. He often thought of the gift in just these terms.

The young doctor was a man of medium height and middle weight. His figure was neat and compact, and his shoulders looked smaller than they were because his head was large. The proportion of his head to his body was that often shown in boys. His hair was thick, with bronze lights in its wayward forelocks, which often fell across his brow when he was animated by interest or excitement. His eyes were a dark gold. They rested large in his ruddy face, bearing upon the world with an expression of light-hearted kindness that was disarming. Anyone who met him judged him offhand a good man. There was nothing mawkish or clammy in his goodness, for in his humor he had a strain of irony and it showed plain in the slightly fastidious curve of the nostrils in his straight short nose, and in the speculative lift of the corners of his generous lips with their curving bevels. He wore a trimmed mustache. From bending over a desk, or a microscope, his back was somewhat rounded. His clothes were well cut but rather boyish— short jacket, close-fitting trousers. His linen collar stood up high, starched, and always freshly clean. In his dark silk cravat every day was a pin of a little fox head in gold with ruby eyes which his wife had given him as a wedding present. The pin always fascinated sick children as he bent over their beds, and sometimes he took it from its silk and handed it to them to think about. He saw how in their imaginations they made more of the little gold fox than could be seen. He kindled. That was what he wanted to do—to see beyond time into the past, or through the body into the inner power that animated it, or beyond the signs of human trouble to its often obscure causes.

With his eye well adjusted now to the tube of light under his control, he estimated a count of the bacilli floating in the field of methylene blue stain—those bright scarlet lines that looked like clipped hairs clustered at random. Then he re- moved the glass slide, numbered it, and filed it in a slot bearing the same number in a small wooden box. In a record book he wrote down his findings, which tomorrow he must report to the patient concerned. He was tired. He stretched and yawned. He could never hold an impersonal attitude toward his cases, and he often felt hollow for a moment or two when he found evidence of the disease he was born to fight. This he always concealed unless he was alone.

Before joining his wife for the night, he put his micro- scope away with what he could only admit was fondness. He set it into its leather case lined in thick yellow plush, closed the little double doors on the front of the case, and brought down the lid which sealed all, clicking the clasp home securely. His weapon. He smiled at a thought.

If he had come west a few years ago, it was probable that his weapon would have been a firearm, and his battle would have been against Indians. People still talked of those days of action. Sometimes they seemed to miss them, even with all their brutal horrors. Much value was always put on action for its own sake. What, he thought, what of the action which he saw in the microscopic field—what passions of action, inscrutable yet powerful? It was against those, with his own weapon, that it was now time to fight, to whatever degree he was able.

As for Indians—after a century of killing them, he thought that perhaps now there would be time for the white man to learn something about them. He referred especially to the Pueblos in their settled towns. He had seen little of them so far, but enough to feel that their life with its obscure movement of mind and person seemed to have been held by time itself in a state of suspension since the days before the coming of the Spaniards three and a half centuries ago. Who knew anything about those days before history? Or for that matter—aside from incidents of warfare between white men and red—anything really about the Indian world since then?

ii.

One day not long afterward during office hours the doctor had a caller who came not for treatment but for acquaintance.

The newcomer wore a black bowler hat, a rusty black frock coat that hardly reached his knees, narrow trousers powdered with dust, and large shoes the worse for wear. He was tall and thin, leathered by exposure to sun, wind, and space. Uncertain of his reception, he was sidelong and diffident until the doctor rose with enthusiasm to the contents of his mind, for here he found a fellow scientist who was as starved for conversation as he was himself. The visitor's name was Adolph Francis Alphonse Bandelier. He had just come back to Santa Fe from a trip among the pueblos. The doctor, whose practice did not as yet require all his time, listened to him talk for the rest of the afternoon. In that first meeting he learned much about his visitor, and found much in him to like and to respect.

Bandelier was at work systematically studying the prehistoric and contemporary life of the Pueblo Indians. He was commissioned to his work by the Archaeological Institute of America. It was the first time any really ordered effort had been made to examine the whole existence of those Indian people. Bandelier seemed to the doctor to be singularly equipped for the job by temperament, training, and experience.

He was born in Switzerland and as a child he was taken to Brazil by his family, when his father accepted a position there. From an early age, he collected specimens—entomological, mineral, botanical. At fifteen he was sent back to Europe to study geology, and at that age had an experience which was inspiring. In Berlin he was received by the greatest student of his time, Baron Alexander von Humboldt. It was a tremendous honor.

The august savant was then eighty-seven. An incredible range of world experience lived on in him. He had known Thomas Jefferson, Goethe, Napoleon, and all the kings of Europe. He had traveled and observed two thirds of the world, from Siberia to South America and Mexico. He was a scientist and an artist; a philosopher and a courtier; a pinnacle of greatness and a model of simplicity. In his studies, no phenomenon stood alone, but each led to others. Goethe once said after hearing Humboldt lecture, "Must one probe into everything?" It was a dazed tribute from one universal mind to another.

In 1855 when young Bandelier went to see him, Humboldt was living in a modest house, painted pink, opposite the main post office in Berlin. There he was engaged in what he called the "most important work" of his life, "the sketch of a physical description of the universe." Such amplitude of vision must stir a sober boy at the outset of his own intellectual life. The old gentleman received callers from the world over, many of them illustrious, and worked away at his immense correspondence, and examined all the latest scientific papers. In his rooms a fine philosophical clutter was to be seen: stuffed birds and other natural history exhibits, folios and books, maps and pictures, study lamps, a live chameleon in a glass box, and, in the midst of it all, the old man who had ridden, sailed, or walked across the world in search of knowledge for its own sake. Everything he saw might help to illuminate everything else he had ever seen. His influence moved whole academies and entire philosophies.

No wonder if the young Swiss scholar felt kinship with such a man, however far apart might be the scale of their worlds and their gifts. Like Humboldt, Adolph Bandelier seemed to retain a "horror for the single fact." He felt also that facts must be personally pursued wherever possible to insure authority. Hearsay was often beguiling but inaccurate. Even the glorious Humboldt, in his five-volume *Political Essay on the Kingdom of New Spain,* published in 1811 after his trip to Mexico, had stated, without having visited Santa Fe, that the Rio Grande was "sometimes covered for a succession of years with ice thick enough to admit the passage of horses and carriages." Observation of the climate was enough to prove the statement untrue. But in any case, in his present work, Bandelier was making every effort to determine his facts for himself.

In just what way? the doctor wondered.

Since 1880, when with his wife Josephine he had come to Santa Fe to study the Pueblo Indians, he had spent many periods living among them in their earthen towns. Their life was expressed to a remarkable degree through symbolism, and, to understand that, it was necessary to encounter the mind behind it, and, to do that, he needed to be among the Indians day and night.

But they received him without reluctance?

For the most part, yes. They were naturally reserved in their behavior, and some pueblos were more conservative than others in their willingness to admit white people. Santo Domingo, in fact, seemed on the edge of a really hostile posture at times when white men tried to enter. But apparently the Indians in general felt they had little to fear from him. It was both easy and hard to explain. For one thing, he always went among them alone.

But armed?

No. Unarmed. He went, dressed just as now, in his black suit and bowler hat, and they let him stay. If his shoes seemed shabby, it was because they had done much work.

So?

Yes, for he walked whenever he went to the pueblos by the river.

He meant, then, that he went all the way from Santa Fe, alone, unarmed, on foot, often spending days together in the wilderness of desert or prairie, to reach his destination? The doctor was stirred with admiration for such courage and simplicity. He could not help wondering aloud whether Bandelier might not have been in danger many times from the Apaches and other Indians who roved about the open lands he must cross in his long walks.

Certainly. Bandelier knew the Apaches were likely to be troublesome. All he could say was that he had never encountered any in a hostile mood.

What would he have done, though, if attacked? After all, he went unarmed.

With the effect of a shrug, the visitor declared that perhaps after all he went not wholly unarmed, for sometimes, against the desert sunlight, he carried an umbrella.

The doctor laughed out loud at that, and Bandelier, with the reluctance of a sensitive man, supposed it might look comical to anyone else. Anyhow, he did live with the Indians, staying in their rooms with them, and making friends with some of the Pueblo men. He found them to have lively minds, a sense of humor, a childlike responsiveness to acts of genuine and disinterested friendliness, and a complete lack of curiosity about any life but their own. And, of course, there were some matters of their own life about which they were unwilling to talk. But from every visit to the pueblos, he returned with more information, more respect and, perhaps in a fashion difficult to describe exactly, even with affection for the Children of the Sun, as they sometimes called themselves.

It appeared further that Bandelier while in Santa Fe

spent hours reading in the archives at the palace. These were preserved in no order whatsoever, and, indeed, were now fragmentary at best; for a great bulk of the records of Spanish and Mexican times had disappeared. The papers of Captain General de Vargas, for example, he described as in "horrible condition." One document written by Vargas had been "stolen by an American." Anyone with a scrap of feeling for history must mourn the disappearance of early Spanish documents from Santa Fe; for the Spaniards, with their legal and administrative sense, had always documented their proceedings, and, if only it were complete, their record of Santa Fe and the kingdom of New Mexico would have provided the fullest account of the earliest civilized life of North America.

In 1880, on first arriving, Bandelier discussed the archives with Governor Wallace, who was "very kind and polite." The governor told him that "the archives were much neglected by his predecessor," who had "thrown them into an outhouse to rot," but that he, Governor Wallace, had "saved them." Bandelier asked him about an earlier territorial governor called Pile who was reported to have ordered the archives destroyed or sold at auction as there was no convenient place to house them. Wallace did not disavow the story, but thought Pile had acted "through ignorance." Bandelier found this difficult to believe, and a day or so later, from the rector of the cathedral, he heard another explanation of Governor Pile's crime against history.

As American commercial interests grew stronger by the day in Santa Fe and the region about it, there was increasing demand for property held by Mexican families. Evidence of grants and deeds for much of such property was preserved in the archives. The scattering of the archives by order of Governor Pile, said the priest, "was done on purpose to destroy Mexican claims." In consequence, much property changed hands to the advantage of the newcomers. Progress had its injustices.

Anyhow, working with what papers were left, Bandelier tried to classify and even translate certain of those which he regarded as of the first historical importance. After more than three centuries of obscure but teeming life, the disorganized experience of Santa Fe was for the first time seen through an intelligence that comprehended enough of it to let it declare a pattern.

As they talked, the doctor was entertained by Bandelier's early impressions of the city in 1880, the year of his arrival. He had slept "with bedbugs" at the Grand Central Hotel. There was "gambling, at hotels, at Mr. Gold's, everywhere gambling places, in the form of 'clubs.'" He found "not very inviting" the custom of "meat (sheep and beef) hung out on the portals." Things were not cheap in Santa Fe. If he wanted a buggy with driver and two horses, it cost him five dollars a day; and if he wanted to take a photographer along to record Indian life, the charge was five dollars a day and two dollars per print. This was one reason why he went alone, on foot, when he visited the Indians now. The consequences of this were sometimes droll, for his shoes wore out fast, of course, and when he sent them to the shoemaker to be resoled he was "thus kept in the room all day." It was clear that the tireless student of man was not affluent. Perhaps he felt some embarrassment about it, for when he mentioned spending an evening at Governor Wallace's, he remarked, "Costly living. Society I don't know." He seemed more at home referring to another social event, when he had been invited to "a singing party in the First National Bank," and said it was a "pleasant evening." Still, he went often to the Wallaces' until they were superseded in office.

One thing he always noted with pleasure coming home with his wife after a party was the atmosphere of the night. The moonlight was often "splendid" and "magnificent," and "in general, the sky here is most beautiful. Owing to the great altitude, the firmament is of remarkable clearness, Jupiter"—it was a detail stated in a way to delight the doctor—"Jupiter presenting a very perceptible diameter." Sometimes in winter, during a full moon, "the snow on the mountains is almost phosphorescent." The night was often full, too, of more homely effects. and Bandelier discussed these also. While at work writing in his parlor, he sometimes heard "ugly music" coming from a "newly opened saloon across the street." On the other hand, he sometimes heard a "serenade to the ladies across the alley," and added, "good voices." The doctor recognized the frankness of Santa Fe's nocturnal life in these musical references.

The city was changing, it must be observed. Bandelier had gone to Mexico in 1881, and upon his return in 1882 he could see differences in even so brief a time. He thought he saw "a better feeling between the Americans and Mexicans than it was before." The city had "grown considerably." New houses had "sprung up, some two story, of stone and brick." Amid all the low, flat adobe structures that had prevailed for centuries, those new buildings in the "territorial style" were conspicuous. There were also some new houses, "one story of adobe," but even these had an innovation—"metallic roofs." Bandelier thought these "very fine and good-looking." It was now a town of "6,500 souls."

If too soon it seemed time for his caller to leave, the doctor hoped he might meet Adolph Bandelier soon again. Particularly, he wanted to hear him speak about his observations among the Pueblos, and gain a sense of the Indian past, the Indian present; for the life of Santa Fe had always been colored by the nearness of the Indian people, and still was.

iii.

In the course of their meetings during the next decade, the doctor and the student of man talked of everything under the sun, but mostly about Indians. Bandelier, the anthropologist and archaeologist, had a mind as serious as it was voracious, and a temperament which, if it was somewhat melancholy, was yet compassionate. In Mexico on his trip in 1881 he had become a Catholic. His study of the Indian life, with its pagan origins lost in ancient time, had an odd double richness. His commentary on that life in all its details was scrupulously objective in its fullness, so that his records brought to the doctor, and to subsequent students of aboriginal man in the Southwest, a foundation of pure knowledge never before available. And then, against this background of scientifically observed and recorded information, he imposed various expressions of his own emotions; for, living with Indians so long as he did, in intimacy and transcendent of much danger, he viewed their life finally with love, and he made upon it various moral judgments closer to the Catholic sense of sin than to the scientist's dispassionate objectivity.

Most of the pueblos with which the doctor became familiar through Bandelier's study were situated in the valley of the Rio Grande, both above and below the region of Santa Fe, which the river, of course, by-passed a score of miles to the west. The Indian towns had their differences of speech, some belonging to one language group, some to another, and their differences of government and social organization. But their similarities in essential matters were so many that it was not inappropriate to consider them all as expressions of a common style of life.

The Pueblos believed they had their origin in an underworld of the earth. All life came up through a sacred underground lake when the first ancestors climbed a fir tree that grew there and that reached into the open world. This place of origin was "in the north." From it the people found their way southward to the river valley where long ago they made their towns. In the center of each town, in the ceremonial kiva, they fashioned a symbolic reproduction of the place of emergence, the *shipapu,* that channel through which the life of memory, and of the underworld, the overworld, and the sky were related to one another. The doctor considered that this represented in all reverence a sort of cosmic womb from which all life came, as Indians had seen life come from woman. The *shipapu* was a small stone-lined pit that could be thought of as a passageway to the ancestral world, and also as a channel by which the spirit in all things was kept alive from the time of creation until any time. All the beliefs, skills, traditions of the people were sanctified by the idea that such ways had "come up with them."

But there was no way to determine from the Indians themselves where and when they had brought their life from the north. The Indians had no written records. They lived only in the present, except in their fears, which were the medium of their government of the future. Had they always lived in the river pueblos? It would have been impossible to say before the labors of Bandelier. But he found and studied certain abandoned cliff dwellings in the blind mountains west of the Rio Grande above Santa Fe, and others even farther west in the Navajo deserts. He discovered artifacts and other objects of use in the ancient caves which had their counterparts in the modern pueblos. From such evidence he deduced that the Pueblos came to the river through a series of migrations—how long ago precisely no one could then say.

Certainly the cliff homes were ancient. The doctor visited some of the sites. He was moved by their utter stillness and their perfect state of preservation; for if the first of these qualities suggested eternity, the second was alive with many suggestions of human life. It was as if someone had left a well-used room where he had been interrupted in his daily concerns by an urgent call from without. He had gone, never to return, leaving much evidence of his busy interests. Cooking bowls and storage pots, corn and bone tools and matting, little stone images of animals or of ideas rubbed smooth to a polish by his worshiping fingers—such objects made this prehistoric man stand forth clearly in the minds of his discoverers.

Why had he gone? It was a question without a clear and certain answer.

The cliffs themselves were places of beauty in which to live, not to mention convenience and safety from possible enemies in the canyons below. There was a richness of color and texture, a grand elegance of the cuts made by wind and water in the smooth face of the cliffs that gave the doctor a pleasure which he could only suppose to be aesthetic. He saw no reason to think the vanished people had found any less pleasure in what pleased him so, and in the same terms—terms which even he could not define clearly. But the people had left their beautiful cities in the cliffs.

Had they been forced to flee before enemies? But there were no signs of conflict. Had they been visited by epidemics? But no excessive burials seemed indicated. Did their water supply disappear? Possibly, in some places, but in others—notably in the Rito de Los Frijoles—live streams still flowed by the uninhabited cliffs. Bandelier had discussed the matter with Archbishop Lamy, whose interest in the Indians had led him to compose a short history of the Pueblos in 1875. The archbishop said he had visited various ruined pueblos, and found evidence of water sources dried up. But in some of these places, he said, "springs were found by digging at considerable depth, and it appeared as if these springs had been artificially closed by the Indians, and even unto like cemented." Water, then, was available at many of the evacuated Pueblo cities.

The great mystery led Bandelier to ask Indians why their ancestors had left the wonderful cliffs. The replies were inconclusive, like the remembrance of dreams. An Indian told him that the Acoma people had come from the north, and some settled at Zia, but were driven out "much disturbed and harassed by venomous insects." The insects seemed to call up concepts of winged furies out of other mythologies. The people hurried on before the poisonous swarm and took up their dwelling on top of the great rock of Acoma. No one could say when.

Behind all such speculation about migrations local to the southwest lay a larger notion which stirred the doctor's imagination as he heard of it. This was the theory that all the North American Indian people had come unimaginably long ago from Asia, crossing the Bering Strait and coming down the western shelf of the cordilleran Rockies until they found, now here, now there, the places of settlement which they still generally occupied. It was strangely impressive to think of so tenacious a movement over so vast a reach of the earth; and—how strong was the persistence of tradition, how deathless was the effort of truth to perpetuate itself—did this not in the largest terms make harmony with the Indian belief that life had come "from the north"? Yet science required evidence. All that could be observed were a certain likeness in the Pueblo people to Mongoloid physiognomy, and in their artifacts a certain suggestion of Asiatic expression in design. Bandelier's discoveries, his recorded observations, must, the doctor knew, create an almost endless suggestibility for later students of his experience.

In their dwellings the Pueblo people displayed a common style of building. Since the coming of the Spaniards, the Indians had built with shaped bricks—adobes—made of earth and straw mixed wet and dried in the pure air and bright sunlight. It was a technique taught by the Franciscan friars who built the first Pueblo churches. But there were remains—some buried, some still open to the eye—that showed walls built up of countless applications of earth puddled into small pieces of structural material each the size and shape of a closed double handful. With these, or with the later adobes, the people made their little rooms which they put together, side by side and one on top of another, in recessive terraces rising, as at Taos, even to a height of five stories. The walls had no windows. Entry was managed through trap doors in the terraced roofs by means of ladders. The communal dwelling, then, was secret and secure, a hive blind to the exterior view, but honeycombed inside with cells arranged in a system of little apartments for separate families. The form of the town had not changed since the Spaniards saw their first pueblos in 1540. What Bandelier and the doctor visited in the 1880's must have been constant in design for more than a thousand years. In the rooms of such a house Bandelier lived with his Indian friends to come by knowledge of them.

He acquired an intimate sense of all their ways. Since the early Franciscans, who could remember any other white man who had been accepted as a companion by the Indians? His interest in their affairs was serious but tactful. He gave them dignity as people, and his unprotected presence among them was a form of confidence which must have moved them. He made several friendships with Indian men and was presently able to ask them direct questions about their beliefs, customs, and traditions. He could not feel that they had given him everything he wanted to hear, but he heard far more than anyone else ever had. Much of what he learned he was working into a scheme for a long book about the Indians. It was to be a novel. In the form of a story he could find, apparently, a proper medium for revealing the truth about the Indians without being constricted by the conventions of a scientific report. It was plain to the doctor that Bandelier had become devoted to much of the Indian life, and in the work of storytelling he would be free to animate his subject with his own emotion, and so give it a life of its own.

He ranged the whole of Indian experience, and put what he knew into systematic notes, and often, in addition, into his diary. Much of this information he shared with the doctor, telling how the Pueblo Indian dealt with his gods who lived in everything, and who must be invoked with visible prayers, such as a stick with feathers bound to it, and the scattering of corn meal or flower pollen, and the performance of massed dances, and the making of sand paintings; and how under the communal life all land was distributed to families by the ruling elders and was held only for use, not for trade or sale; how the town was organized into cults (named for the seasons) which took turns in conducting the major ceremonies of the year; and how other observances, such as the administration of war, and the defeat of witches, and the curing of the sick, were under the care of men's secret societies established for each purpose.

In the family, it was the woman who kept and transmitted property from one generation to the next, and who built walls, made pottery, wove cloth, and ground corn. Man married into her family, and, if one of the two must abandon a married home, it must be he. His work was to govern, to make war, to perform vital ceremonies by which nature's life was continued, to farm the fields, to hunt animals, and to initiate boys into the crafts and secrets of these duties.

In the acts of such a life Bandelier saw, for the most part, decorum and restraint. It was a Pueblo ideal to be a part of the group rather than to stand forth an individual. Any eccentricity would be met by the worst of penalties— ridicule. Emotions were held in check, and all things were done without innovation, in the old ways that had "come up" with the Indian people. It was interesting, and it was sad, that the effects of Christian teachings of the friars over so many centuries had all but vanished. The pueblos still had their mission churches and the archbishop did his best to provide pastors or regular priest visitors, but stronger still seemed the ancestral ways, however amenable the Indians might be to Christian observance on occasion. Did it seem that, to their unlimited number of gods, they had simply added yet one more, the Christ of the Spaniards, without granting Him supremacy over the others? The old ways still were the strong ones. Some of these were matters of shame to Bandelier.

Though some of his Indian friends denied it, the priest at Santo Domingo told him that certain of the massed dances "by men and women" were danced naked, "even in open air," and that on such occasions the pueblo was well guarded by Indian sentinels stationed outside. In November in 1880 he saw a day-long dance at Cochiti which he called "nothing else than a theatrical performance accompanied by and interrupted with dancing." He went several times during the day—it was a fine day—to the plaza to see the performance.

The men were dressed only in a *maxtlatl,* or loincloth, bracelets, anklets, and collars. Their hair was tied back, topped with a tuft of corn leaves. White, black, brown, or

copper-colored paint covered their skin, and some had designs painted on their bodies, and "one particularly ugly
devil" was transformed by "ashy gray" with a "large open
hand" in dark pigment on one side of his body. He thought
the faces were "particularly ugly." If the body was darkened,
the face was painted white, "or the reverse." The women
were fully dressed and their faces were painted. The
general dance step was "a very light trot, and therefore
slow." All about the general mass of dancers were others
whom he called "skirmishers." These were the *koshare,*
the clowns, the spirits of mockery and mischief. It was
these whose antics shocked him. He could hardly describe
what they did, even to the doctor, a medical man and a
scientist. One of the skirmishers repeatedly rolled in the
dust and was dragged by other performers till he was completely naked. Then followed "an exhibition of obscenities
hard to describe," which was received with the "greatest
delight" by more than a hundred spectators, "men, women,
girls and boys, Mexicans, and Indians," who looked on
"with the greatest ingenuity and innocence." Not even the
women showed the "slightest indecent look," but all applauded "the vilest motions." Bandelier was "terribly
ashamed." The acts which he witnessed were variations of
sexual expression by men and women alike, all "performed
to greatest perfection," at which "everybody laughed." Before it was all over, he left.

That was not an isolated instance. Later he heard of
similar performances at Laguna pueblo, and again at Cochiti he saw the *koshare* rehearsing for another festival,
in "an exact repetition" of what he had seen before, but
with some additions, also. The "filthy, obscene affair" included other "jokes" by the *koshare* in which they drank
urine from privy jars, ate excrement and handfuls of earth,
ashes, and clay, and washed each other's faces in such dirt.
How could such things be? In the home life which he
saw, the Indians showed no inclination to private acts of
such nature. All their improprieties seemed openly public,

like the "figures of clay" he had come upon at Tesuque north of Santa Fe, "chimneys, etc.," of which he had seen many recently made, and "very obscene."

Reflecting upon such reports, the doctor, while he could understand and respect Bandelier's sense of outrage, wondered if perhaps the Indians, in their ritual eroticism, might not be recognizing, in ways sanctioned by all, those dark impulses which were buried in human nature, and which in more civilized races sometimes rose to plague individuals in private with tragic results. Perhaps the Indians, by ridiculing them in public, dissipated their troubling effects, permitting in ceremony that which must be denied in secret. To be sure, these were only speculations, not supported by any substantial evidence.

Bandelier was interested to learn of other Indian practices that combined with forms of worship a living instrument of danger. His informant was a priest who worked among the river pueblos, from whom he obtained much information that Indians had been unwilling to reveal. In this instance, Bandelier was convinced "of the existence, in caves," of huge rattlesnakes which the Indians fed "with rabbits and sacred meal." Near the pueblo of Sandía, in the mountain foothills, lived a great rattlesnake which the Indians revered. One day it came from its cave to a grove near the pueblo. It was soon discovered there. In excitement and concern the people gathered to recapture it. They closed about it with noise, fed it rabbits and sacred meal, and finally induced it to return to its hole in the rocks. The priest saw its trail. It looked "like the trace of a big timber."

Similarly, at Isleta, a sacred serpent, attended by a guardian who fed it rabbits and meal, escaped one day when the sentinel was negligent. Some Indian girls saw it and raised an alarm. Men came and at last returned the great snake to its hole. But later it escaped again, leaving a heavy track which led to the Rio Puerco many miles away. It was never found again, and the people of that town gave up the custom of keeping a reptile deity.

The priest went one day to Jemez Pueblo with an Indian companion. In a mesa near the pueblo the Indian going ahead by himself discovered a pit closed over by "a plate of rock." Taking away the plate, he found an enormous rattlesnake coiled below. He ran to tell the priest and brought him to the cave but when they got there, the snake was gone—whether deep into the cave, or free on the mesa, they did not know. But if the priest may have thought the Indian was making a story for him, he was soon convinced of its truth, for on looking close he saw near the lip of the pit little tufts of rabbit fur, and eagle feathers tied together in little bunches as worshipful offerings, and he knew he was looking at a shrine. "In presence of these facts," said Bandelier, "I can hardly doubt the fact that big snakes are sometimes kept and treated as fetishes by the Pueblos." He heard another snake story. A priest of San Juan while saying mass one day presently noticed under the altar "an enormous rattlesnake coiled up." If Indians had seen it too, they had evidently given no sign. Which gods? What reverence? Whence powers?

Bandelier thought about the Indian claim that extraordinary powers resided in certain magic songs. When these were sung with all proper observances, marvels resulted. Power was inherent in the song, and such a song was handed down in memory as a treasure. An Indian told him how years ago the Pueblos with a ritual chant could grow and ripen a corn plant in one day, "between *sunrise* and *sunset*." When he asked further, he was told that the song was now lost, but his Indian informant added that the Navajos had the song, and still performed the wonder. The subject was brought up by another friend, a Mexican, who was "thoroughly informed" about Pueblo life. He not only confirmed the fact that Indians still kept large rattlesnakes as Bandelier had heard, but also he "positively" asserted that he himself had "seen the corn plant grown and raised through incantation." The information certainly belonged in any study of the Indian, and Bandelier noted it for what it was worth.

So also he cited Indian practices with the peyote bean. Pueblos used it, and, though he did not observe their doing so, he learned about its properties among the Suma Indians near El Paso. They mixed the peyote with grape brandy "in order to make the latter still more intoxicating." The Indians claimed that peyote had magic powers—as a love potion it changed "men into horses and other animals." In any case, he concluded that peyote was "strongly narcotic, like opium," and that the Indians used it with brandy when they wanted to "get drunk pleasantly."

The more the doctor learned from Bandelier about the Indian people during the 1880's, the more certainly if slowly he came to an observation of his own upon the subject. With his study of the Indian nature, the tragic sense of life entered for the first time into the doctor's view of Santa Fe and its history as part of the great West. For a time he thought this conclusion might have arisen from association with Bandelier, who himself seemed to have the dignity of the tragic view. But the more he learned, the more he felt that the tragic was inherent in Indian life, and did not rise simply from interpretation.

For the Indian was the most religious of all creatures he had ever heard of, and his every act of every day was linked to prayers of propitiation to his ancestral gods. And yet these gods were incapable of response, for they were locked in the material substances of nature—rocks, trees, mountains, feathers, springs, animals, reptiles, the sun, the moon, and the stars. As all nature seemed hostile and needed persuasion, the Indian seemed to confront everything in fear. To be ruled by fear, the doctor thought, was to live by holding your breath, as it were. The Pueblo Indian as an individual strove to be above all else inconspicuous, lest he attract the malign attention of gods or witches. His whole scheme of communal life appeared to be a demonstration of this attitude. He was submerged among his people, and only when he acted together with them to create a society, a dwelling, or a prayer did his existence show its power.

Still, like Bandelier, the doctor was moved to respect much of what he came to know of the Indian uses of environment; and he began to collect objects of Indian make, such as pottery and ornaments and the small wooden dolls representing the supernatural *kachinas,* or visitant gods; and gradually he acquired a fine collection. He spoke of it with humor as his "museum." In time, Bandelier's systematic work and the doctor's sympathetic response to it made others at Santa Fe conscious of the Indians in a new way. If it had aspects of fantasy—those reticent lives and vanishings and unchanged survivals—the Indian tradition gave to Santa Fe something hard to define but easy to feel. Was it a certain spirit? Even, as some citizens might ardently put it, a certain vibration? Whatever: once revealed by the devoted researches of Bandelier and those who responded to his labors, like the younger archaeologist Edgar L. Hewitt, it was there, evidently, to stay.

Considering prehistoric Indian remains in all their ghostly eloquence, and seeing Indians of the modern day still following closely the ways of their forbears, the doctor thought of the smallness, and the tenacity, of man against all the immense and immensely beautiful and impersonal land.

iv.

If in the beginning the doctor thought of staying in Santa Fe for only a few years, the idea gradually lost its force. His practice grew, attended by encouraging success with the regime of treatment he prescribed for tuberculosis. His patients were taken in at Saint Vincent's Hospital, and sometimes the archbishop dropped in to see them during his own tours of the corridors. The hospital was always crowded, and a new wing was required by the mid-1880's. The doctor soon had other colleagues in the city, and he began to wonder if one day still other hospitals might not be needed—perhaps a sanatorium devoted wholly to the care of tubercular patients, who came in greater numbers every year.

It always gave him personal as well as professional satisfaction when his patients could be released from the hospital to live in boardinghouses, and by small adventures of authorized daring—little walks about town, a meal in a hotel, an evening at a party—could find their way back to self-reliance and health. It was not long until the tubercular patients became a recognized segment of the population. Their increasing and changing numbers were responsible for much of the city's new prosperity.

For after centuries of a sleepy isolation, Santa Fe began to show a spirit of enterprise. An eastern editor making a tour in the early 1880's gave it as his opinion that, in the modern world, Santa Fe could "sleep no more and hold her place." He noted that "other villages" in New Mexico "have existed from time immemorial but all communication with the outside was through Santa Fe." The railroads, the telegraph were animating other towns in the old province and, if Santa Fe was to keep pace, she must exert herself. But it was clear that she would do so in her own way, and without losing the character that had made her unique throughout so many centuries.

Even so, the devices of modern life were in local use. The telephone had come to town in 1881, soon after gaslights and steam power. A photographer had his tent in an open lot with a sign reading *"Galeria de Photografo,"* and clients could be taken either formally, in front of a painted canvas drop showing marble pillars and draped curtains, or informally, mounted in open air upon a burro. Store space was at a premium. The doctor heard that a store measuring thirty by seventy feet in a good location brought a monthly rent of $150. Clerks were paid from $50 to $150 a month. There were "several merchants doing a business of one million to two million dollars a year in some of those flat mud houses." The Palace Hotel, recently completed in two stories and "finely furnished," charged four dollars a day for a room.

But along with all such bustle and progress, it was just as true, to the doctor's delight, that the affairs of government, the courts, the territorial legislature were still conducted in Spanish and English, with interpreters. Juries, for example, were "composed of Mexicans and Americans, and, as the average Mexican never learns to speak English, an interpreter is engaged to translate sentences as fast as spoken. This is annoying to the spread-eagle, highfalutin style of the American lawyer, who is repeatedly checked in his upward flight, to give time for the echo of the interpreter. This custom may destroy the howl and flourish of the lawyer, but the loss is more than made good by the deliberation and directness it gives his argument."

The plaza continued to be the center of the city's public entertainments, and the doctor and his wife, like everyone else, went promenading there to see what could be seen. The palace had been renovated during the time of Governor Wallace, and its long portal was upheld by evenly spaced square pillars with scrollwork corbels, all painted white. Along the top of the whole front was a low white balustrade of wooden pegs, surmounted by white wooden urns in line with each pillar below. The effect was oddly classical, thought the doctor, and very pleasing. The plaza's other three sides were lined with covered walks. Some of the buildings had two stories, and these carried galleries on the second-floor fronts. The park in the center of the plaza was enclosed by a white wooden picket fence over which the thick boughs of cottonwood trees cast cool deep shade. The hexagonal bandstand in the park on the palace side had a pagodalike roof rising to a finial with a carved urn. The edges of the hexagon were finished with wooden lace under whose points, on grand occasions, bunting in the national colors hung in wide swales.

There, on Sunday, Tuesday, and Thursday, from six to seven o'clock in the evening, the regimental band of the garrison played concerts. The musicians were negro soldiers and their conductor was a German bandmaster. They played martial airs, overtures, potpourris from grand operas and light operas, waltzes, and florid paraphrases of virtuoso pieces. The repertoire in 1883 included the waltz from *Die Fledermaus*, the "Fatiniza March" and "Mandolinata."

The uniformed bandsmen—all but the drummers—wore white cotton gloves throughout their concerts. A German visitor was astonished at this practice, and commented upon it to the doctor.

"That one could perform, gloved, on a wind instrument," he declared, "as was the case here in Santa Fe, was new to me. When I expressed my surprise to the bandmaster, and told him that in Germany even at Court concerts and Court balls the musicians never wore gloves," the German conductor, he said, "already much Americanized, answered: 'You see, as far as fine civilization goes, we in New Mexico are ahead of you.'"

There were other things to see. One was the daily guard mount at the garrison. It had interest as an entertainment, but, as the doctor saw, it had more: it was an occasion of pride in the Army. Now and then a circus came to town and the audience was augmented by people from the villages and ranches for miles around. Every year on the Fourth of July public festivities lasted all day and most of the night. Bandelier said they were "all right, as long as you keep out of it." The doctor smiled at this, for he had seen him at the horse races on one such occasion. When, in due course, baseball was organized at Santa Fe in 1887, Bandelier commented on the "great baseball excitement in town and great foolishness in consequence. The people," he said, "seem crazy," and added that it was "a perfect shame." He preferred moments of private entertainment with a certain decorum, and, if possible, an intellectual or at least an artistic tone.

Occasionally the doctor joined Bandelier to attend the evening meetings of the German singing society and *Turnverein* which took place in the First National Bank. Other evenings of song were held in private houses. Again with some regularity, a group of friends drew together for intellectual exercises. Sometimes Bandelier was the host at home, when he would read aloud from the manuscript of his long novel about the Pueblo Indians. He called it *The Delight Makers*—a phrase which was a translation of the word *koshare,* which signified those spirits of mischief some of whose antics he had found so shocking. His audience was not always all he could hope for—they seemed only curious about the subject matter of his book, and it struck him that "they could not sufficiently appreciate the literary part and exigencies of the work."

Other members of the group had their turns. One evening an amateur archaeologist lectured on the Pueblo Quemado which was situated in the Potrero de las Vacas, and Bandelier was obliged to note that "on the whole the lecture was a very shallow thing, superficial and buncombe." On another evening, the friends heard a lecture on phrenology, and again, "a highly interesting paper on the origin of the House of Anjou." Bandelier was offended by the program of still another meeting, when a member read a paper on "Development in Christianity," in which the reader "assailed Infallibility and the Immaculate Conception." It seemed like a direct attack upon Bandelier's devout Catholicism. "There was little delicacy" in the affair, he thought, and he suspected a plot animated by "foolish ideas of changing my religious opinion," as he said. The doctor was sympathetic and gave what reassurance he could to his brilliant friend, only cautioning him not to drink so much coffee, since he complained of "nerves" afterward and inability to sleep. Presently, when summoned to a meeting of the group, "to assist at a reading," Bandelier declined, "but went to the archbishop instead.—I cannot" he said, "afford to be with society that had no other object but entertainment."

With Archbishop Lamy he found both intellectual and spiritual comfort. He often went to Tesuque to visit the archbishop at the Villa Pintoresca, with its "most delightful scenery." There he could talk of Indian antiquities. The archbishop dined with him and spent many evenings in town, when Josephine—"Jo"—Bandelier made supper. The doctor and his wife were sometimes included in such evenings, for between the prelate and the medical man a good friendship had developed.

In 1885, it was something of a shock to the doctor, as to all the city, when the archbishop announced his retirement. After thirty-five years of exhausting work over his vast territory, the old priest had received permission from Rome to give his office into the care of his coadjutor, Archbishop Salpointe, who had come from Arizona, where he had been vicar apostolic. There was hardly an aspect of life in all the territory of New Mexico, and particularly in Santa Fe, which had not felt the generous and civilizing influence of Archbishop Lamy. As he officially stepped down from his throne, a number of his major undertakings were still growing toward completion. These included the expansion of Saint Vincent's Hospital, and the building of the cathedral and the chapel of Our Lady of Light at the convent of Loretto. He was a man after the doctor's own heart; for if he had retired, this did not mean that he would be idle. In 1886 he set off on a trip to Mexico to beg contributions toward the work on the cathedral. He journeyed ten thousand miles, mostly on horse or muleback. Late in the same summer, the cornerstone was laid for the new wing at the hospital. The doctor, with his other medical colleagues in town, attended the ceremonies, which were performed by the Papal Delegate to the United States assisted by three other bishops.

In the same year, on Sunday, December 12, which was the feast of the Virgin of Guadalupe, what seemed like a portent for the whole future appeared in Santa Fe. It was, as always, a day of processions and special services in the cathedral and all the other churches of the capital. Suddenly the city was alive with a throng of new visitors. "They infest every part of the town," noted Bandelier. They were "six to eight hundred excursionists" who arrived by train, and took to the streets to watch the processions swaying slowly past with sodality banners, candles, thuribles, and a statue of the Guadalupana, all brought up at the end by the clergy, including the prelates of the archdiocese. Railroad trains now ran from the Atlantic to the Pacific, and, as

America went traveling on transcontinental excursions, Santa Fe became an inevitable stopover where tourists could see unchanging reminders of Spain and Mexico in the United States, and Indians in native dress displaying wares for sale, and the old churches which perhaps more than any other signs gave a foreign flavor to the Royal City of the Holy Faith of Saint Francis of Assisi.

The feast of Saint Francis was kept every year on October 4. On that day in 1887, the doctor was passing through the plaza at dusk. Bonfires of short sticks of piñon wood were laid in little hollow squares along the curbings, and, as he watched, they were lighted by boys with torches of burning pine. Firelight sprang alive on the shops and houses, and looking up toward the cathedral at the head of San Francisco Street he saw a procession come slowly forward from the cathedral doors. The marchers carried candles through the sharp autumn air. Voices singing plaintive Spanish hymns rose on the evening. The doctor asked a bystander what occasioned the religious fiesta, and was reminded that it was Saint Francis's Day. He was not a Catholic, but, as he loved the city and its people, and paid respect to those things which they loved, he stood to watch the whole procession.

For he knew that the brothers of Saint Francis had come here from Spain and Mexico more than two and three-quarter centuries before, to bring their knowledge, their labor, and their mercy to the Indian people. From Bandelier's study among the documentary remains of the Spanish past in Santa Fe, he knew what mortal danger and disappointment the Franciscan friars had suffered without desisting from their labors so long as they were permitted by government to remain in New Mexico. A few years ago the Franciscan order had been welcomed back to Santa Fe. He was glad to be among those paying honor to their founder that evening. Quite unexpectedly he was rewarded by what he saw as the end of the procession drew near to him. There, wearing a long black cloak over his prelatic violet, walked Archbishop Lamy, old, thin, and frail, to keep the feast of a man and a saint in whose company the doctor thought him a proper figure.

v.

On January 3, 1888, "the best physicians of our city," as Archbishop Salpointe later expressed it, were summoned by him to Archbishop's House for consultation upon a patient suddenly ill. It was Archbishop Lamy. Staying at his lodge in the country, he had been seized by an inflammation of the chest. A carriage was sent to bring him to town. He was put to bed in the high square room with plaster heads of cherubim in the ceiling and his old cases of books all about where he had lived so long. The sisters of Loretto came to nurse him. Among them was their Mother Superior, who was his niece Francisca Lamy. The doctor saw soon enough that the old man was suffering from pneumonia. The consulting physicians gave him proper treatment, and he began to recover. But soon he fell back into fever and long periods of unconsciousness, and, more significantly, his own conviction when awake that his time had come to die. He asked for the last sacraments, which were administered to him by Archbishop Salpointe, who granted also the indulgence *"in articulo mortis."* When the awesome and comforting ritual was done, the old archbishop said to his successor,

"Thank you. I was able to follow word for word the prayers you said for me. Pray always, for I feel that I am sinking."

He did not again speak so distinctly, though in a day or so the doctor and his colleagues thought his condition was improving once more, if slowly. Archbishop Salpointe felt safe in leaving on the train during the night of February 12 for an engagement at Las Vegas. The doctors had done all they could. Sisters of Loretto took turns, two by two, in keeping vigil in the sickroom. The convent gardener slept in a room nearby in case his help might be called for,

for the archbishop was so weak that he could not turn himself.

At half-past five in the morning on February 13, Mother Francisca heard her uncle stir. Though he did not speak, she knew what he wanted. She called the gardener and they adjusted him "as best they could in his bed." Toward seven o'clock—the doctor was given a full report later—something made the gardener tell Mother Francisca that it would be well to call a priest. She could find none immediately, since all the priests were saying their masses. But finally one came and, after a glance, began at once to recite the prayers for the dying. He had hardly done when a smile came over the face of the old archbishop "as though," said Mother Francisca, "he received some heavenly vision." He died in ease at a quarter of an hour before eight o'clock that morning. He was seventy-four years old. He had been a priest for fifty years, a bishop for thirty-eight. In a few minutes the bells of Santa Fe began to toll for him.

In mitered state, robed in pontifical vestments of scarlet satin and gold, gloved, wearing his episcopal ring, and holding a crucifix, he was laid in state on a high catafalque in the chapel of Our Lady of Light at the Loretto Convent, which—in his last act of pontifical dignity—he had dedicated eight weeks before, just upon its completion. He was surrounded by eighteen lighted candles. The sisters had covered the candlesticks and all the ornaments of the chapel with black crepe. The unlighted candles of the main altar were dressed with spirals of black cloth, and a black and silver frontal hung below. In the candlelight his face was strongly marked by shadows—a statement of bone and cavity through the close-drawn veil of flesh. His expression was gently serious, and it made many of those who passed by his bier—there were thousands in the next two days—it made the doctor and many others remember, in contrast, the strong sweetness of his smile.

On the morning of February 16 the city turned out into

the streets to mourn their old friend when borne by six priests and led by Archbishop Salpointe his body was taken in procession to the cathedral. The march proceeded from the Loretto Chapel to Cathedral Place, over to Palace Avenue, around the plaza and up San Francisco Street into the main doors of the church that became his tomb. The pontifical requiem mass began at half-past eight and lasted until noon. The cathedral was filled with a great crowd. The doctor was present. It was extraordinary, the feeling of power in prayer that was released by those who wept for the archbishop. The doctor was moved by something that, in his scientific terms, eluded description. At the end of the mass, the body of the archbishop in its shining vestments was lowered into a vault before the epistle side of the high altar.

With him was buried, the doctor thought, a whole epoch of Santa Fe. What survived him would survive merely to increase and improve—the impulses of organized and civilized life that had come with the archbishop's faithful energy. Men after him must simply do what they could to shape the future in the ways he had shown them.

vi.

Three years later the doctor lost a closer friend when Adolph Bandelier left with Josephine his wife for Peru in 1891, to study prehistoric remains and explore Spanish archives. The doctor heard from him, and shared his news. Jo Bandelier died soon after arriving in Lima. It must have been a frightful blow for Bandelier, who was already somewhat embittered and lonely in his thought. But, two years later, he married Fanny Ritter, of Zurich, who was in Lima, and for the next ten years the Bandeliers worked in Peru and Bolivia as historians and archaeologists. Fanny Bandelier was a brilliant scholar and collaborated with her husband in translating documents and drawing up his papers. In 1903 they moved to the United States, to pursue their documentary study of the Spanish Indies in the learned societies and institutions of New York and Washington for eight years.

A scholarly foundation gave Bandelier his greatest opportunity in 1911, when he was appointed to conduct research in Spain among the archives of the Indies. He was by now going blind, and it was a blessing that his wife was able so expertly to help him in the examination and translation of documents. They spent a preliminary year in Mexico, and then sailed for Spain. In 1914 the doctor at Santa Fe was grieved to hear of the death of his friend and—yes—his teacher, at Seville.

He smiled to remember his qualities. Bandelier never lost his delight in the marvels of nature, and recorded much of what he talked about with his friends. In 1886, for example, he had been excited to see at 8:50 one August evening how "the sky suddenly lit up for about ten seconds," and he thought it was "possibly a meteor above the clouds." It was stormy all night. In the following year he mentioned "an uneasy night," and declared that, though he could not be sure, he thought he detected at a little before two in the morning "two very slight earthquake shocks." A month later there was another demonstration in the sky at night. It was a great illumination of about five or ten seconds— extremely brilliant bluish electric light, he said. "It lasted longer than lightning and was brighter . . . fearfully intense glare." About five minutes afterwards he heard a "very distinct rumbling noise." Several other people had noted the same thing, including the doctor. Was it a meteor? If it was a meteor, it had exploded over San Ildefonso and "did not reach the horizon."

With the coming of autumn each year, Bandelier was always inspired by the appearance of slopes of gold on the mountains, when the aspen groves turned their color. No matter how hard the country—and on his long walks alone from Santa Fe to the river pueblos the land was often hard to him, so that he was "unwell" or "completely worn out" —he never seemed to lose his feeling for its beauties.

But Bandelier could also be displeased at certain effects

of life in Santa Fe, and was never shy about expressing his irritation to the doctor. The years 1888 and 1889 were hot and dry, and the drouth made Bandelier furious. "Let anybody speak to me of the *climate of Santa Fe!*" he exclaimed. "It is the meanest, the most abject, the dryest, the most abjectly windy spot upon earth. Not fit," he went on, "for people to honor it with their presence." The doctor had to raise his eyebrows at such vehemence. But there was more—a theory of cure for tuberculosis which must interest the doctor, even delivered as it was in a sort of comic fury. "Not a single man or woman can live here," said his friend, "unless he or she is in a dying condition, when it may occur that the hellish, fiendish winds blowing here give him some strength through the gymnastics they force upon his lungs." The east wind off the plains, hauling immense clouds of dust from as far away as Kansas, depressed Bandelier.

The behavior of Bandelier's fellow creatures sometimes made him cross, especially their noises—two bands playing at the same time during a circus performance, firecrackers on the Fourth of July, the commotion attendant upon elections. Elections particularly infuriated him. During the presidential campaign of 1888, he remarked that "in town everybody is crazy on elections," and insisted that it was "absolutely disgusting in every respect." He saw politics and drunkenness together, and he could not wait for the elections, "a perfect nuisance," to be over. The town was filled with "election fools" for days before the polling day. When the day finally came he saw "carriages with 'intelligent voters'" driving past to the polls at a schoolhouse near his home. He said "this system of popular suffrage is a mean farce." What would he have made of the popular excitement, with all the noises of jubilee, that swept the city in 1912 when, after sixty-four years as a territory of the United States, New Mexico was signed into the Union by President Taft?

But by then Bandelier was in Spain, and two years later he was dead.

To recall him not so much in his works of great achievement, or his tempers, but at his little comforts and satis-
factions was, to the doctor, the fondest of all the duties of
memory—how he used to enjoy going to the Brewery with
a crony for the afternoon to drink beer while Jo had her
Kraenzchen at home for her lady friends; how he used to
go to the plaza to hear the Cavalry band and to the garrison to see guard mount; how he would walk out to Tesuque
to gossip with the old archbishop about Indians who lived
a thousand years ago; or how, when his specimen of *cereus
grandiflora* was about to bloom, he would notify his friends
to come in the evening to watch the petals unfold, at which,
"Beautiful sight!" Bandelier would exclaim.

vii.

In the years soon following the Statehood Act of 1912,
the doctor achieved the realization of a purpose which perhaps symbolically, he sometimes thought, united three of
his truest interests.

These came together in the building of a sanatorium on
a beautiful site below Santa Fe's mountain rim. The purpose of the new building answered his professional vocation, for the hospital was devoted exclusively to the treatment of pulmonary tuberculosis. Its location expressed his
feeling for Santa Fe, where he had made a good life with
his family, and where his work had borne successful outcome in more cases than he could have hoped for. And
its appearance acknowledged his sense of the New Mexican
past, for it was designed in an architectural style that called
upon both the Pueblo Indian habit of construction and
that of the Mexican house and patio.

Out of the diversities of Santa Fe's long history, a modern
style of living began to emerge. Becoming aware of her
past, Santa Fe began to preserve her image in the works
of the present. It was, for the doctor, in whatever part he
helped this application of design to occur, the fulfillment
of a true strand of his own nature.

X

The Chronicler: 1915 and after

i.

IN ITS FOURTH CENTURY Santa Fe remained a city of arrivals. Many of those arriving stayed to contribute their special purposes to the stratified society visible there. Many moved on to other marvels elsewhere. And some—like the present chronicler—often went and returned, seeing changes in the city's modern life as they occurred.

ii.

In the last years before 1920, it was still a small town, and its character, as the chronicler first saw it in his youth, was still largely Mexican. His impression was that of many earlier travelers—one-story houses built of adobes scattered about on sandy hillsides the color of sunburned skin. Walls and perspectives did not shut away the great countryside in its immediacy. Wherever he looked up the street he could see mountains rising, and many of the chief streets made him think that they had their origin in water courses cut by mountain freshets. As they prefigured flow, so they led down to the level plaza, which in its first design was the last ordered plan created for the city by its Spanish founders. The plaza was a rectangle, and all its purposes originally were official. Private life began just beyond its limits. How wayward, how independent this was still seemed visible in the twentieth century. If the streets straggled into the hills following the path of water influenced by gravity, they showed in the disposition of their houses how strong was the Spaniard's desire for isolation and privacy.

Only a few streets illustrated the break in native tradition which had come with the conquest and later the ownership of the city by the United States. Palace Avenue was one of these, with its mansions of brick or stucco in the conventional American taste of the late nineteenth century. Saint Vincent's Hospital—enlarged many times since the first efforts of Archbishop Lamy—was a large three-storied building in the heart of town near the cathedral. About the state capitol, with its yellow brick walls and silver-painted dome in the Beaux-Arts manner popular with official architects, other streets lined with red brick houses and white-slatted front porches carried the American accent in building. Public utility plants, brick warehouses, an occasional railroad hotel stood by the tracks of the spur line from Lamy, and proclaimed the technological energy of the Americans which when it went to work in Santa Fe brought more changes in a few decades than the city had ever known before in all its centuries.

But, if the Mexican style still dominated all, even this, by 1920, was not pure and uncomplicated; for the Mexican style had two aspects which in their contrast seemed plain enough. One was that of the old, traditional, unself-conscious Mexican way, with its adobe-enclosed expressions of life unchanged in any essentials for many generations. The other was that of a restored Mexican character, which reflected the hope of new Anglo-American residents that they might save the Latin airs of the city by giving to new gestures in its life the feeling and effect of old ones.

For, as many people of taste and sensibility moved to town in the twentieth century, they were captivated by its flavor, unique in American cities, of a foreign culture showing a tradition unbroken since the seventeenth century. Somehow they must find a medium through which to save the image of that tradition. Their need was answered by the vision and the talent of a group of Santa Fe citizens led in the beginning by Dr. Sylvanus Morley, who worked to bring together the past and the present there in a tactful union of native traditions: the Pueblo Indian, the Spanish, the Mexican, with all their flavor, and the American, with all its technological solutions of efficiency and comfort.

The result was an eclectic style for the building arts in Santa Fe which was a valid expression in its use of native habits of construction. The first creations in what came to be called the "Santa Fe style" of architecture leaned toward the Pueblo Indian manner, and yet this in itself carried historical modifications introduced by the earliest Franciscans in the mission chapels among the Indian towns. Thus the Art Museum (built 1917) in its over-all idiom recalled the Pueblo massing of walls, terraces, and recessions; while the museum auditorium by itself was derived largely from the church of Saint Stephen at Acoma, which was as much Spanish Franciscan as it was Pueblo Indian. The modern statement of such architecture was accepted with admiration by residents and visitors alike, and became the necessary mode of almost all new construction at Santa Fe in the twentieth century.

It was not without its stylistic dangers. One difficulty that accompanied the use of Pueblo Indian styles in building lay in the matter of scale and proportion. A pueblo was made like a hive, to contain and accommodate dozens or hundreds of families. It was, so, a massive concretion of cells grown to meet needs that were cumulated gradually. But all too often a modern house put together in its image seemed to illustrate misplaced emphasis—a single house trying to look like a whole pueblo.

In the 1920's the native style was given a new direction by the architect John Gaw Meem, who had come to Santa Fe as a tubercular invalid and who remained in his recovery to produce a great list of buildings. He was an architectural designer of utmost integrity and an artist of delicate and well-nurtured taste. In his adaptations of the local heritage, he turned increasingly to the Spanish colonial style, which had a lighter grace of line and substance, and yet was as true to the environment as his earlier works in the Indian manner. As the city expanded, its new dwellings and public buildings made increasing use of the gifts which Meem gave to his fellow residents: a sense of harmony with their surroundings, both historical and immediate, and the means of expressing it.

In an unspoken cooperation and agreement about matters of taste and style, the past of Santa Fe was consciously perpetuated by its modern inheritors. The result was the modern city in all the pride of its special character, combining Indian, Spanish, and Mexican ways with American ingenuity.

iii.

Of these living energies it was, even so lately as 1920, primarily the Spanish-American which animated the social atmosphere of the city. The ways of the newcomers were yet only edges on the old Latin substance. The city not only looked Mexican, it felt and acted Mexican, in a natural manner. There was not yet an organized necessity to produce native ways of behavior and style for commercial reasons.

In all its lyric spontaneity and, too, its flaring temper on occasion, the native manner was at large. It was observed with delight by new colonists, whom it must convince that here was the place for them, whether they happened to desire a combination of freedom and the picturesque, or the health of the air, or the splendor of the land. In that town, set in that country, a colonist could be convinced in a few hours, by the simplest symbols and examples.

He would see the black-shawled old women creeping to the cathedral for vespers through a pellucid dusk. He would listen to the sounds of Mexican popular music, yelled by wandering young men in the dark, who in their unself-conscious pleasure gave a rude authority to the songs in all their harmonic poverty of endless thirds, their poison-candy-box sweetness of melody and sentiment, their insinuations of human animality. Late at night he would hear the native dogs of Santa Fe barking across the city's runnels and hills in a dialogue that would end only with the dawn. Someone might tell him of the Penitent Brothers—that order of Latin men who still re-enacted the Passion of Our Lord on its anniversary in Holy Week, practicing self-flagellation and—he hoped with a thrill that it was true—crucifying one of their number at the climax on Good Friday. The charm of manner and physical frankness of the Latin young people must attract him, and so must the dignity and occasional scandalous hilarity of their elders. If he was there in the month of May, the waft of scent from countless lilac bushes sweetened the whole air of the city; and if in the winter, the poignant incense of burning piñon wood. Perhaps he had never seen such brilliance of color in any other land-scape of mountain and plain; never such starlight, trembling so near, or such a moon upon mountains so near and noble.

As Santa Fe was marked by Mexico, so must these seem Mexican also. It was here, in the foreign, the picturesque, in combination with the dazzling properties of land and sky, that the first modern colonists of Santa Fe found what they were looking for.

iv.

They were artists.

Between 1910 and 1920 both Taos and Santa Fe attracted the foundation of artists' colonies. The appeal of both places lay in a striking localism of subject matter and in the landscapist's medium of natural light, which in those high plateaus was so clear and brilliant.

People of sensibility almost always felt powerful reactions

to the atmosphere of the southwest. This was enriched at Santa Fe by the traditions of centuries of social life strong in energy, emotion, and local style. The artists who first discovered Santa Fe in the twentieth century were sure they had found a wholly fresh range of material to be observed and recorded. In the courses of a very few years their paintings gave evidence of the existence of a "School of Santa Fe."

Quantities of pictures appeared year after year, now representing Mexican adobe houses each with its string of bright red chili peppers, or again showing groves of quaking aspen trees yellow in the mountain autumn, or again canyons of pink earth grown with silvery chamiza bushes, or grand thunderheads looming above light-struck deserts, or blue mountains, or old Latin faces runneled by age until the painter must be reminded of brown eroded earth, or combinations of earth forms and light resulting in massive abstractions, or—in a variety of expression—the life of the Pueblo Indian.

In the Pueblo Indian the United States found its last romance with aboriginal America. The Pueblo was the only Indian who lived in a condition unchanged as to essentials since prehistoric times. When the conquering Americans were obliged to segregrate Indians upon government reservations, the Pueblo was spared the indignity, for he had already lived through centuries in his own cellular towns. The government confirmed his ownership of ancestral lands and left him for the most part to his ancestral ways. His character was fixed and his traditions were secure. Much of what he did to place and sustain himself in nature had aspects of formal beauty. Much of his life was strange. The colonial artist could not resist him and his world as subject matter.

So Indians were painted in a profuse variety of heroic contexts, until a kind of pictorial trade slang was established —lone Indian figure in a blanket looming against distant horizon; Indian by firelight; Indian flutist at dusk on top of pueblo; Indian hunting in the snow; Indian pottery-makers at work; Indian weavers weaving; Indian, alone or in group, dancing or drumming in ceremonial. Such local subject matter, of course, was sometimes beautifully handled by artists of superior gifts. The subjects found a wide market.

But nonobjective styles of painting presently came to Santa Fe, as to every settlement of artists, and the famous subject matter which had drawn painters there in the first place now lost some of its point. Painters soon came under the stern necessity to paint what they felt by themselves instead of what they saw more or less in common with less-informed persons; and the landscape, with its social novelties, became a point of departure for pictorial abstractions. Nothing could create more uncertainties than an artistic, a literary, a scientific, or an intellectual fashion. The grand certainty of Santa Fe remained objective—the landscape and its overwhelming quality, which almost amounted to a sufficiency in itself as an aesthetic statement.

The nervous organizations of the natives—Indian and Latin—had withstood centuries of that landscape which to those of Anglo blood and professional sensibility was so vastly affecting. The natives inherited the country and used it in honesty as people who made their lives directly off its yield. Its incidental magnificence remained, for them, incidental. If they wanted anything picturesque they looked anywhere but out of the window.

But the Anglo-colonials coming to the landscape discovered the spirit of the place. However satisfying this might be to personal life, it was not in every case adequate to professional needs. The penalty came when painters themselves confessed in their work that to paint novelty was not enough. Further, to paint abstractions in the face of the local subject matter might be obedient to fashion but was irrelevant to place. The day had to come when a new string of chili peppers, a new aspen tree, another adobe bake oven, a sternly distorted mesa, a prismatically cubed pueblo, an Indian with striped blanket and black and white olla, were received with a groan by cultivated dwellers; and the innocent and honest curiosity of the tourist, so scorned by artistic circles, appeared preferable alongside the search of the artist for something new to paint which brought him to Santa Fe—as if something familiar where he came from were not quite good enough for any creature of talent.

The life of any artistic renaissance in America was brief. It was so with that period of the Santa Fe art colony when discoveries were being made about the local scene in its relation to art, and when on all sides appeared rapturous signs of human emancipation—gentlemen with beards and ladies with velvet blouses and spiritual labels worn by both like scapulars reading Painter, Poet, Lover, Peasant, Decadent.

Yet these ardent workers created a far-reaching influence. By their works and their own particular conventions of living they achieved a new celebrity for Santa Fe. The tourist trade began to grow in response to their images of life there. They, the pioneers, created a mecca for younger artists who came in turn to reinforce the colonial character. The United States was notoriously lacking in societies of artists in all fields. The American artist growing into his vocation had few places where he could go to find himself accounted for as a human being and as a workman among others of his passion and his faith who had already proved themselves. Contact with a living tradition was what he needed and, generally, could not find. Santa Fe after 1915 was able to receive artists in swelling numbers, and—always in rivalry with Taos—to provide a justifying experience for those who otherwise might live without meaning or integration in the society of their country.

So, however might flow the mutations of artistic style in relation to the physical environment of Santa Fe, the population of its artists remained and increased; for in the end they stayed to live there not because of local subject matter but because they had found a way of life for themselves that was rewarding. By their general originality of temperament and their conspicuousness of style, they constituted a new and meaningful strain of citizens in the society of Santa Fe. Between 1915 and, say, 1930, they had more effect

on the social scene than anybody but the Latin population.
The writer took his place in Santa Fe along with the
painter. Men and women of letters came to live there because of the beauty of the natural surroundings and because
of the informal manners of the local society. Of these only
a few worked with success upon themes of New Mexican
life—for example, Witter Bynner in his Indian Earth poems
and such rhapsodies as his *Dance for Rain at Cochiti*; and
Oliver La Farge in his *Laughing Boy*. Miss Willa Cather
never lived long in Santa Fe, but in her brief visits found
the material and the spirit to make her portrait sketch of
Archbishop Lamy in her novel *Death Comes for the Archbishop*. Ruth Laughlin is one of the few literary figures
native to Santa Fe. Her best known works deal with her
city. For the rest, writers at Santa Fe pursuing their work
as novelists, poets, or dramatists usually dealt with ideas
and subjects which they brought with them. Joining with
the painters as citizens, they helped to make a lively effect
upon the old city, especially at the time of the annual fiesta,
when Santa Fe celebrated the reconquest by Captain General
de Vargas and also held carnival for several days in honor of
the modern tourist.

v.

Both the ancient and the modern life of Santa Fe and its
ambiente were brought into a state of high organization
for the entertainment of the tourist. Until World War II,
the tourist trade was the largest annual business of New
Mexico. If there was much to show the tourist, it had to be
made presentable for him in the way of exhibits, natural
or arranged, and his comfort had to be insured through
hotels and transportation and good roads. Efforts in all these
concerns were designed at Santa Fe to bring him face to face
with the leading exhibit of all, which was the Indian.
The traditions of the Pueblo Indian were revived on two
levels, so to speak, and the first contributed greatly to the
second. First of all, the Indian's great buried past was

brought to light through the scientific labors in anthropology and archaeology of such experts as Edgar L. Hewitt, Sylvanus Morley, A. V. Kidder, Lansing Bloom, and Kenneth Chapman. Bandelier's intimations and discoveries were opened out into a comprehensive theory of Indian life, and the great age, dignity, and mystery of this could not fail to interest anybody who heard of it however briefly. The silent cliff cities, the still-living pueblos up and down the valley of the Great River were revealed as important historic possessions of the United States. In consequence, all appropriate forces —federal and state governments, chambers of commerce, the Santa Fe Railroad with its Fred Harvey System—went to work to make the Indian spectacle accessible to the traveling public.

Not only the Indian past was revived; but the Indian present was given new energy. Led by Dr. Hewitt and his associates, the Indians were shown how to revive their ancient arts and crafts. It seemed like a sensitive and generous thing to do—to help the Indian in his process of inevitable acculturation by giving him the means of exhibiting and selling his old skills which had fallen into decline. It was true that things once made wholly for use were now made for sale; and it followed that, in a shift of purpose in their making, something was lost of spirit and quality in the piece of pottery, the silver jewel, the woven blanket, the carved fetish, the worked buckskin which resulted. But the society of which the Indian must one day, however far in the future, became a full member was essentially a commercial society. Was he to be denied his chance along with the rest to make money out of his knacks?

It was a question which agitated many people in Santa Fe, where partisanships were swift to come on any issue, and violent in their sway, and shrill of claim. Champions of the Indian in his tribal integrity complained that if he became a manufacturer of curios, he would soon be a lost soul among his own kind. Others replied that he would be better served if he had a chance to earn a little money to raise his standard of living into closer conformity with that of the white Americans. The reply to this was that before the white Americans did so much about the Indian they would do well to purify the values of their own society.

Controversy even struck the Indian revivalists in their own sphere of duty. At a certain pueblo near Santa Fe where the revival of pottery was a lively success, rivalry sprang up between two Indian craftswomen—some issue over the use of glaze in a certain style. The Indian town was so riven by the affair that hostility divided its two plazas—the North and the South. Here was trouble enough. But Santa Fe sponsors of Indian work now entered the quarrel, and feeling ran as high among cultivated groups in the capital as it did in the Indian town. White Americans fell to fighting over Indians instead of against them. Socially it was an improvement, and, in any case, if prosperity was the goal, this was more or less achieved by the pueblo as travelers increasingly bought its products of native crafts.

The establishment of the Museum of New Mexico with its many branches reflected the growth of interest in Indian life, the Spanish past, and the fine arts at Santa Fe. All the local expressions of culture found their outlet in the lively program of the museum. Exhibits of prehistoric Indian life, including models of excavated Pueblo ruins, told the traveler what he would presently be seeing in actuality. Historical objects from the Spanish period showed him what he could hope to find in modern crafts work in the shops of the city. The historical museum's most impressive and moving exhibit was its own building, for this was the palace of the governors itself, in its fourth century, at the north side of the plaza. There to be seen, if the traveler could see them, were the shadows of other times in Santa Fe. In the painting galleries of the art museum he saw shows by the living artists of Santa Fe, and of all New Mexico, any of whom could have hanging space for the asking, without being subject to standards of selection on the part of museum staff or jury—a practice which could put a brilliant painter like Randall Davey in an alcove next to one occupied by the works of people who assembled collages of dried bark, leaves, grasses, pollen, and other abstract bits of vegetable mold into landscapes popular as souvenirs.

A hundred years ago the end of the trail from Missouri to Santa Fe was marked by a hotel on the plaza called La Fonda. In the 1920's a large and luxurious new hotel of the same name was planned for the same spot by a group of local stockholders. It was designed in the Santa Fe style, to be furnished throughout according to the taste of the Spanish colonial arts and crafts revival. But by themselves the city's investors could not finance such a plan, and the project was saved only when the Fred Harvey Company, which operated many other hotels along the line of the Santa Fe Railroad, took it over. Rather like a major power acquiring a colony, the Harvey Company entered Santa Fe to operate La Fonda in a sort of benevolent despotism as the social center of the capital. It was also the grand station for tours to the Indian country. Indians and tourism became big business in the twentieth century. The Harvey Company maintained fleets of limousines and buses, staffed by couriers trained in knowledge and elocution, to conduct travelers to the pueblos, ruined or living.

Where the Harvey enterprises led, the motoring public of the country followed on their own, as travel by car on constantly improving highways became a national habit between the two world wars. In their hundred thousands, the travelers came every long summer season. Santa Fe after three and a half centuries was still the chief center of communication with the Indian country which the motorist was seeking. Obliged, then, to pass through the capital, he saw that in itself it was an exhibit. He roamed the plaza and the narrow earthen streets. He encountered Indian vendors of pottery, jewelry, blankets. He walked through the cathedral and thought of its builder and perhaps of Miss Cather's story. In the hotel lobby at evening, he saw Indian dancers going through some of their ceremonial steps, accompanied by chant and drum. He was enveloped by the atmosphere of Santa Fe. Imperceptibly, in a process lasting through years, the city had converted its history into an asset of commerce. As such, it was seen by the traveler as a mixture of the true and the contrived, the dignified and the vulgar, the beautiful and the cheap.

No aspect of it showed such mixtures more strongly than the annual fiesta, held in late summer to commemorate the return of De Vargas in 1692. The truest reference to the captain general's real strength could be found in the procession that started in the cathedral on the Sunday evening of the fiesta week, and wound its way by the light of candles borne by marchers all the way to the Cross of the Martyrs on a hill overlooking the city from the north. The business houses of the plaza made a custom of turning out their electric lights during the progress. The city street lamps were dark. At the end of the line always came the Archbishop of Santa Fe, following through candlelighted dusk the tradition and observance of his first great precursor.

For the rest, the fiesta was given over to hilarity, though an historical pageant with figures from the Reconquest was played in a serious tone, and modern Santa Feans of Spanish blood rode in the parade dressed in velvet and armor. Their accouterments looked like imitations of the real thing; they themselves did not look like imitations, even though with touching enthusiasm they subscribed to the commercial good cheer of their Anglo-American fellow citizens. The artist-writer group of the city helped with decorations, firework concerts, and the creation of a great effigy symbolic of gloom and care, which was burned on the opening night of the festivities. People danced in the streets. Indian and Spanish costumes were loyally undertaken by almost everyone. The Santa Fe High School band in a sort of frantically sassy style gave virtuoso performances of Latin tunes. The hotels were overrun. In the season of late summer, the skies were bright as white gold by day and immensely and closely starred by night.

The Indian was not neglected. His dances were offered by selected groups from various pueblos; and in the fiesta parade, his teachers at the United States Indian School sponsored floats on which young Indians rode, smiling and full of pep, wearing varsity sweaters, and sanctioning in innocent good manners the slogans printed on large placards above them. One, showing a vocational machine shop worked by Indian youths with a white man posed as their teacher, read this way: "Papoose want um be Big Chief Machinist." Another, showing a young Indian astride a stuffed bucking horse, read: "Me 'um' enjoy riding Mustang." In the young Indian's acceptance of his conqueror's comic-strip view of him, the conquest was complete.

Older Indians were not lost altogether. Where she sat in the portal of the palace, selling her little rows of painted clay dishes and necklaces of dyed corn, an old Indian woman was addressed by a prosperous Texan who knew the kind of salesmanship that had produced his affluence.

"Now, lissen," he said to her while she kept her sober face unchanged, "you goan have to *smahl* if you goan sell anythin today, you know that?"

When she failed to see him, he shook his finger in her sad old face and went rapidly away. In the summertime, coming for cool weather and the charm of a dried mud city in high altitudes, Texans achieved an illusion of conquering Santa Fe as tourists if so long ago they had failed to conquer it as soldiers or politicians.

vi.

If it was the colorful layers of its society which made Santa Fe prosperous, the administrative job inseparable from prosperity got done by conscientious businessmen who were like businessmen anywhere. They formed a large segment of the local population, and with no claims to creative distinction in any direction they saw to the banking, the shopkeeping, the power supply, and the general order of the city. Most of them were of Anglo-American stock, though a liberal salting of Spanish-Americans gave its complexion to business life, and perhaps especially to politics and government, municipal and state.

The state legislature met in Santa Fe every two years,

from January to March, in regular session. Then from all corners of the immense state came cattlemen and sheep ranchers, businessmen and lawyers, as the elected representatives of the people of New Mexico. Here was always a chance for a particularly developed Latin talent to express itself. Since most legislation was arranged by conference and committee, there was rich opportunity for the use of confidential messengers or go-betweens. With patience and ingenuity men of Spanish blood exercised their hereditary gifts for labyrinthine government every two years at Santa Fe. Their Anglo-American colleagues were more direct about the job. They congregated in hotel lobbies or corridors and blunderbussed their way through political argument, compromise, concession, and agreement. The state capitol was always filled with crowds during the legislative session. Business was conducted with a general air of urgency under pressure. There was much to consider in a very short time.

Since the 1930's one obstacle to speedy conclusion of public business had been removed. This was the use of both Spanish and English in the conduct of legislative debate, with spoken interpretation from one tongue into the other. But—true to its cultural mixture—New Mexico sent many legislators of Spanish blood to the house and senate at Santa Fe, and behind closed doors, in committee rooms, in bars and hotels, Spanish was the language in which much of the public will was expressed on its way to becoming state law in English.

It was curious how little public effect the apparatus of business, both commercial and governmental, had on the general aspect of the city. What showed more plainly were the workings of other stripes of the local society—the strong free character of the artist-writer group, the ageless and unchanging flavor of the Latin heritage, the deeply rooted and quiet presence of the Church, and finally the growing luxury class of colonists who were establishing themselves in the intimate canyons and on the immediate foothills.

Business was allowed to go its humble way of supporting

the convenience of all the other local groups until it might have the misfortune to antagonize one of them by some enterprise of profit or progress. And then it heard all about itself in resounding terms. If, for example, paving and street lighting were proposed by the practical administrators for an old, dark, dusty, or muddy street lately come into use as a main traffic lane, swift objection was sure to rise from those who had come to Santa Fe to escape modern progress. Controversy flourished in Santa Fe, engendered by the presence together of so many egocentric individuals and the many contrasting groups in which they found an approximation of identity. Outcry and all its ingredients of gossip, slander, scandal, and satisfying self-expression seemed a natural right of the emancipated citizen of Santa Fe. The climate—the altitude—appeared to increase the capacity for emotional discussion of all issues, private or public, until they became common news. To an uncommon degree, free opinion not only set the tone but actually accomplished the corporate work of life in Santa Fe.

vii.

World War II was a sort of historical divide or watershed in the growth of modern New Mexico. Its effects were immediate and—it would appear—permanent in Santa Fe.

For, by a decision of national policy, Santa Fe suddenly had a new neighbor in the city of Los Alamos, thirty miles away. It was a mushroom city, built from zero, on an ancient and famous mesa where previously had stood only a well-regarded school for boys. The site was compatible with the government's need for total security in its development of nuclear fission experiments for the purpose of creating the atom bomb as a weapon to be used in the war. In a matter of months the laboratory city on the mesa had grown to a population of many thousands, some of whom lived in newly built quarters there. But a great number of the Los Alamos population of scientists, technicians, and workers had to find houses elsewhere. Santa Fe was the nearest city. It was about doubled in size to a population of 30,000 in response to the social needs created by the war and afterward sustained. Before this time, colonists had come to find their places, if not always in an orderly fashion, still in an individual gesture which the old city could absorb with little shock. Now the new society came en masse, bringing with it the color and style of any general cross section of American life from the well-salaried levels of industry, administration, government, and university. What must become of the rarity of Santa Fe, the flavors of its many clearly defined traditions, the unique and incomparable values of air and scene that had always impressed arriving travelers?

As the city had taken the shocks of 1821, 1846, and 1862, she took the latest one. All the processes making their way slowly along before the war were now pushed rapidly ahead in their ordained directions by the war's demand of great, sudden, impersonal growth. For a long time the Mexican tradition had been turning from something thoughtless and real into something modified by commerce; and now it swiftly became still more commercial. The tourist value of the Indian gained even more in notoriety and attraction through the sudden expansion of its local public, as it were. The luxury hotel at the end of the Missouri trail was now too small and had to be doubled in size by the addition of a new wing erected on property in Cathedral Place purchased from the archdiocese. The artist-writer group was a third of a century old as an institution, however its individual members might vary in age; and, if its first radiant days of originality and discovery were long spent, the group continued to attract new recruits who, compared with their forerunners, came quietly.

Business, legislation, the technology of running a city, faced with new problems and imperative demands to supply utilities and keep order in a period of frantic growth, now had their way. New streets, power lines, pavements, parking meters, and other signs of modern civic amenity appeared amid the foothills at the end of Santa Fe Plain. With World War II a new industry came to displace the tourist trade as New Mexico's leading business. It was the whole complex of activities operated by the federal government of the United States. The money it poured into the state through construction, maintenance, and salaries made possible in many a New Mexican city the achievement of municipal improvement on a scale never before expected there. For the first time in its history, Santa Fe gave signs of general prosperity, and even, in a certain expanding part of its population, of wealth.

viii.

It was imported wealth, for the most part.

The migration to Santa Fe of people of leisure began before World War II, and increased in numbers and pace after it. Some of them stayed the year round; some "divided their time" between Santa Fe and other backgrounds. Many of those who came to live built Spanish Colonial houses of much beauty, or took ancient Mexican houses and with fine effect converted them into dwellings in which every luxury and rarity of furnishing took its place comfortably against old plain walls of plastered adobe. A new accent of living—the accent of high fashion—came to Santa Fe. The population in its various interests throughout its history had always seemed very knowing. The city had always been, not only a political capital, but a center of opinion and an example of style. Now, with the increasing drift of a luxury class into town, the airs of national, and even international, chic began to tell in the local scene.

Santa Fe became one of those subcapitals of the world's fashion, a city special in character, known by "everyone"— a designation meaning a small segment of the world's people who were famous for their riches, or talents, or style, or beauty, or wit, or all these together. By the mid-twentieth century "everyone" had been to Santa Fe or had heard of it, as in various times "everyone" had been familiar with Biarritz, or Palma de Mallorca, or the Lido, or Juan-les-Pins, or Prades. Superimposed on the old Mexican tradition, and the solid commercial and administrative structure, and the artistic factions of town, this luxurious element even with all its inner diversities showed a collective knack for the glittering and the conspicuous in its social life. The older sections of the local society accommodated it with a resilience that had survived many historical changes. A local newspaperman caught the spirit of Santa Fe in its social laminations: "Everybody wishes the Joneses well; nobody worries about keeping up with them." Santa Fe remained true to its tradition of tolerance. With more disparities and contrasts among its citizens than most small cities could show, it yet granted them coexistence harmonious to a high degree.

It was always difficult to fix upon the particular stimulus amid all the general charms which had most to do with bringing modern colonists to town. Some spoke of the altitude, with its bracing effect; others of the air, the light, the color all about. Yet beyond these something else could be felt. It was an insinuation of freedom in behavior, not in any publicly unsavory terms, but rather in an opportunity for an individual man or woman to live a life of free expression. In modern times, was this the most significant—and perhaps the most Latin—of attractions about Santa Fe?

For if the Mexican, and his Spanish ancestor, had an elaborate code of convention by which to live, it was often a mere formality which could be referred to when dignity called, but which need not otherwise limit the expression of individual life in its liveliest fancies. Throughout centuries the citizens of Santa Fe had expressed their individual natures with fiery emotion that was on occasion the despair of government. Conquered and colonized by a Puritanical invader, the Mexican energy could only subside. But it must take a long time for the subsidence to be complete; and, meanwhile, enough of the old Latin flair for independence of behavior was left to serve as an invitation to men and women in search of social freedom.

They were those who to be happy must feel free to enact in public their private image of themselves if it differed from the image required by conventional society. The early American frontier made more allowance for such an impulse than the modern nation. The frontiersman, the mountain

man, was almost officially an eccentric. The American faith
postulated equality—and liberty. If equality tended to make
an anonymous crowd, then liberty must include the guarantee that the individual should be free to make himself stand
forth from the crowd if he wanted to, like the man whom
Audubon saw on the levee in New Orleans acting out for
his own satisfaction a one-man drama. His right to create a
spectacle was sanctioned by his fellows. It was not entirely
plain what he strove to represent, but that it was wonderfully
odd was clear. He was dressed in a great-brimmed hat, a
green coat, yellow nankeen pantaloons, a pink vest, and a
fancy shirt. A live baby alligator nested in a bunch of
magnolias on his breast. He carried a loud silk umbrella
and a cage of birds. He ranged through the riverside throng
singing in Scotch dialect. When he talked, his speech was
American. There were few places in modern America where
he would have felt at home. Santa Fe was one—perhaps the
only one.

It was a haven for free souls in almost any incarnation
imaginable. Some were described as "rich Greenwich Vil-
lagers," others as "high-level D.P.'s." The complicated nervous organization required for creation in the arts—a
condition to which human history owes many of its most-
treasured achievements—was often found in a type of man
or woman called "a sensitive" in the jargon of Santa Fe.
To the unimaginative observer, the appearance and behavior of such people often suggested that they were occupied with affectations, trivialities, self-dramatized missions.
In truth, they were more often than not, to whatever degree
their talents allowed, committed to the lonely and difficult
task of searching out fundamental human values.

In some cases the visible ravages of the vocation were more
comic than impressive—educated women reverting consciously to peasant attitudes in their search to feel and to
know the essential womanhood which most women elsewhere seemed able to take for granted in themselves; men
of the arts complicating the cultivation of the artist's pure
vision with intellectual theory; Easterners dressing up in

rodeo clothes and so helping the process of making the West "western" by making it self-consciously regional; non-native women in stage make-up of heavy sunburn and adaptations of Indian dress, such as one seen on a summer day, in the lobby of La Fonda.

She wore a squaw-bang haircut with braids hanging down to her waist. Her blouse was loosely fitted and covered with brightly embroidered flowers. Her skirt was the long, fully pleated skirt of the Navajo woman. Many strands of Navajo silver beads hung about her neck, and looped earrings of turquoise wampum dangled to her shoulders. On her feet were moccasins solidly covered with sparkling sequins. Her fingernails were painted to resemble mother of pearl. A cigarette thickened by lipstick was held shoulder high in one hand and in the other was flashed a gold cigarette case with a monogram in diamonds or brilliants. Moving against the robust background of the Santa Fe Rotary Club on its collective way into lunch, her apparition was one which Audubon would have recorded. The private drama which she was enacting with unintended comic effect was that of a woman enlarging beyond tact the arts and lures of feminine sexuality.

ix.

Among the twentieth century colonists of Santa Fe were always those who dramatized their own moral emancipation. They descended upon the city with visible attributes of fashion and knowledgeability and soon found the group to which their gifts accredited them, whether in the arts or the rituals of well-to-do society. They adopted those local airs in dress and style of living which were picturesque and, in their usages, relieved of convention. Conspicuous not so much by their number as by their intensity, they sometimes eclipsed the traveler's view of the general human scene.

These immigrants showed in their attitudes and airs that they had come in search of something. If they were in search of freedom and peace, like many another, here the hint was strong that the terms were sexual and egocentric.

Not able, for whatever inner or outer reason, to get along at home elsewhere—in marriage, business, or society—how well did they get along in the new place of freedom and peace? The idling, the drinking, the philandering that they proclaimed gave signs of continued unrest. If they came for license they found it no more happy than law.

Their make-up of sunburn, real or cosmetic, induced a spurious health—reassurance from without. Their quests for expression however exotic were so patent as to be at times embarrassing, like a re-enacted dream. They presented an open conspiracy of hedonism. The girls and women displayed a hard, predacious animality that recalled the vision of womanhood seen in movies. It was a burlesque of freedom and as a spectacle it was an invasion of that reticence of vision which any beholder had a right to own undisturbed. The men all too often impersonated something—art, cowmanship, literature, the well-connected remittance man. Yet their public hunger for an allowed conventionality, if it was a bore to some observers, was to others an occasion for an act of charity in their thoughts.

So again Santa Fe with its long tradition of sanctuary showed that there could be accommodation for citizens of any character so long as they did not affront more than public amusement at harmless nonconformity.

All this produced an animation in occasions and events that seemed to belong especially to Santa Fe, where social news had a particular electricity to it. Speed, shock, and the impact of incredible fact about local residents ruled conversation, especially at lunchtime in the various restaurants of La Fonda, where during the season tables were always at a premium. There the opinion-makers of Santa Fe looked to see who had just arrived in town, and who was with whom, and what for, and at a guess for how long; until it seemed that works, in a community of art-committed people, had been sacrificed to relationships, as if to prove that the only way to transcend incandescent mountains and skies lay, not in long hard work with pigment or word, but in the immediate soul-purging medium of gossip: outcry: havoc.

Such humors were fugitive.

Behind them rested the lives and works of Santa Fe in all the variety of their enduring traditions from longer ago.

EPILOGUE:

PAST AND
PRESENT

XI

The Survivals

i.

FOR MANY ASPECTS—great or small—of modern Santa Fe
bear survivals of the old city's earlier periods of significant
change. They can be read back through historical time, until
the sense of unity and the claims of tradition are satisfied
by a design which returns to make its end where it found
its beginning.

ii.

In the late nineteenth century, when the doctor of medicine came to New Mexico, he was the prophet of a movement in medical therapy. Santa Fe—with other Southwestern
cities—became famous for the benefit of its climate in
treating tuberculosis. For a time the population of "health-
seekers" contributed more than any other group to the
prosperity and fame of the city. Even if other groups of colo-

nists later eclipsed them, and if sanatorium life disappeared from the scene, a great number of patients still come for the benefits of the climate in Santa Fe, which the doctor in his time first administered.

In his time, too, the work of Adolph Bandelier in the study of Indian life led directly to the opening of public interest in the prehistoric Indians and their living descendants. The complex and lucrative tourist commerce of today grew out of the work, performed to achieve other ends, of Bandelier and his scholarly successors, such as Hewitt, Kidder, Bloom, and Chapman. Perhaps a more fitting monument to their labors is the Museum of New Mexico, with its many departments. The historical archives of the Museum owe much to their first serious reader, Bandelier himself, and to Governor Lew Wallace, who saved what he could of the collection of documents already scattered, lost, or sold by his predecessors.

iii.

From the lifetime of the German bride of 1870 Santa Fe still knows influences. Her own social effect, with its imported graces and charms, has its echo in many houses there today. The business world of her husband has its direct descendants in many firms still flourishing. When Governor Wallace for his own interest and pleasure made drawings of what he saw about him in New Mexico, he became the prototype of hundreds of artists to follow.

The sense of Archbishop Lamy and all his works still reaches over Santa Fe today like a blessing. The religion which he restored in New Mexico retains its dignity and humble universality. Every school, public or private, is the heir of his energetic faith in education; for he was the first to found academies and colleges, and he was a sponsor and then an overseer of the first public school system in the state. Hospitals and asylums today reflect his own gestures of mercy and charity—the first to reach all people at Santa Fe. His love of his city and the monuments of its own past survives in most moving form in the old palace of the governors—for, one time when progressive-minded citizens were talking of demolishing the palace to make room for something more modern, the archbishop protested, and by his influence aroused others to defend and save the old building. When he led the movement to bring the railroad to town he sponsored the coming of all the machinery of modern civilization. But first of all he owned and shared a civility of heart which—who knows to what degree?—may have given the modern city its tradition of hospitality to so many kinds of human interest.

iv.

From the invasion of 1846, when the young United States lieutenant came to town as a conqueror, the whole power and accent of the United States in its ownership of Santa Fe reaches into today. Many a man since has come to be cured of his ills, has stayed to survive them, and has enriched the blessed place of his recovery by his mature work. He married the culture of his new land, figuratively and, in many cases, literally, like the lieutenant himself. Many of the great Spanish and Mexican families of Santa Fe are linked in marriage and business with Anglo-Americans.

v.

The Missouri trader of 1821 released several traditions for later times. He was one of the earliest men of enterprise— though a curiously prim one—to bring to Santa Fe the "commerce of the prairies," in the phrase of Josiah Gregg, whom he most resembled in type. Santa Fe had its birth as a "new emporium" in his time, when the old sleepy commerce of the Spaniards and Mexicans that had faced south for centuries turned suddenly to face eastward toward the energetic United States. All of Santa Fe's subsequent history and much of its present character bears the marks of this development.

The trader was one of the first travelers to make close observations about what he saw in Santa Fe and—like so many to follow him into today—to write and publish a book about it. Much of what he recorded could be applied to his city now—florid politics in the manner of that Governor Armijo whom he watched with fastidious fascination, and a certain laxity in social behavior which though it shocked him seemed to be taken with a shrug by the residents. Finally, like some modern literary travelers, though drawn to Santa Fe, he was evidently unable to remain there for long. But, so long as he was able, he always returned.

vi.

From the example and power of the matriarch of the eighteenth century, the Latin-American family of Santa Fe today takes its character. Perhaps the family is still as poor as it would have been in her day. Perhaps its children have less opportunity than the economically more privileged children of the Anglo-American colonists. Perhaps the degree and quality of education in the family do not always seem impressive. No matter. Through the power of the mother, even in a patronal society, the native intelligence, shrewdness, and relative indifference to material things as measures of human worth, the matriarch survives. Her power is not emphasized; it merely continues, like a stream from a source unending.

She is visible in every Spanish-American woman taking her way to mass in her black rebozo, a nameless being made invincible by faith. The unassailable dignity of that possession is the legacy above all others which the matriarch and her people pass on through the generations. It is a dignity that permits them, when in modern times they are dispossessed by newcomers of their old place as owners of the city and all its kingdom, to be unaware of their dispossession. In a superb indifference to any essential change the matriarch's descendants conduct themselves as though Santa Fe still belonged to them. And it does—though not to them alone, for as good citizens of the United States, they own the city jointly with the successors of their conquerors of a century ago. The matriarch disapproved of change; her heirs often seem not to notice it before their eyes.

vii.

If Santa Fe ever knew glory, it was in the time of the alderman of 1691, and its champion was the Captain General de Vargas. It was essentially a glory of character, and the character was the captain general's. His memory is a proud possession today. It moves those who remember his story as they walk about his capital. He is the grand example of a true public servant. As pacifier of the Pueblo Indians he left a great gift both to them and to his own people. It was peace of the same sort as that which prevails today between the Indian people in their ancient ways and the modern owners of the once royal city.

viii.

In the time of the bannerman, Santa Fe earned its first battle wounds, of which the city, the kingdom, nearly died in 1680. Retreating to El Paso before the fury of the Pueblo rebellion, the colony time and again threatened to dissolve. But certain members within, and certain officials far away in Mexico, refused to permit the northern capital to vanish. The colony lost at El Paso made its way home again up the Great River to re-establish its capital city. Throughout its whole chronicle Santa Fe, as a corporation of society, has encountered periods of abrupt change; and through tenacity has always survived.

The shocks of the twentieth century—social, artistic, political, industrial—may not be comparable with those earlier challenges that threatened the very life of the city; but they have been met, and with grace.

ix.

The father president of 1635 still walks in Santa Fe in the person of any Franciscan priest now stationed there. A recent archbishop of Santa Fe was a Franciscan. Friars of his order are at work all over New Mexico as parish priests and missioners. When occasion demands, they enlarge their duties to include publicly the task of social critic, like the father president when he raged against the governors for their mistreatment of Indians long ago. Such action is no more popular now with worldly men than it was then. But the point of view of the friars remains a fixed one. They have always left it to truth to prevail.

In much of the adaptation of Indian architecture to modern uses, the ingenuity of the father president and his early brothers is reflected. Indians could build little rooms well enough; but the friars required very large ones for their churches. Adapting Indian methods and materials and refining these with his own knowledge, the mission friar created a style which is repeated today in many new churches and public buildings. What the father president built, he considered necessary and useful. It is doubtful whether he regarded his result as having beauty. But beauty has been found in it today, and later builders have meant to perpetuate it in new examples of the style born of the friar's purpose and his own belief in it.

x.

The young royal notary coming to the dark little capital in 1620 to serve his exile brings to mind the adventure of any fallible heart beating its way through any beginning.

Every day at Santa Fe seems like a beginning, so fresh the strike of breath in that air, so clear the endowment of sight in that light. The royal notary's gesture was the common one of man giving his work, duty, and, when needed, his life to the land.

It remains as the all-enclosing image beyond histories and passions—the land of Santa Fe Plain, where, in days long before the arrival of the first royal Spaniards, Indians met the Sun on his dancing ground.

THE END

BIBLIOGRAPHY

BIBLIOGRAPHY

All source materials, whether published or unpublished, primary sources, general works, periodicals, or drawings, are here grouped in a single alphabet.

ADAMS, ELEANOR B. "Bishop Tamarón's Visitation of New Mexico in 1760, *New Mexico Historical Review.*

ALEXANDER, HARTLEY BURR. *North American (Mythology)* Vol. 10, *Mythology of All Races,* Louis Herbert Gray, ed. Boston: Marshall Jones Co., 1915.

ALTAMIRA Y CREVEA, RAFAEL. *A History of Spain from the Beginnings to the Present Day,* Translated by Muna Lee. New York: D. Van Nostrand Co., 1949.

ARMIJO, MANUEL. *Decrees.* Ms., Santa Fe, New Mexico, Historical Society, Museum of New Mexico. (Excerpts quoted by permission of Museum of New Mexico.)

—— *Letter to General Kearny, Written in Apache Canyon, August 16, 1846.* Original document. Henry E. Huntington Library, San Marino, Calif.

ARNY, F. M., *et al. Centennial Celebration . . . July 4, 1876.* Santa Fe: Williams and Shaw, 1876.

BANCROFT, HUBERT HOWE. *History of the North Mexican States and Texas.* 2 vols. San Francisco: A. L. Bancroft and Co., 1884.

BANDELIER, ADOLPH F. A. *The Delight Makers.* With an introduction by Charles F. Lummis. New York: Dodd, Mead and Co., 1916.

—— *Diaries, 1880-1890.* 10 vols. Ms., Santa Fe, Museum of New Mexico. (Excerpts quoted by permission of Museum of New Mexico.)

—— *Final Report of Investigations among Indians of the Southwestern United States, Carried on Mainly in the*

Years from 1880 to 1885. Part II. Papers of the Archaeological Institute of America. American series, IV. Cambridge: John Wilson and Sons, University Press, 1892.

——— *Hemenway Southwestern Expedition: Contributions to the History of the Southwestern Portion of the United States.* Archaeological Institute of America, American series, V. Cambridge: John Wilson and Son, 1899.

——— *Historical Documents Relating to New Mexico, Nueva Vizcaya, and Approaches Thereto, to 1773.* Collected by Adolph F. A. Bandelier and Fanny R. Bandelier. 3 vols. Edited . . . by Charles Wilson Hackett, Washington, D.C.: Carnegie Institution, 1923.

——— *Historical Introduction to Studies among the Sedentary Indians of New Mexico.* (In *Papers of the Archaeological Institute of America, American Series,* 1.) Boston: A. Williams and Co., 1881.

——— and EDGAR F. HEWITT. *Indians of the Rio Grande Valley.* Albuquerque: University of New Mexico Press, 1937.

BENAVIDES, ALONSO DE. *Fray Alonso de Benavides' Revised Memorial of 1634.* . . . Edited by Frederick Webb Hodge, George P. Hammond, and Agapito Rey. Albuquerque: University of New Mexico Press, 1945.

BENNETT, JAMES A. *Forts and Forays: A Dragoon in New Mexico, 1850-1856.* Edited by Clinton E. Brooks and Frank D. Reeves. Albuquerque: University of New Mexico Press, 1948.

BENT, CHARLES. *Letters, 1839-1846.* Ms., Santa Fe, Museum of New Mexico, Read Collection. (Excerpt quoted by permission of Museum of New Mexico.)

BLACKMORE, WILLIAM. *Diary.* Ms., Santa Fe, Museum of New Mexico.

CARROLL, H. BAILEY. *The Texan Santa Fe Trail.* Canyon, Texas: Panhandle-Plains Historical Society, 1951.

CHAVEZ, ANGELICO. "First Santa Fe Fiesta Council, 1712," *New Mexico Historical Review.*

——— *Our Lady of the Conquest.* Santa Fe: Historical Society of New Mexico, 1948.

CLELAND, ROBERT GLASS. *This Reckless Breed of Men, the Trappers and Fur Traders of the Southwest.* New York: Alfred A. Knopf, 1950.

CONNELLEY, HENRY. *Proclamation,* 9 September 1861. Santa

Fe: New Mexico Historical Society, Museum of New Mexico. (Excerpt quoted by permission of Museum of New Mexico.)

CONNELLEY, WILLIAM E. *Doniphan's Expedition.* Topeka: Crane and Co., 1907.

COOKE, PHILIP ST. GEORGE. *Conquest of New Mexico and California, an Historical and Personal Narrative.* New York: G. P. Putnam's Sons, 1878.

CRANE, LEO. *Desert Drums, the Pueblo Indians of New Mexico, 1540-1928.* Boston: Little, Brown and Co., 1928.

CREMONY, JOHN C. *Life among the Apaches.* Tucson: Arizona Silhouettes, 1951.

DEFOURI, JAMES H. *Historical Sketch of the Catholic Church in New Mexico.* San Francisco: McCormick Brothers, Printers, 1887.

DICKEY, ROLAND F. *New Mexico Village Arts.* Drawings by Lloyd Lozes Goff. Albuquerque: University of New Mexico Press, 1949.

. . . . . *El Palacio.* Santa Fe. v. 29; v. 31.

EMORY, WILLIAM H. *Notes of a Military Reconnaissance.* With introduction and notes by Ross Calvin. Albuquerque: University of New Mexico Press, 1951.

FALCONER, THOMAS. *Letters and Notes on the Texan-Santa Fe Expedition, 1841-1842.* . . . With introduction and notes by F. W. Hodge. New York: Dauber and Pine Bookshops, 1930.

FULTON, MAURICE GARLAND. *New Mexico's Own Chronicle, Three Races in the Writings of Four Hundred Years.* Adapted and edited by Maurice Garland Fulton and Paul Horgan. Dallas: Banks Upshaw and Co., 1937.

GARRARD, LEWIS H. *Wah-to-yah and the Taos Trail.* Edited by Ralph P. Bieber. Glendale: Arthur H. Clark Co., 1934.

GIBSON, GEORGE RUTLEDGE. *Journal of a Soldier under Kearny and Doniphan, 1846-1847.* Edited by Ralph P. Bieber. Glendale: Arthur H. Clark Co., 1935.

GOULDING, WILLIAM R. *Journal of the Expedition of the Knickerbocker Exploring Company of the City of New York from Fort Smith Overland to California. March 10 to September 18, 1849.* Ms., New Haven, Yale University Library, Coe Collection. (Excerpt quoted by permission of Yale University Library.)

GREGG, JOSIAH. *Commerce of the Prairies.* Edited by Max L. Moorhead. Norman: University of Oklahoma Press, 1954.

HACKETT, CHARLES WILSON. *Revolt of the Pueblo Indians of New Mexico and Otermin's Attempted Reconquest, 1680-1692.* Introduction and annotations by Charles Wilson Hackett. Translations of original documents by Charmion Clair Shelby. 2 vols. Albuquerque: University of New Mexico Press, 1942.

HAMMOND, GEORGE P. *Narratives of the Coronado Expedition, 1540-1542.* Edited and annotated by George P. Hammond and Agapito Rey. Albuquerque: University of New Mexico Press, 1940.

—— *Don Juan de Oñate, Colonizer of New Mexico, 1595-1628.* Edited and annotated by George P. Hammond and Agapito Rey. 2 vols. Albuquerque: University of New Mexico Press, 1953.

HANKE, LEWIS. *The First Social Experiments in America, a Study in the Development of Spanish Indian Policy in the 16th Century.* Cambridge: Harvard University Press, 1935.

—— *Spanish Struggle for Justice in the Conquest of America.* Philadelphia: University of Pennsylvania Press, 1949.

HERODOTUS. *Histories.* Book VIII. With an English translation by A. D. Godley. Loeb Classical Library. London: William Heinemann, 1921.

HEWITT, EDGAR L. *Ancient Life in the American Southwest.* Indianapolis: Bobbs-Merrill Co., 1930.

—— and BERTHA P. DUTTON. *The Pueblo Indian World.* . . . Albuquerque: University of New Mexico Press; Santa Fe: School of American Research, 1945.

HOLLISTER, OVANDO J. *Boldly They Rode, a History of the First Colorado Regiment of Volunteers.* With an introduction by William McCleod Raine. Lakewood, Colorado: The Golden Press, 1949.

HORGAN, PAUL. *Great River, the Rio Grande in North American History.* 2 vols. New York: Rinehart and Co., Inc., 1954.

HOWLETT, W. J. *Life of the Right Reverend Joseph P. Macheboeuf, D.D.* Pueblo, Colorado: 1908.

HUGHES, JOHN TAYLOR. "Diary," in *Doniphan's Expedition,* by Connelley. Topeka: Crane and Co., 1907.

HULBERT, ARCHER BUTLER. *Southwest on the Turquoise Trail; the First Diaries on the Road to Santa Fe.* Denver and Colorado Springs: Stewart Commission of Colorado College and the Denver Public Library, 1933.

JAMES, THOMAS. *Three Years among the Indians and Mexicans.* Edited by Walter B. Douglas. Saint Louis: Missouri Historical Society, 1916.

JONES, HESTER. *El Palacio.* v. 38.

KELEHER, WILLIAM A. *Turmoil in New Mexico. 1846-1868.* Santa Fe: The Rydal Press, 1952.

KENDALL, GEORGE WILKINS. *Narrative of the Texan Santa Fe Expedition.* . . . 2 vols. Facsimile reproduction of the original edition. Austin: The Steck Co., 1935.

KUBLER, GEORGE A. *The Religious Architecture of New Mexico in the Colonial Period and Since the American Occupation.* Colorado Springs: The Taylor Museum, 1940.

LAMY, MOTHER FRANCISCA. "Letter, Santa Fe, 15 February, 1888," *La Semaine Religieuse,* 1888, Diocese of Clermont-Ferrand, Puy-de-Dôme, France.

MAGOFFIN, SUSAN SHELBY. *Down the Santa Fe Trail and into Mexico, 1846-1847.* Edited by Stella M. Drumm. New Haven: Yale University Press, 1926.

MELINE, JAMES F. *Two Thousand Miles on Horseback, Santa Fe and Back.* New York: Hurd and Houghton, 1867.

New Mexico Historical Society. Museum of New Mexico. *Aguilar papers.* Ms. (Excerpt quoted by permission of Museum of New Mexico.)

―――― *Archives, Spanish period.* Twitchell Collection. Ms.: numbers 2, 7, 13, 17, 20, 26, 31, 36, 44, 48, 57, 63, 88, 94, 113, 117, 131, 132, 141, 154, 157, 169, 177, 179, 186, 193, 197, 205, 215, 220, 221, 240, 246, 252, 267, 275, 279, 280, 331, 336, 351, 353, 358, 376, 400, 472, 476, 481, 513, 514, 521, 526, 530, 550, 559, 598, 618, 622, 626, 636, 646, 647, 675, 711, 714, 756, 758, 771, 776, 780, 793, 816, 817, 818, 857, 882, 919, 938, 987, 1027, 1052, 1055, 1085, 1093G, 1094, 1097, 1098, 1099, 1102, 1105, 1106, 1110, 1118, 1120, 1148, 1149, 1159, 1191, 1198, 1230, 1232A, 1233, 1238, 1250, 1255, 1258, 1260, 1262, 1272, 1273, 1311, 1313, 1314, 1328, 1334, 1335, 1337, 1340, 1342, 1376, 1384, 1386, 1712, 1730, 2366. (Excerpts quoted by permission of Museum of New Mexico.)

New Mexico Historical Society. *Bustamente papers.* Ms. (Excerpts quoted by permission of Museum of New Mexico.)

―――― *Chacon papers,* numbers 1712, 1730.

―――― *Read collection (Charles Bent letters).*

. . . . . *Niles National Register,* Dec. 4, 1841.

Old Santa Fe Association, Inc. *North Side of the Ancient Plaza, Santa Fe.* 1948.

PATTIE, JAMES O. *Personal Narrative of James O. Pattie of Kentucky.* Edited by Reuben Gold Thwaites. Cleveland: Arthur H. Clark Co., 1905.

PHILIBERT, SISTER M. *A Miraculous Staircase in a Mechanical Age.* Santa Fe: Schifani Brothers Printing Co., 10th ed., 1952.

PIKE, ZEBULON MONTGOMERY. *The Expeditions of Zebulon Montgomery Pike . . . during the Years 1805-6-7.* Edited by Elliott Coues. 3 vols. New York: Francis P. Harper, 1895.

PINO, PEDRO BAUTISTA, *et al. Three New Mexican Chronicles.* . . . Translated with introduction and notes by H. Bailey Carroll and J. Villasana Haggard. Albuquerque: The Quivira Society, 1942.

PRATT, ORVILLE C. *Diary of an Overland Journey from Fort Leavenworth to Los Angeles, June 9 to October 25, 1848.* Ms., New Haven, Yale University Library, Coe Collection. (Excerpts quoted by permission of Yale University Library.)

READ, BENJAMIN N. *Illustrated History of New Mexico.* Santa Fe: New Mexican Printing Co., c. 1912.

RIDEING, WILLIAM H. *A-saddle in the Wild West.* . . . New York: Appleton, 1879.

RITCH, WILLIAM GILLET. *Article Addressed to the Editor, New York Herald, Concerning Establishment of Archbishopric of Santa Fe, June 21, 1875.* Ms., Henry E. Huntington Library, San Marino, Calif. (Excerpt quoted by permission of the Huntington Library.)

SALPOINTE, JEAN BAPTISTE. *Soldiers of the Cross. Notes on the Ecclesiastical History of New Mexico, Arizona and Colorado.* Banning, California: St. Boniface's Industrial School, 1898.

. . . . . Santa Fe *Daily New Mexican. 1868:* July 14; *1872:* August 22, 29, 30; September 6, 7, 19, 20; October 16, 18, 23, 28, 31; November 4, 5, 22; December 9, 14, 20; *1873:* August 13; *1874:* December 7; *1918:* July 15.

. . . . . Santa Fe *Weekly Gazette*. *1866:* July 28; October 20, 27.

SCHLAGINTWEIT, ROBERT VON. *Die Santa Fe und Südpacificbahn in Nordamerika*. Köln, Edvard Heinrich Mayer, 1884.

SMITH, WILLIAM A. *Diary: 1865-1866*. Ms., Santa Fe, New Mexico Historical Society, Museum of New Mexico. (Excerpt quoted by permission of Museum of New Mexico.)

TELLER, WOOLSEY. *The Santa Fe Trail to California. Letters of Woolsey Teller Written on the Trail and in California in Description of His Trip Across the Plains and in the New Eldorado*. Ms., New Haven, Yale University Library, Coe Collection. (Excerpts quoted by permission of Yale University Library.)

TERRA, HELMUT DE. *Humboldt: The Life and Times of Alexander von Humboldt, 1769-1859*. New York: Alfred A. Knopf, 1955.

THOMAS, ALFRED B. *The Plains Indians and New Mexico, 1751-1778*. Albuquerque: University of New Mexico Press, 1940.

TWITCHELL, RALPH EMERSON. *The Leading Facts of New Mexican History*. 2 vols. Cedar Rapids: The Torch Press, 1911.

—— *Old Santa Fe, the Story of New Mexico's Ancient Capital*. Santa Fe: New Mexican Publishing Corp., 1925.

—— *The Spanish Archives of New Mexico*. 2 vols. Cedar Rapids: The Torch Press, 1914.

VARGAS ZAPATA LUJÁN PONCE DE LÉON, DIEGO DE. *First Expedition of Vargas into New Mexico, 1692*. Translated, with introduction and notes, by J. Manuel Espinosa. Albuquerque: University of New Mexico Press, 1940.

VIGIL, DONACIANO. *Speech Made before New Mexico Assembly, May 16, 1846*. Original document. Henry E. Huntington Library, San Marino, Calif.

—— *Speech Made before New Mexico Assembly, June 22, 1846*. Original document. Henry E. Huntington Library, San Marino, Calif.

VIGIL Y ALARID, JUAN BAUTISTA. *Proclamation by Acting Governor Vigil y Alarid, Santa Fe, August 1846, to the Citizens of Santa Fe*. Original document. Henry E. Huntington Library, San Marino, Calif.

WALDRIP, WILLIAM I. "New Mexico during the Civil War," *New Mexico Historical Review*, XXVIII, No. 3 (July 1953).

WALLACE, LEW. *Drawings*. (Photostats.) Santa Fe, Museum of New Mexico.

WALLACE, SUSAN E. "Among the Pueblos." *Atlantic Monthly,* LXVI (1880), August.

WARNER, LOUIS H. *Archbishop Lamy, an Epoch Maker.* Santa Fe: New Mexican Publishing Corp., 1936.

WEBB, JAMES JOSIAH. *Adventures in the Santa Fe Trade, 1844-1847.* Edited by Ralph P. Bieber. Glendale: Arthur H. Clark Co., 1931.

. . . . . *Weekly New Mexican Review,* February 16, 1888.

WHITFORD, WILLIAM CLARKE. *Colorado Volunteers in the Civil War; the New Mexico Campaign of 1862.* Denver: The State Historical and Natural History Society, 1906.

WHITMORE, JAMES E. *Diaries, 1860-61.* Ms., Santa Fe, New Mexico Historical Society, Museum of New Mexico. (Excerpts published by permission of Museum of New Mexico.)

INDEX

INDEX

Abiquiu, 105
Acapulco, 114
Acoma, and people, 289, 312
adobe, 14, 122, 131, 290, 310, 311
Agua de Santo Domingo; mission and pueblo, 23-24
Agustín, Emperor of Mexico, 143, 153-55, 156
Alarid, Juan Bautista Vigil y. *See* Vigil y Alarid
Albert, Prince, 252
Albuquerque, 101, 233, 237, 239-40, 247
Altamira, Marquis of, 104
Americans in disfavor, 184-88, 221
Analco, 58, 109, 128
animals, domestic, 115
Antonio (town crier), 100
Anza, Juan Bautista de, 128-29
Apache Canyon, 199, 238
  battle, 239
Apaches. *See* Indians
Archaeological Institute of America, 281
archaeology and the Indian, 281
Archbishops. *See* Lamy; Salpointe
archdiocese, establishment of, 262
architecture, 311-13
archives, 284
Archuleta, Colonel Diego, 205, 218, 219
Arillaga. See Paredes y Arillaga
Aristotle, 31
Arizona, 248, 262, 265, 302
armament (1804), 136
Armijo, Manuel, 178-91, 197-200, 204, 207, 228, 338
  displacement, 191
arms and armor, 11
  illness, 210

Army of the West, 214, 216, 277
Arroyo Hondo, 220, 247
Art Museum, 312
artists and writers, 314-18, 326
Atchison, Topeka and Santa Fe Railroad, 272, 319, 321
atom bomb, and Los Alamos, 325-26
attack on city (1680), 49-53
attire. *See* clothing
attire and property of Captain General de Vargas, 74-76
attractions, social, 328-29
authors and artists, 314-18, 326

bailes, 260-61
Bajada, La, 4, 68, 207
ball (1846), 205-06
Bandelier, Adolph Francis Alphonse, 280-309, 319, 336
  death, 307
  Delight Makers, The, 291, 300
  departure from Santa Fe, 306
  study of Indian life, 286-87, 291, 300
Bandelier, Fanny, 306-07
banner, royal, 54-55, 59
Barcelo, Gertrudes (La Tules), 175, 218
Barrancas, Las, 52, 53
battles; Apache Canyon, 239
  Glorieta Pass, 239
  Santa Fe, 73
bells, 21, 159, 201-02
Ben Hur, a Tale of the Christ, by Lew Wallace, 271
Bent, Charles, 218-20
  murder of, 220
  proclamation by, 219
Benton, Thomas H., 199
Bent's Fort, 214

353